COLLECTOR'S ENCYCLOPEDIA OF

Barbie DOLL

Exclusives

IDENTIFICATION & VALUES

1972–2004

THIRD EDITION

J. MICHAEL AUGUSTYNIAK

COLLECTOR BOOKS
A Division of Schroeder Publishing Co., Inc.

On the cover:

Top right box: Montgomery Ward's 1972 The Original Barbie

Back row: Hard Rock Café Barbie, It's My Birthday Barbie, Secret of the Three Teardrops Barbie, Burberry Barbie

Third row: My Li'l Valentine Nikki, Feelin' Groovy Barbie, My Scene Delancy, 1977 Harley-Davidson Barbie, Boot Camp Barbie, Enchanted Halloween black Barbie

Second row: P.B. Store Green Dress Barbie, Redhead Joyeux Barbie, Angelic Harmony Hispanic Barbie, 2004 February Amethyst Barbie

Front row: The Tango Barbie and Ken

Cover design by Beth Summers
Book design by Allan Ramsey

SEARCHING FOR A PUBLISHER?

We are always looking for knowledgeable people considered to be experts within their fields. If you feel that there is a real need for a book on your collectible subject and have a large comprehensive collection, contact Collector Books.

Collector Books
P.O. Box 3009
Paducah, Kentucky 42002-3009
www.collectorbooks.com

Copyright© 2005 by J. Michael Augustyniak

Contents

Avon Sterling Silver Rose Barbie Doll

Contents

P.B. Store Black Leather
Dress Barbie Doll

David's Bridal Unforgettable
Barbie Doll

Preface

"She has lived in different eras and visited different cultures. She has brought to life our most beloved fairy tales and worn costumes of pure imagination. . . Barbie doll has marked the passage of time with her beauty, her style, and the memories she provides. She is a fashion queen and the girl next door. A princess, a model, a bride, and a ballerina. To millions of fans she is more than just a doll. And that is why we love her. Because to so many, she means so much."

— Barbie Collectibles Catalog

Introduction

he Collector's Encyclopedia of Barbie® Doll Exclusives was designed to be just that — a thorough and complete encyclopedia featuring every department store special, every store promotional doll, and every Barbie doll and fashion retail exclusive released since 1972, the traditional cut-off year for "vintage" collectors. The most desirable of dolls, from extremely valuable and rare exclusives offered through Sears, Kellogg's, and Montgomery Ward in 1972, to the very latest releases appearing in stores for Christmas 2004, are all featured in this book, which is a permanent visual record of all of the elusive offerings from over three decades and over 100 retailers! No other book on collectible dolls has ever been as ambitious in its scope, nor as complete in supplying photos, information, and current values for each and every exclusive doll ever produced, from forgettable dolls worth less than $10 to rare vintage treasures commanding over $1,000. Collecting exclusive Barbie dolls is a hobby for every budget, since one can collect customized dolls selling for under $10 that are exclusive to discount department stores, or one can spend hundreds of dollars per doll on rarities from the Japanese P.B. Store.

The Barbie doll exclusives phenomenon goes back decades. In 1972, Montgomery Ward was the first retailer to commission an exclusive Barbie doll to commemorate its 100th year in business. Department store specials began appearing in finer stores in 1975; department store specials were either unique Barbie dolls, fashions, or toys offered exclusively to upscale retailers in the U.S., or regular children's-line dolls packaged with a special gift for the child. For Sears' 100th anniversary in 1986, Mattel created an exclusive Barbie doll for that store, and soon other retailers began to commission their own customized Barbie dolls — special dolls created exclusively for particular store chains. The appeal of such dolls to retailers is obvious — the customer has to shop at their stores in order to buy dolls found nowhere else!

By 2005, over 100 different retail outlets have called unique Barbie dolls their own! This is a source of both delight and frustration to collectors, who must tirelessly pursue the latest special edition, occasionally from obscure retailers nowhere near their homes. The author hopes this book will be an invaluable resource in the seemingly endless search for elusive exclusives.

Pricing

$\mathcal{V}$alues listed in the book are for individual **Never Removed from Box (NRFB)** dolls. This means that the dolls are still perfectly intact and undisturbed inside their original boxes, just as they left Mattel. Box condition is a consideration with collectible dolls, since many collectors prefer to leave their dolls inside the boxes, and Mattel's packaging usually allows the dolls to be appreciated without being removed from their boxes. This is especially true for recent dolls like Wal-Mart's Birthstone Barbie dolls, which have large box windows that show the dolls and fashions completely. Keeping NRFB Barbie dolls' boxes in the best condition possible will ensure maximum resale value, and the grading system that rates toys' packaging and contents on a scale of 1 (worst) to 10 (best) is slowly gaining acceptance among doll collectors, with grades of C 1 to C 10 found more and more often with sales listings.

Conversely, box condition is a non-issue for a growing number of collectors, since many Barbie dolls produced prior to 1999 were produced in such great quantities that they are easily found today, often at prices below Mattel's original suggested retail. Mattel's commitment to trimming production numbers has been a drastic — and much needed — effort to ensure that Barbie remains the most collected doll in the world. It is incredible that Mattel has produced exclusive versions of dolls for F.A.O. Schwarz in quantities of 1,000 dolls or less in the last few years.

Even with vastly-reduced production numbers, Mattel's policy of distributing surplus dolls through Mattel Toy Clubs or Mattel Toy Stores has caused values to fall on those dolls, which inevitably find their way to eBay and diminish the value of all the dolls purchased at full retail. Thankfully, Mattel is working harder to match production numbers with demand.

Dolls removed from boxes for display and then replaced are **Mint in Box** and are worth between 25 to 50 percent less than an NRFB doll.

Dolls without boxes but in mint condition with all original accessories are worth approximately 30 percent of an NRFB doll, although some dealers report getting as much as 50 percent.

Incomplete dolls and played-with dolls, as well as otherwise mint dolls affected by smoke or fading, are valued at the seller's discretion.

The values in this book have been compiled and averaged from numerous dealer lists and catalogs, collector and dealer advertisements, Internet sales, and regional and national doll shows and conventions. The values are intended to be used only as a guide to a Barbie doll's worth. Prices may be higher or lower depending on the national economy and the political climate.

Barbie Doll Head Molds

Barbie doll is known for always changing her appearance. She has adopted numerous head molds in the last 46 years. From her creation in 1959 through 1966, she used one basic head mold (altered for the Fashion Queen and Miss Barbie dolls). From 1967 through 1976, she used four different head molds (the 1959 original was used for the Montgomery Ward, Twist 'N Turn, Stacey, and Steffie dolls). Many new head molds have debuted since 1977, offering more variety and ethnic diversity. Shown below are the different head molds used by Barbie that are found in this book.

1959 Barbie

1967 Twist 'N Turn Barbie

1968 Stacey

1972 Steffie

1977 SuperStar Barbie

1977 Supersize Barbie

1977 Superstar Barbie Fashion Face

1979 Kissing Barbie

1981 Oriental Barbie

1983 Spanish Barbie

1986 Diva

1988 Christie

1991 Asha

1991 Nichelle

1991 Shani

1992 Mackie Neptune Fantasy

1992 Teen Talk Barbie

1992 Teresa

1999 Fantasy Goddess of Africa Barbie

1999 Generation Girl Barbie

1999 Lara

2000 Lea

2002 Tango Barbie

2003 My Scene Barbie

1975 **Barbie's Apartment**. This special set combines the regular line Country Kitchen and Studio Bedroom playsets that were sold individually with a room-setting backdrop. A fabric cat and elephant pillow are among the accessories that are included. $150.00.

1975 **Hawaiian Barbie** has brown eyes and uses the Steffie head mold. This is the first Hawaiian Barbie, and her box features the cursive Barbie signature logo. Accessories include a lei, a grass skirt, a ukulele, and a surfboard with sail. $80.00.

1976 **Beautiful Bride Barbie** has green eyes and rooted eyelashes. Rooted eyelashes would not be used again on a U.S. Barbie doll until 1992. Her wedding ensemble was boxed and sold separately as Fashion Originals #9419, another department store special of 1976. She is hard to find. $220.00.

1976 **Ballerina Barbie On Tour!** contains the 1976 Ballerina Barbie doll dressed in her original white and gold tutu, along with a pink practice outfit and Snowflake Fairy costume. She has newly designed dancer's arms and uses the 1967 Twist 'N Turn Barbie doll head mold. $115.00.

Arm/Flower/Pearl variations.

1976 **Barbie Classy Corvette.** Barbie doll has owned many Corvettes over the years but this was her first — a canary yellow vehicle with racing stripes and her *B* logo on the hood. A mobile phone, tape deck with three cassettes, and suitcase with luggage rack are included. **$75.00.**

Barbie Fashion Originals are top-of-the-line designer fashions; in 1976 Mattel released four Fashion Originals to upscale stores as department store specials. Several new fashions were introduced each year through 1980.

1976 #9419 $120.00.

1976 #9421 $125.00.

1976 #9422 $95.00.

1976 #9424 $95.00.

1977 #9470 $125.00.

1977 #9972 $95.00.

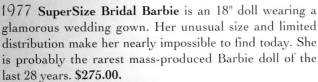

1977 **SuperSize Bridal Barbie** is an 18" doll wearing a glamorous wedding gown. Her unusual size and limited distribution make her nearly impossible to find today. She is probably the rarest mass-produced Barbie doll of the last 28 years. **$275.00.**

1977 **SuperStar Barbie In the Spotlight** contains SuperStar Barbie doll wearing her original hot pink gown along with two regular-line Best Buy fashions, a blue gown #9626 and a silver and pink jumpsuit with jacket #9624. SuperStar Barbie doll debuts the new smiling-face head mold used on the majority of Barbie dolls from 1977 – 1999. She also introduced the permanently-bent glamour pose arms, and she is the first Barbie doll since 1966 to wear earrings. She has a silver wrist tag with the Mattel logo on one side and "Made in Taiwan" on the other. **$150.00.**

1976 - 1982 **Hawaiian Barbie.** The same basic version of Hawaiian Barbie appeared in Mattel's Department Store Division catalogs until 1982. Mattel declared that she was their most popular department store special. Such a long production run resulted in several variations over the years. Beginning with the 1976 version, the Barbie name logo on the box changed from the older cursive signature style to a more modern, glamorous Barbie logo. The 1978 version's lei was changed to cloth instead of plastic and her makeup was given a softer look. Her fabric print outfit has been found in several variations: tulip print, daisy print, black print, and blue print. **$60.00.**

1977 SuperStar Barbie Beauty Salon features a reclining swivel chair, working faucet, hair dryer, and three-way full-length mirror. **$50.00.**

1978 Barbie Designer Originals Wedding Belle fashion, although not a department store special, is the same gown worn by the 1978 Beautiful Bride Barbie. **$38.00.**

1978 Beautiful Bride Barbie is a SuperStar Barbie doll redressed in a lovely ivory lace wedding gown. **$110.00.**

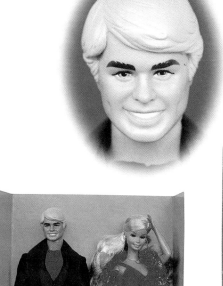

1978 SuperStar Barbie & SuperStar Ken is an extremely hard-to-find set containing the regular-line SuperStar Barbie and SuperStar Ken dolls with the addition of wrist tags. SuperStar Ken has a handsome new head mold and a new body with swivel neck, bent arms, and a swivel waist. **$225.00.**

13

1978 **Fashion Originals #2667.** This department store special was repackaged as a regular line Designer Original in 1979 called Sleek 'n' Chic. **$65.00.**

1978 **SuperStar Barbie In the Spotlight** appeared with slight differences from the 1977 version. The liner behind the doll is now dark purple and the wrist tag is deleted. **$130.00.**

1978 **Fashion Originals #2670.** This Fashion Originals was repackaged as a regular line Designer Original in 1979 called Golden Firelight. **$60.00.**

1979 **Fashion Originals #1022.** **$45.00.**

1978 **SuperStar Barbie In the Spotlight** is a revamped version of the 1977 set minus the doll's wrist tag but with two different Best Buy fashions: #2562, a blue blouse and pants with silver net jacket and #2564, a silver and pink skirt and jacket. **$140.00.**

1979 **Fashion Originals #1021.** **$45.00.**

1979 **Fashion Originals #1023. $45.00.**

1979 **Ballerina Barbie On Tour!** set has the same outfits as the 1976 On Tour! set, but Barbie doll's hair is now pulled to the side, and she has a tiny red dot in the corner of each eye. Four different Snowflake Fairy costume variations have been found with this 1979 set. **$110.00.** Sets in which Barbie doll wears a red foil "TAIWAN" wrist tag are more desirable. **$125.00.**

1979 **Hawaiian Ken** has the 1968 Ken doll head mold with unique black hair and brown eyes. He has a surfboard, towel, bead necklace, plastic lei, and print shorts, which have been found in two variations. **$45.00.**

1979 **Hawaiian Ken** is shown here with *blue* eyes — a rare variation since Hawaiian Ken dolls were supposed to have brown eyes to reflect a Hawaiian native. **$100.00.**

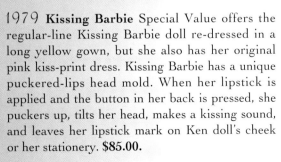

1979 **Kissing Barbie** Special Value offers the regular-line Kissing Barbie doll re-dressed in a long yellow gown, but she also has her original pink kiss-print dress. Kissing Barbie has a unique puckered-lips head mold. When her lipstick is applied and the button in her back is pressed, she puckers up, tilts her head, makes a kissing sound, and leaves her lipstick mark on Ken doll's cheek or her stationery. **$85.00.**

1979 **Me & Barbie Birthday Party** features a yellow room setting with a party game and spinner, a table and two chairs, bubble solution, and gifts. This set was also available through the Montgomery Ward catalog. **$45.00.**

1980 **Malibu Barbie The Beach Party** consists of a Malibu Barbie doll with a red foil "TAIWAN" wrist tag in a pink swimsuit unique to this set, vinyl carry case with window, surfboard, table with umbrella, chair, hibachi, beach bag, hat, towel, snorkel, face mask, swim fins, comb, and lotion bottle. The accessories included with this set were sold separately in The Beach Scene Play Pak #2319. Malibu Barbie debuted in 1971, and a swimsuit Barbie doll has been available every year since then. This Malibu Barbie uses the SuperStar Barbie head mold, while most of the 1970s Malibu Barbie dolls have the Stacey head mold. **$80.00.**

1980 Barbie Fashion Originals #1445. $38.00.

1980 **Barbie Fashion Originals** #1446. $40.00.

1980 **Beauty Secrets Barbie Pretty Reflections** offers Barbie doll with realistically poseable arms that contain wires for bending in any position, jointed wrists, and a button in her back that makes her arms move slightly. This set is special because it contains a full-length three-way mirror that is a pink version of the one from the Barbie Beauty Salon. **$75.00.**

1981 **Golden Dream Barbie Special** includes a regular-line Golden Dream Barbie with Quick Curl hair that contains tiny wires for super styleability, along with a gold-trimmed white faux fur coat and gold clutch purse. **$65.00.**

1982 **Pink & Pretty Barbie Extra Special Modeling Set** contains the regular-line doll with the addition of a TV camera and stage light (previously used in the Sears SuperStar Barbie Photo Studio), pink sunglasses, autograph book, and photo cutouts. **$85.00.**

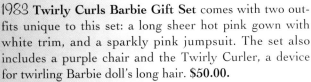

1983 **Twirly Curls Barbie Gift Set** comes with two outfits unique to this set: a long sheer hot pink gown with white trim, and a sparkly pink jumpsuit. The set also includes a purple chair and the Twirly Curler, a device for twirling Barbie doll's long hair. **$50.00.**

1983 **Hawaiian Barbie** was sold in a smaller box than previous Hawaiian Barbie dolls. She wears a new darker-print bikini and skirt, has a garland in her hair, and comes with a ukulele and a windsurfer. **$35.00.**

1984 **Hawaiian Ken** uses a new Hispanic head mold created for the Hispanic versions of the 1983 Sunsational Malibu Ken and the 1984 Sun Gold Malibu Ken. These are the only three dolls to use this handsome head mold. Hawaiian Ken wears a colorful shirt and shorts that match Hawaiian Barbie doll's swimsuit, and he has a surfboard. **$30.00.**

1984 **Loving You Barbie Gift Set** contains a child-size purse along with stationery supplies and a stamper. Red hearts cover her overskirt and sleeves. Loving You Barbie is considered by many collectors to be one of the most beautiful Barbie dolls of the 1980s. **$68.00.**

1985 **Happy Birthday Barbie Party Gift Set** offers the regular Happy Birthday Barbie along with 15 party supplies including a doll-size tablecloth, a card for the child, a child-size birthstone ring, and a heart pendant. The pretend cake with 16 candles, party hat, plastic cat, gift boxes, and tableware were originally created for the Me & Barbie Birthday Party playset. **$36.00.**

19

1986 **Deluxe Tropical Barbie** has an extra skirt/wrap, hat, carry bag, and camera. Her surfboard is the same type as used for the Hawaiian Ken dolls. She boasts of having "the longest hair ever!" **$25.00.**

1987 **Feelin' Groovy Barbie**, sold originally for $25.00, was the most expensive department store special offered by Mattel, yet she sold out quickly because of her outstanding quality. She uses the Steffie head mold with black hair, has pale skin and red lips, and wears a pink minidress with a matching long skirt under a jewel-tone jacket with faux fur trim. She is the first U.S. Barbie doll to carry the designer's name on the box front. Mattel used the original Barbie signature logo on the box front to further distinguish the doll. The success of Feelin' Groovy Barbie led to more expensive collector series Barbie dolls. **$85.00.**

Store Promotional Dolls

1974 **Barbie's Sweet 16** celebrates the sixteenth birthday of Barbie doll, using her original patent date of 1958 as her birth year. Barbie doll has a blonde shag hairstyle and wears a pink party dress with white polka dots. Her limited special offer is a bonus fashion: a yellow tank top with a "Sweet 16" logo and denim shorts. She also comes with a compact, brush, comb, and four barrettes with lilac and strawberry fragrance stickers. The box back has an offer for a Barbie necklace, chewing gum, and an iron-on patch, available by mail until May 1, 1975, and a coupon for a free Howard Johnson's birthday dinner. Later Barbie's Sweet 16 dolls omit the extra shorts and tank top fashion. $150.00.

1976 **Deluxe Quick Curl Barbie** with Free Jergens Children's Toiletries features Barbie doll with Quick Curl hair (tiny wires are rooted with the doll's hair to make it easily styleable). She wears a long blue dress with a white shawl and "pearl" necklace. A long blonde fall, brush, comb, curler, two ribbons, and two bobby pins are also included. Her limited special offer is a Jergens Barbie Bath Set featuring a two-ounce pink bar of soap and a one-ounce bottle of Barbie Bubble Bath. $88.00.

1977 **SuperStar Barbie** debuts a newly sculpted head with open-mouth smile; this face has been used for the great majority of playline Caucasian Barbie dolls sold since 1977. Her body is also redesigned, with a swivel head, ball-jointed arms that are permanently bent at the elbows (so she can "pose like the models do"). SuperStar Barbie has sunstreaked blonde hair and wears a hot pink satin gown with a silver and pink boa, sparkling necklace, earrings, and a ring. She is the first Barbie doll sold wearing earrings since 1967. This is the earliest SuperStar Barbie to appear on the market, offering a free golden star-shaped SuperStar necklace for the child. A posing stand is included. $120.00.

1978 **SuperStar Barbie** promotional doll wears a shimmery evening dress in one of two color schemes: pink with silver highlights or ruby with metallic ruby highlights. Both dresses have a silver sequin collar, marabou boa, silver sequin hat, and sparkling earrings, necklace, and ring. A white star-shaped posing stand is included, and a free golden Sparkling SuperStar haircomb with rhinestones is a gift for the child. **$175.00.**

1978 **SuperStar Ken** has "the movie star look" with his blue jumpsuit with attached red dickey, belt with silver star-emblem buckle, silver "Ken" bracelet, silver watch (set at 8:25), silver-rimmed red sunglasses, and a red ring. He has a newly sculpted head that swivels and a redesigned body with permanently-bent arms, a swivel waist, and ball-jointed arms and legs. With his blonde hair and dimples, SuperStar Ken has often been compared to Robert Redford. This promotional version offers a golden sparkling SuperStar ring for the child. **$70.00.**

1979 **Pretty Changes Barbie** with Free Barbie Play Perfume features Barbie doll wearing a satiny yellow jumpsuit with a sheer white and yellow overskirt, matching floppy hat, and a scarf with flower. Also included are a yellow and white long-sleeved overblouse, white picture hat, a brunette fall, and a long blonde fall. The box back says, "From disco to dressy, Barbie has lots of different looks." Early promotional dolls come with a 1.2 fl. oz. bottle of Barbie Play Perfume, packaged inside a small box taped to the side of the doll's box. Three distinct hairstyles were used for this doll: straight hair, full hairstyle with loose curls, and tightly-curled hair. **$57.00.**

AAFES 1996 **Sweet Daisy Barbie** was only available at military base stores for $24.00. She wears a blue daisy-print dress with a denim top over a pink shirt and a blue hat with a daisy on the brim. **$15.00.** The prototype doll has a red hat and a black and white gingham skirt with blue and red flower designs. **$65.00.**

AAFES 1997 **Ponytails Barbie** (white or black) wears a red top with a black and white skirt featuring two buckles, and she has a red ribbon in her hair. One matching barrette is included for use in the doll's or the child's hair. **$15.00.**

AAFES 1998 **Making Friends Barbie** (white or black) wears a pink minidress and denim vest. She comes with a telephone, sunglasses, and an address book for the child. **$14.00.**

AAFES 2000 **Boot Camp Barbie** (white or black) wears a camouflage uniform and comes with khaki-look shorts and a t-shirt — authentic-looking government issue (GI) gear complete with dog tags and boots. Stickers are included to add to her t-shirt and jacket to indicate her branch of the service (U.S. Army or U.S. Air Force), as well as her rank. The box back states, "Check out the shine on her boots. She's learning what it takes to be in the military!" **$25.00.**

AAFES 1999 **Your Pen Pal Barbie** (white or black) wears cuffed denim jeans and a butterfly-logo striped top. Three postcards and 21 stickers are included. **$14.00.**

24

AAFES 2001 **Paratrooper Barbie** (white or black) wears a green military flight outfit complete with a parachute that tucks into her backpack, a helmet, dog tags, and boots. She comes with boxes of "SUPPLIES," "BROWN RICE," a "FIRST AID KIT," "DRIED FRUIT AND NUTS," and "CHICKEN AND VEGETABLE SOUP." $22.00.

AAFES 2002 **Aviator Barbie** (white or black) wears an authentic flight suit and jacket, complete with sunglasses, a scarf, and a helmet with flip-down shades. The box remarks about Barbie, "A top graduate of military flight school, she's one of the best and brightest. Not only is she in top physical condition, she's aced subjects like science and engineering." $20.00.

Ames 1991 **Party in Pink Barbie** has green eyes and wears a pink minidress with lacy skirt, black leggings, and extra black halter top. The outfit pieces mix and match for eight looks. Mix and match wardrobes are used on many exclusive Barbie dolls since such outfits are viewed by parents as a better value than a doll in a single-look fashion. **$16.00.**

1992 **Barbie Magic Talk Club Friends' Fashions #2552** is Party in Pink Barbie doll's outfit in a different color scheme, with the addition of a microphone and a computer chip that allows the wearer of the dress to talk and sing at the Magic Talk Club. **$10.00.**

Ames 1992 **Denim 'n Lace Barbie** wears a denim jacket and skirt with white lace accents, white floral leggings, a hat, and a floral-print top. Her bag matches her top. **$14.00.**

Ames 1992 **Hot Looks Barbie** is a second Ames doll for 1992 wearing a blue and pink outfit that coordinate for ten different looks. **$14.00.**

Ames 1993 **Country Looks Barbie** is dressed in casual red, white, and black western attire with a bandanna and red boots that allows for eight different country looks. **$12.00.**

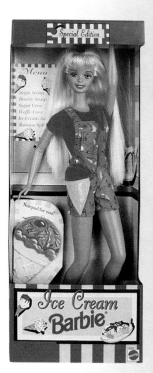

Ames 1998 **Ice Cream Barbie** wears ice-cream-cone-and-cherry-print purple overalls, a pink t-shirt, white socks, and purple shoes. She comes with an ice cream cone–shaped purse and a notepad. **$12.00.**

Ames 1997 **Ladybug Fun Barbie** wears a white ladybug t-shirt, ladybug-print black and white skirt with matching scarf, ladybug purse, and white sneakers. A ladybug barrette is included for the child. **$12.00.**

Ames 1999 **Magna Doodle Barbie** wears a blue and white striped shirt and red shorts. She comes with a miniature Magna Doodle–style keychain. The doll was originally planned as a Hills exclusive, but Ames acquired the Hills chain. **$14.00.**

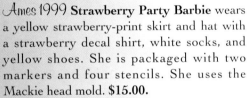

Ames 1999 **Strawberry Party Barbie** wears a yellow strawberry-print skirt and hat with a strawberry decal shirt, white socks, and yellow shoes. She is packaged with two markers and four stencils. She uses the Mackie head mold. **$15.00.**

Ames 2000 **Floating Flower Fun Barbie** wears a colorful checked and floral-design swimsuit with a pink foam skirt. The child can make a pop bead bracelet or decorate Barbie doll's skirt with flowers. **$14.00.**

Ames 2000 **Extreme 360° Barbie** is dressed for in-line skating and skateboarding. A helmet, wrist guards, elbow guards, and sneakers are included. She has the Generation Girl head mold. **$16.00.**

Applause 1990 **Barbie Style** was sold in greeting card shops. The Barbie name logo on her box lid and *B*-print designs on her white satin dress are Mattel's first attempt to modernize the Barbie logo used since 1976. **$20.00.**

Autogrill Toys 1996 Barbie Pez Autogrill Toys is an exclusive for the Autogrill Toys stores of Italy. Barbie doll wears a black knit top with a red plaid skirt, red pantyhose, an apple necklace, a red headband, and black boots. The same basic doll was sold in different packaging in the U.S. in 1996 as School Spirit Barbie, but this Italian doll has only one belt buckle on her skirt while the U.S. version has two belt buckles. **$35.00.**

Applause 1991 **Applause Barbie** wears an elegant silver lamé gown with pink trim and white tulle. Sold during the 1991 Christmas holiday season, this doll is often called the Applause Holiday Barbie. **$24.00.**

Avon 1996 **Winter Velvet Barbie** (white or black) wears a rich blue velvety top and silver design skirt. Collectors notice a similarity in the basic style of this gown and the one worn by the 1995 International Happy Holidays Barbie. Avon identifies its black dolls as "African American" on the boxes. **$20.00.**

Avon 1996 **Spring Blossom Barbie** (white or black) is the first Barbie doll sold by Avon, although Avon did sell other 11½" fashion dolls in the past. Barbie has a satiny purple top with pink dotted overskirt and yellow hat, and she carries a yellow basket of flowers on her arm. **$15.00.**

Avon 1996 **Barbie Fashions** are three regular-line Fashion Avenue fashions specially packaged for Avon in plastic bags containing each fashion wrapped in pink tissue paper with a golden *B*-logo seal. **$10.00 each.**

Avon 1997 **Color 'n Wash My Hair Barbie** is a rare Avon doll created by Mattel's Philippines licensee. She wears a sparkly pink and white fashion and comes with a towel and bottle of pink hair coloring that washes out with water. She is very similar to the U.S. playline Foam 'n Color Barbie although her fabric and makeup differ from the U.S. doll's. **$50.00.**

Avon 1997 **Spring Petals Barbie** (blonde or black) wears a floral and gingham dress with a bow at her waist and a matching headband. She carries a bouquet of flowers. **$12.00.**

Avon 1997 **Spring Petals Barbie**, brunette, is Avon's first Caucasian brunette Barbie doll. She has the SuperStar Barbie head mold. **$15.00.**

1996 Barbie Fashion Greeting Cards You're Special! uses the same print material as worn by Avon's Spring Petals dolls. **$8.00.**

Avon 1997 **Barbie Fashions** are a second series of outfits wrapped in pink tissue paper and sealed inside plastic bags for Avon. These fashions include a pink and blue ski suit with boots, skis, and poles, a golden dress with gold and white jacket with faux fur collar, white pantyhose, pumps, and a purse, and a satiny red dress with black bows, pantyhose, sheer black wrap, and black pumps. **$10.00 each.**

Avon 1997 **Winter Rhapsody Barbie** (brunette, blonde, or black) is second in Avon's series of winter-themed dolls. She wears a dark pink and black taffeta skirt with golden threads topped with a fitted pink velveteen jacket with faux fur collar and sleeves and a golden ribbon choker. **$18.00.**

Avon 1997 **Barbie Doll as Mrs. P.F.E. Albee** honors the first General Agent hired by the California Perfume Company, founded in 1886 and known as Avon since 1920. Persis Foster Eames Albee was born in 1836 and was 50 years old and married with two grown children when she accepted the job as a door-to-door perfume saleswoman, the first Avon lady. Initially offering just one product, the Little Dot Perfume Set (five bottles of different scents), Mrs. Albee dressed elegantly for her customers and was associated with Avon for 25 years. Barbie doll wears a purple jacket with matching skirt, jabot, hat, and shoes, and she comes with a tiny California Perfume Company brochure that says, "highly concentrated odors extracted from flowers." **$50.00.**

Avon 1998 **Barbie Doll as Mrs. P.F.E. Albee** second edition is attached to a box liner depicting a 19th century Victorian home, after she has just completed a successful sale. She carries her product in her valise. Dressed in an elegant pale yellow and pink skirt, jacket, fancy hat, and white gloves, Mrs. Albee, as the box states, proves that "to be successful, one must look the part." Both Mrs. Albee dolls use the Mackie head mold. **$42.00.**

Avon 1998 **Spring Tea Party Barbie** (blonde, black, or brunette) wears a satiny, ribboned bodice, a long skirt with sparkly layered tulle, and a hair bow. Her box states that tea is the most popular drink in the world after water. Package cutouts include tea biscuits, finger sandwiches, placemats, name cards, an invitation, and a rag doll. **$15.00.**

Avon 1998 **Winter Splendor Barbie**, white, wears a velvety black bodice, black gloves, and a long red gown that drapes to her right. **$24.00.**

Avon 1998 **Winter Splendor Barbie**, black, uses the Asha head mold with light skin tone, unlike all previous black Avon Barbie dolls which have the Christie head mold with dark skin. **$26.00.**

Avon 1997 **Barbie Bedroom and Barbie Dining Room** are furniture and accessory sets sold by Avon in pink Barbie-logo boxes featuring a photo of Barbie, a list of contents, and the *Avon* name. **$20.00 each.**

Avon 1999 **Lemon-Lime Sorbet Barbie** is from a set of two Avon Barbie dolls wearing fruit-themed, scented fashions. She is listed as African American and uses the Mackie head mold with light brown skin and green eyes. Lemons and slices of limes adorn her sheer skirt, and extra green and white checked capri pants are included for a different look. A lemon necklace is included for the child. **$16.00.**

Avon 1999 **Strawberry Sorbet Barbie** wears a pink strawberry-scented fashion with extra pink and white checked Capri pants. A scented strawberry necklace in included for the child. The box back folds out into a cardboard picnic table. **$14.00.**

1999 **Fruit Fantasy Barbie** was created for the foreign market as a playline doll with no association with Avon, even though this blonde doll is identical to Strawberry Sorbet Barbie. Instead of the extra Capri pants, Fruit Fantasy Barbie comes with a bottle of strawberry fragrance. Both Fruit Fantasy Barbie dolls were sold at U.S. KB stores in 2001. **$14.00.**

1999 **Fruit Fantasy Barbie**, brunette, was made for the foreign market and comes in a unique peach gown. She is Caucasian and has the Mackie head mold with brown hair. Mattel opted to replace the Lemon-Lime Sorbet Barbie with this doll in the Fruit Fantasy series. She comes with a peach necklace for the child and a bottle of peach fragrance. This peachy doll is a great complement to Avon's fruit-themed pair. **$16.00.**

Avon 1999 **Avon Representative Barbie** (white, black, or Hispanic) is dressed in a stylish suit with black stockings. The jacket color is unique to each ethnic version. Each doll holds an Avon bag. The box states that the doll is a tribute to the ideals and vision of the corporation, which are "to be the company that best understands and satisfies the product, service and self-fulfillment needs of women globally." The Caucasian doll has the Mackie head mold, the African American doll has the Nichelle head mold, and the Hispanic doll has the Teresa head mold. White or Hispanic, **$35.00**; black, **$65.00.**

Avon 1999 **Snow Sensation Barbie** (white) wears a powder blue floor-length ballgown with white faux fur trim. Her miniature snow globe plays a melody from *The Nutcracker Suite*. She has the Mackie head mold. **$24.00.**

Avon 1999 **Snow Sensation Barbie** (black) has the Asha head mold with light skin and side-glancing eyes. **$27.00.**

Avon 2000 **Angelic Inspirations Barbie** (white or black) wears a glittery golden gown with golden wings and tiny rosettes at her waist and in her hair. Her dove chirps when its lower beak is pressed. Four inspirational cards are included. **$35.00.**

Avon 2000 **Blushing Bride Barbie** (white or black) wears a sophisticated wedding gown with subtle silvery accents, with white roses at the waist and in the bouquet, and a tulle veil. **$22.00.**

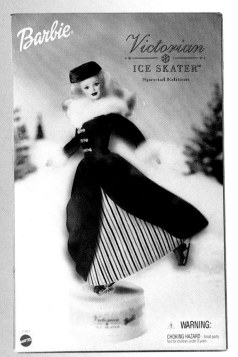

Avon 2000 **Victorian Ice Skater Barbie** wears a full, sweeping skirt with a satiny underskirt. When Barbie doll is placed upon the music box stand base, a turn of the key causes her to twirl around as a Victorian-era waltz plays. **$24.00.**

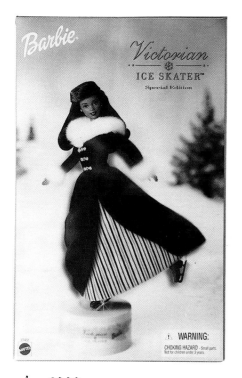

Avon 2000 **Victorian Ice Skater Barbie**, black. **$24.00.**

Avon 2001 **Ballet Masquerade Barbie** (white, black, or Hispanic) wears a costume with a shimmery brocaded bodice with rich colors and embellished with feathers, reflecting the dazzling beauty of nature. A Harlequin mask is included. **$24.00.**

Avon 2001 **Flower Mania Barbie**, a grocery store doll in the U.S., was an Avon exclusive in England. She is virtually identical to the U.S. grocery store Flower Mania Barbie, except the charm necklace included with Flower Mania Barbie was not included with the Avon doll, and her box back includes the "AVON GUARAN-TEE" and lists the Avon Cosmetics address in England. **$20.00.**

Avon 2001 **Ring in the New Year Barbie** (white, black, or Hispanic) wears a golden tapestry-inspired print swirling in the dark blue of her full skirt. A white faux fur wrap complements the white faux fur trim on her bodice, and a strand of golden beads with a blue "jewel" and pumps complete her ensemble. When the button on her golden 2001 ornament is pressed, "Auld Lang Syne," the Scottish melody written by Robert Burns and translated "Old long since" or "Old times long past" in English, plays. **$25.00.**

Avon 2001 **Timeless Silhouette Barbie** (white or black) wears a satiny pink dress decorated with black silhouettes of ponytail Barbie dolls in various poses. She has a velvety black bodice with satiny pink trim, short white gloves, a "pearl" necklace, and a black and pink tulle wrap. **$23.00.**

Avon 2002 **Angelic Harmony Barbie** (white, black, or Hispanic) is a vision of celestial splendor in her pink iridescent gown with golden trim and graceful ribbons. She has a rose on her bodice, and a golden halo sits atop her head. She holds a golden trumpet that she will use to welcome the day. Note the metallic golden strands in her hair. **$27.00.**

Avon 2002 **Simply Charming Barbie** (white, black, or Hispanic) wears a delicate floral-print gown with a flower at her waist and a picture hat with tulle trim, evoking images of a garden in full bloom. A gold-toned bracelet with a picture hat charm is included for the child. **$24.00.**

Avon 2002 **Sterling Silver Rose Barbie** (white, black, or Hispanic) was designed by Bob Mackie. She wears a velvety purple gown with a dramatic silver and purple rose at the shoulder, a tulle train, and long, purple satin gloves. Note her beautiful platinum and purple hair. The Hispanic doll uses the Lea head mold. **$65.00.**

Avon 2002 **Winter Reflections Barbie** (white, black, or Hispanic) wears a satiny white gown with glittery over-skirt and white faux fur trim. Her bodice and sheer sleeves are decorated with silvery sparkles and glittery snowflake designs, and her hair ornament features a metallic silver snowflake. **$22.00.**

Avon 2003 **Glamorous Gala Barbie** (white, black, or Hispanic) wears a rich red gown accented with a gold-tone filigree flourish and a faux fur stole. $27.00.

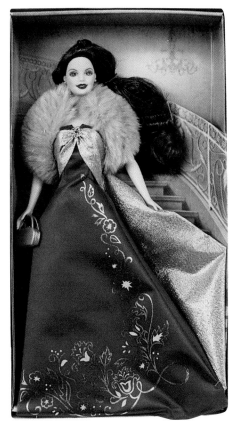

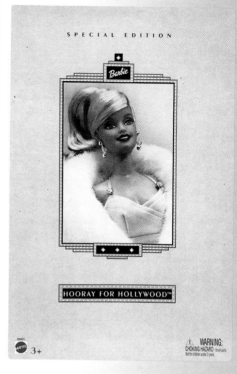

Avon 2003 **Hooray for Hollywood Barbie** (white, black, or Hispanic) is a silver screen starlet during Hollywood's Golden Era. She arrives for the premiere of her movie "Sweet Romance" wearing a sleek golden gown, a white stole, black gloves, and gold-tone shoes. A golden purse, a clapboard key chain, a movie program, and movie tickets are included. **$29.00.**

Avon 2003 **Victorian Tea Barbie** (white, black, or Hispanic) wears a lovely satiny white gown with a pink floral pattern and a straw hat with flowers at the brim, "pearl" stud earrings, and pumps. Her plastic tea set is complete with a tray, a teapot, a sugar bowl, a creamer, two cups, two saucers, and two spoons. **$24.00.**

Avon 2004 **Talk of the Town Barbie** (white, black, or Hispanic) wears a classic crisp white jacket with a tapered-waist silhouette and a full black skirt with white dots. She has a "pearl" necklace, a black hat, and a white poodle on a leash. The Hispanic version uses the Generation Girl Barbie head mold. **$30.00.**

Barbie Bazaar 2004 **Chinoiserie Red Sunset Barbie** from the Silkstone Barbie Fashion Model Collection has a long, side-part flip hairstyle and wears short cherry-red pajamas. She was initially offered free to 600 subscribers purchasing a two-year subscription to Barbie Bazaar magazine, and then the remaining 2,500 dolls of the 3,100 dolls produced were sold at BarbieCollector.com. **$100.00.**

Ben Franklin 1977 **Barbie Plus 3** doll has a Stacey head mold and comes in an orange swimsuit, with three extra Best Buy fashions included (#9153, #9160, and #9161). The original price was $3.88 for the set. **$85.00.**

Best 1980 **Barbie Shopping Spree.** These inexpensive fashion assortments were packaged exclusively for catalog showrooms, including Best. **$24.00.**

Best 1978 **Malibu Barbie Fashion Combo** features a regular Stacey-head Malibu Barbie wearing a pink swimsuit. She is packaged with unique mix and match fashion pieces: a long pink dress, a dark floral-print skirt, and a yellow halter top. Malibu Barbie Fashion Combo was also sold at Service Merchandise stores. **$65.00.**

Best Buy 1999 **Detective Barbie** wears black pants with a red shirt, a denim vest, and sneakers. She comes with everything needed to solve a mystery: a crime computer, a video camera, a wrist watch, a cell phone, binoculars, a flashlight, sunglasses, a magnifying glass, fingerprint cards, a notebook, a pencil, a pager, and clue cards. She uses the Generation Girl Barbie head mold. **$24.00.**

Biedermeier 1999 **Wiener Biedermeier Barbie** is a very limited edition of 100 dolls produced for the 170th anniversary of the Beidermeier store of Vienna, Austria, founded in 1829. She is a re-dressed Austrian Barbie wearing a nineteenth-century brown and gold gown with pink trim, a rose at the bodice, and a picture hat with ribbon. She has a hangtag that reads, "fashion dreams by E. Stelzer Vienna" on the front, and the doll's individual number is on the back. **$275.00.**

Big Lots 2003 **Date at Eight Barbie** wears a floral-print summer dress with a matching plastic purse. Blonde Barbie was available in a blue, pink, or orange dress, black Barbie was available in a blue dress, and brunette Barbie was available in a green dress. **$6.00.**

Big Lots 2003 **Fashion Fantasy Barbie** has a mix-and-match wardrobe including two tops, purple lamé pants, a pink skirt, three pairs of shoes, two pairs of sunglasses, three purses, and a shopping bag. **$10.00.**

Big Lots 2003 **Garden Surprise Barbie** (blue or purple) wears a long gown decorated with a garden scene. The large flowers on her gown are actually pockets which can hold her purse or beauty accessories. **$15.00.**

Big Lots 2003 **Stylin' Hair Barbie** (white or black) and Teresa wear belted floral and circle-print dresses with boots. When the hair extensions are sprayed with cool water, they change color. Four hair swirls, four flower hair clips, and three hair extensions with gem clips are included. **$11.00**.

Big Lots 2003 **Summer Garden Barbie** wears a satiny summer floral-design dress with a matching purse. Blonde Barbie was available in blue, pink, or purple dresses, while brunette Barbie was available in a yellow dress. **$8.00**.

Big Lots 2003 **Trendy Touches Barbie** (blonde or brunette) wears a dress with shoe, purse, sunglasses, and flower icons. Three pairs of shoes and two purses are included. **$10.00.**

Big Lots 2003 **Weekend Style Barbie** wears a retro zig-zag style dress with headband and boots. Blonde Barbie was available in blue, green, or orange dresses, black Barbie was available in a purple dress, and brunette Barbie was available in a red dress. **$6.00.**

Blokker 1996 **Blokker Barbie** commemorates the 100th anniversary of the Blokker organization in the Netherlands. The doll is dressed in Toys "R" Us 1994 Quinceanera Teresa doll's dress, and she wears a "Blokker 100 year" hangtag. She is hard to find. **$42.00.**

Bloomingdale's 1994 **Savvy Shopper Barbie** was designed by Nicole Miller. Barbie doll wears a black velvet minidress under a Barbie doll icons-print coat, and she comes with a Bloomingdale's shopping bag. She originally cost $65.00. **$35.00.**

Bloomingdale's 1995 **Donna Karan New York Barbie** (blonde or brunette) wears a black mock turtleneck, sarong skirt, a red fringed shawl, opaque black hose, a mock lizard belt, and a beret. She carries a purse, black sunglasses, and a Bloomingdale's shopping bag. These dolls were originally $65.00. **$38.00.**

Bloomingdale's 1996 **Calvin Klein Jeans Barbie** wears a denim jacket and skirt, Calvin Klein logo crop top, CK logo cap, and a black bra and panties. She has brown eyes. A CK windbreaker is included. Bloomingdale's originally sold her for $70.00, but Mattel offered her for $33.00 in the 1997 Barbie Collectibles specialty catalog. **$25.00.**

Bloomingdale's 1996 **Barbie at Bloomingdale's** wears a hot pink satin baseball jacket over a gray "Bloomie's"-logo sweatshirt and leggings. She carries a Bloomingdale's shopping bag. She originally cost $36.00. **$16.00.**

Bloomingdale's 1997 **Ralph Lauren Barbie** is called "the most sophisticated Barbie ever" in Bloomingdale's advertising. She wears a double-breasted navy blazer with Ralph Lauren crest, navy knit turtleneck bodysuit, gray flannel pleat-front pants, alligator-look belt, and lined camel hair overcoat. She carries a Blackwatch handbag. She originally retailed for $85.00. A Ralph Lauren Ken wearing a similar suit and coat was created but never released by Mattel. **$55.00.**

Bloomingdale's 1998 **Oscar de la Renta Barbie** is the first U.S. Barbie doll sold wearing an original gown by the famous designer, who has designed under his own label since 1965. Barbie doll wears a golden brocade bustier overlaid with chocolate-colored lace, lace sleeves with faux fur cuffs, a golden brocade gown with tulle underskirt, topaz-colored jewelry, and a chocolate brown lace stole. She retailed for $89.00. **$55.00.**

Burbank Toys 1973 **Barbie Christmas Gift Set** is exclusive to the United Kingdom's Burbank Toys and contains Quick Curl Barbie with an extra carded Best Buy fashion. The artwork on the packaging depicts Barbie doll with gray hair, gray eyes, and pink skin. The box back states that "Barbie is the world's most famous fashion model. She loves to be the first to wear the latest clothes and fashion accessories." This set is very historic since it is the first time that "Christmas" is used on a Barbie doll's box front. **$200.00.**

Burbank Toys 1973 **Barbie Christmas Gift Set** is shown here with several different styles of Barbie Best Buy fashions that were included in these sets. **$200.00.**

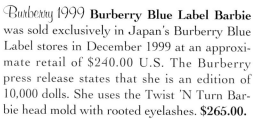

Burberry 1999 **Burberry Blue Label Barbie** was sold exclusively in Japan's Burberry Blue Label stores in December 1999 at an approximate retail of $240.00 U.S. The Burberry press release states that she is an edition of 10,000 dolls. She uses the Twist 'N Turn Barbie head mold with rooted eyelashes. **$265.00.**

Cheerios 1995 **Cheerios Presents Barbie My First Fashions** was a Canadian Cheerios promotion. This fashion was offered free for three UPC symbols from Cheerios' boxes. **$15.00.**

Chicago Cubs 1998 Chicago Cubs Fashion Avenue is a special fashion given to the first 10,000 females who attended the Chicago Cubs vs. Houston Astros game on August 23, 1998, Barbie Day at Wrigley Field. A satiny blue Cubs jacket with matching cap, jeans, shoes, and a Chicago Cubs pennant are included, along with a card of authenticity. **$32.00.**

Chicago Cubs 1999 **Chicago Cubs Fan Barbie** wears a Cubs striped top, blue shorts, white socks, blue shoes, and Cubs cap. The doll was a gift to the first 10,000 females at the Chicago Cubs vs. Kansas City game on July 20, 1999. A card of authenticity is included. **$50.00.**

Chicago Cubs 2001 **Chicago Cubs Fan Barbie** was a gift to female fans attending the August 9, 2001, Barbie Day game featuring the Chicago Cubs vs. Colorado Rockies at Wrigley Field. The doll wears a Cubs uniform similar to the 1999 edition's, but the 2001 doll has the newer Generation Girl Barbie head mold while the earlier doll has the SuperStar face. **$45.00.**

Chicago Cubs 2003 **Chic Barbie** was a gift to female fans attending the Thursday, July 24 Barbie Day game featuring the Chicago Cubs vs. Philadelphia Phillies at Wrigley Field. She is a foreign-market doll wearing a short pink dress covered with holographic silver circles, but the Cubs sticker was added to her box window. **$30.00.**

Child World/Children's Palace 1982 **Barbie Special Value Gift Pack** includes six carded fashions inside a pink child-size purse with "Genuine Barbie Fashion" sticker. The illustrated checklist on the package back shows that this Gift Pack assortment includes four of 38 Barbie fashions, one of 10 Ken fashions, and one of six Skipper fashions. **$30.00.**

Child World/Children's Palace 1986 **Barbie Special Value Gift Pack** features a newer assortment of six carded fashions inside a pink child-size purse with "Barbie" sticker. Even though six fashions are included, only five dolls are pictured on the box front. The photo checklist on the package back reveals that typical assortments include four of 25 Barbie fashions and two of 10 Barbie Fashion Extras. **$30.00.**

Child World/Children's Palace 1989 **Dance Club Barbie Doll & Tape Player** combines the playline Dance Club Barbie doll with a real child's tape player and microphone. A cassette tape of Dance club music is included. **$22.00.**

Child World/Children's Palace 1990 **Barbie** in Disney character fashions, white or black, is the first Barbie doll to wear a Mickey Mouse ears hat. She is dressed in a Minnie Mouse T-shirt, a pink skirt with pink and white shorts, and a denim jacket. An extra pair of pink pants is included to interchange with her checkered shorts. Black Barbie has the Christie head mold. **$20.00.**

Child World/Children's Palace 1990 **Dance Magic Barbie & Ken Gift Set** is a special shared by Children's Palace and several other retailers. Dance Magic Barbie and Dance Magic Ken were sold individually in the regular children's line. Both dolls have transforming white dance costumes. Barbie doll's lips and Ken doll's hair change color with water. **$25.00.**

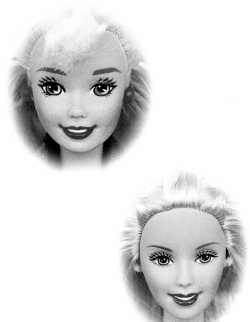

Chuck E. Cheese's 1996 **Chuck E. Cheese's Special Edition Barbie** wears a denim jeans outfit with white T-Shirt featuring the Chuck E. Cheese logo. She holds a bag bearing the Check E. Cheese's logo. $15.00. The Mattel sample doll in white cardboard packaging was created for vendor approval. **$50.00.**

Chuck E. Cheese's 2001 **Chuck E. Cheese's Special Edition Barbie** wears a pink Chuck E Cheese's logo top with a denim skirt. She comes with cardboard tokens, tickets, and pizza. She uses the Generation Girl Barbie head mold, while her predecessor has the SuperStar head mold. **$20.00.**

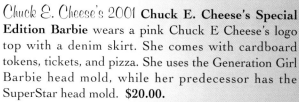

Cole's 1996 **Miss Barbie** was manufactured by Richwell Phils in the Philippines and was sold exclusively in Australia by Cole's grocery stores. She wears a plaid skirt and scarf with a red top. She is of comparable quality to the U.S. grocery store exclusive dolls. **$28.00.**

Coronet 1997 **Coronet Collector's Edition Barbie** Figurine is a mail-in premium offered on Coronet packages. **$5.00.**

Cracker Barrel 2000 **Country Charm Barbie** wears jeans, a red and white gingham shirt with vest, and shoes. A Cracker Barrel menu, a miniature game of checkers, a road map, and a backpack are included. The first Cracker Barrel store opened in 1969, and currently more than 420 locations in 40 states are open. **$24.00.**

David's Bridal 2004 **Unforgettable Barbie** (blonde or black) wears a reproduction of David's Bridal's most popular wedding gown. The box back states that Barbie "embodies all the splendor and romance of eternal love" in her glorious, shimmering gown with gloves. **$55.00.** The earliest Caucasian brunette dolls to reach stores have blue eyes, while later dolls have brown eyes. Brunette with blue eyes, **$80.00;** brunette with brown eyes, **$60.00.**

Deco-Pac 1990 **My First Barbie**, black, was offered in the same manner as the white doll, but in a differently labeled carton. She has the Christie head mold. **$25.00.**

Deco-Pac 1990 **My First Barbie,** white was the Deco-Pac company's first Barbie doll used as a cake topper in bakeries. The doll is similar to the 1990 play line My First Barbie, but the Deco-Pac My First Barbie white dolls were sent to bakeries inside plastic bags, packed into a carton of six dolls bearing stock #96085. The carton is essential for maximum value. **$25.00.**

Deco-Pac 1991 **Specialty Deco-Pak Barbie**, white, wears a pink ballerina outfit and is designed to sit atop a cake. Photos from Deco-Pac incorrectly picture the 1991 My First Barbie Deluxe Fashion Gift Set doll sitting on a cake, but the actual Deco-Pak Barbie has different hair, makeup, and clothing and came in a white box with the Barbie logo. Boxed dolls are hard to find since many dolls wound up on cakes, and bakeries discarded the boxes. Earlier versions of this doll have smaller ballet slippers. For the rest of the decade, Deco-Pac would only offer Barbie figurines, not dolls, as cake toppers. **$38.00.**

Deco-Pac 1991 **Specialty Deco-Pak Barbie**, black, is also packaged in a white box; only the stock numbers differentiate unopened dolls' boxes. The black doll is actually more common, since many bakeries reported running out of the white doll first, while the black doll could still be found in some bakeries as late as 1996. She has the Christie head mold. **$32.00.**

Deco-Pac 2003 **Deco-Pak Barbie** (white or black) is the first Deco-Pac Barbie doll in a decade! Barbie doll wears an iridescent white minidress with molded-on pink slippers. She has a pink *ankle* tag with the illustration of a birthday cake along with consumer information. A pink plastic tube is used to hold Barbie doll's legs inside the cake, and a "Limited Edition Barbie" sticker is included. The white Barbie comes with a pink "Barbie" ring for the child, and the black Barbie comes with a purple "Barbie" ring for the child. **$45.00.**

Diamond Comics Distributors 2004 **Barbie** as Catwoman depicts the felonious feline, Selina Kyle, who debuted in DC Comics Batman #1 in 1940. She wears a shiny purple catsuit topped with a striking cape, and she has sculpted hands featuring cat claws. A black belt with a silvery buckle, black boots, black gloves, a black ribbon choker with a silvery charm, and a purple and black mask with cat ears complete her costume, and she brandishes a whip. She has long black hair, green eyes, purple lipstick and eyeshadow, and arched eyebrows for a menacing look. **$82.00.**

Disney 1993 **Disney Fun Barbie** is advertised as "the coolest guest ever to visit the Magic Kingdom." She wears a short yellow and black top, matching shorts, and a Mickey Mouse ears hat, and she carries a pink Mickey Mouse balloon. **$30.00.**

Disney 1994 **Disney Fun Barbie** Second Edition wears a pink "leather" jacket, a mouse-ears-and-polka-dot-print white skirt, and a Mickey Mouse ears hat, and she carries a yellow Mickey Mouse balloon. **$28.00.**

Disney 1994 **Mickey's Toontown Stacie** is Barbie doll's little sister dressed in checkered shorts with a matching jacket and a "Mickey's Toontown" t-shirt. She carries a yellow Mickey Mouse balloon. **$26.00.**

Disney 1995 **Disney Fun Barbie** Third Edition wears a Mickey Mouse t-shirt, blue Mickey Mouse print skirt, red vest, and a Mickey Mouse ears hat, and she carries a red Mickey Mouse balloon. **$25.00.**

Disney 1996 **Walt Disney World Barbie** wears a white T-shirt, silver lamé jacket, black skirt, and a Mickey Mouse ears hat, and she carries a red Mickey Mouse balloon. Her silver jacket has the Mickey Mouse magician logo with "25," and her backpack has "25" on it. The tie-in to Walt Disney World's 25th anniversary increases her desirability. **$28.00.**

Disney 1997 **Disney Fun Barbie** fourth edition wears Mickey Mouse denim overalls with a belt, a black and white striped shirt, and a Mickey Mouse ears hat. She carries a red balloon and a black purse. **$24.00.**

Disney 1998 **Disney's Animal Kingdom Barbie**, white, is exclusive to Walt Disney World. Barbie doll wears a safari fashion with Disney's Animal Kingdom logo on her shirt as she serves as guide through Disney's Animal Kingdom. She carries a canteen and binoculars. She has the Mackie face. **$20.00.**

Disney 1998 **Disney's Animal Kingdom Barbie**, black, uses the Nichelle head mold with light skin tone. She is much more limited than the Caucasian version and is the first ethnic Barbie doll made exclusively for the Disney corporation. **$25.00.**

Disney 1998 **Disney Fun Barbie Fifth Edition** wears a red dress with belt and black shirt, a red and black jacket, black shoes, and a Mickey Mouse ears hat. She comes with a red Mickey Mouse balloon and a yellow purse. **$24.00.**

Disney 1998 **Disneyland Resort Vacation with Barbie Tommy Kelly Ken Gift Set** includes Barbie with a Mickey Mouse Disney land sweatshirt, black denim skirt, and video camera; Kelly with a mouse-ears headband, polka-dot red dress, and autograph book; Ken with a Disneyland t-shirt, black denim shorts, red Disneyland cap, and Disneyland guide book; and Ken's brother Tommy with red and white striped shirt, black denim shorts, a Mickey Mouse ears hat, and a yellow Mickey Mouse balloon. This set was sold at Disneyland. **$65.00.**

Disney 1998 **Walt Disney World Resort Vacation with Barbie Tommy Kelly Ken Gift Set** is identical to the Disneyland set except that all *Disneyland* names on the clothing, autograph book, guide book, and box have been changed to *Walt Disney World*. This set was sold at Walt Disney World. **$65.00.**

Disney 1999 **Walt Disney World 2000 Barbie** (black) uses the Christie head mold. **$22.00.**

Disney 1999 **Walt Disney World 2000 Barbie** (white) wears a silver lamé miniskirt, a 2000-logo blue top, a red cap with silver lamé brim, socks, and red high-top sneakers. A cardboard picture frame is included for the child. **$20.00.**

Disney 1999 **Barbie** Disney Fun Fashions contains five fashions featuring Mickey Mouse or the mouse ears design, three pairs of shoes, a back pack, and a cloth mouse ears hat. **$20.00.**

Disney 2000 **Barbie** Fun Fashions features five complete fashions, three pairs of shoes, a backpack, and a mouse ears hat. **$18.00.**

Disney 2001 **Disney Favorites Barbie** (white or black) has her short hair in pigtails held with Mickey Mouse ears bands. She wears a red, white, and black dress with the Mickey Mouse ears silhouette on the bodice, cuffs, and hem, white socks, and red boots. She carries a water bottle and a cloth Walt Disney World bag filled with cardboard souvenirs. Black Barbie uses the Christie head mold. **$30.00.**

Disney 2001 **Disney Celebration! Barbie** (white or black) celebrates the 30th anniversary of Walt Disney World in a black bodice with red Mickey Mouse ears silhouettes, a silver skirt with black Mickey Mouse ears designs around the hem and a red ribbon bow at the waist, black pantyhose, black pumps, and a red wrap lined in silver. **$28.00.**

Disney 2003 **Walt Disney World Resort Four Parks One World Barbie** (white or black) wears a red shirt with a Mickey Mouse ears silhouette, a long skirt covered with pink, red, and black Mickey Mouse-ears silhouettes, and a black hat. She carries a tote bag with cardboard souvenirs. **$27.00.**

Disney Europe 1992 **Disney Weekend Barbie** was designed for the Euro Disney theme park. She wears a one-piece black and white dress featuring Mickey Mouse on the bodice and a Mickey Mouse ears hat. **$35.00.**

Disney Europe 1993 **Disney Weekend Barbie** wears a green and pink Minnie and Mickey t-shirt with pink skirt and Mickey Mouse ears hat, and she has an extra Daisy Duck pink and yellow shirt with yellow shorts. **$38.00.**

Disney Europe 1993 **Disney Weekend Barbie & Ken Deluxe dolls** wear the same fashions as in 1991's Toys "R" Us exclusive Barbie & Friends Gift Set, but the Ken doll in this set uses the more recent 1992 Ken head mold. **$55.00.**

Disney Europe 1995 **Disney Fun Barbie** wears blue Mickey Mouse print pants and jacket with a pink and white shirt with matching hairbow. She carries a pink Mickey Mouse purse. **$25.00.**

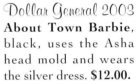

Dollar General 2003 **About Town Barbie** is the first inexpensive exclusive produced for the Dollar General stores. She sold for $5.00 and was available in a blue dress, a pink dress, or a silver dress. **$10.00.**

Dollar General 2003 **About Town Barbie**, black, uses the Asha head mold and wears the silver dress. **$12.00.**

Dollar General 2004 **Pretty Flowers Barbie, Christie, and Teresa** wear green dresses with a purple floral-print and ladybug design or pink dresses with an orange floral-print and bumblebee design. Note the wrist tags identifying the dolls. **$8.00.**

Eaton's 1973 **Barbie & Ken 11-Piece Pool Set** from Canada is labeled "Manufactured exclusively for Eaton's" on the box front. The set contains an inflatable round orange pool, two air mattresses, one lounge chair, one inflatable ball, two inflatable swim rings, two inflatable chairs, and two terry beach towels. Surprisingly, Barbie doll is not even shown in the box photo — only Ken, Francie, and P.J. dolls are pictured. **$36.00.**

F.A. Hoffman, Idee & Spiel 1995 **Steppin' Out Barbie** is the 100th anniversary doll for the F.A. Hoffman, Idee & Spiel store in Germany. Dressed in a satiny pink dress with black collar, cuffs, and hat, the doll and box are identical to Target's 1995 Steppin' Out Barbie. **$22.00.**

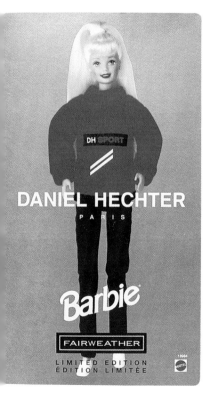

Fairweather 1997 **Daniel Hechter Barbie** is a Canadian exclusive for the Fairweather store. Daniel Hechter Barbie wears a red top with the DH Sport logo, black leggings, and white tennis shoes. She comes with black sunglasses and a DH Sport nylon carry bag. **$25.00.**

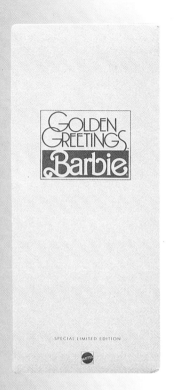

F.A.O. Schwarz 1989 **Golden Greetings Barbie** is F.A.O. Schwarz's first exclusive Barbie doll. The store, named for co-founder Frederick August Otto Schwarz, opened in 1862 and released its first catalog in 1876; it sold Barbie dolls since her 1959 debut. The F.A.O. Schwarz advertising for this doll reads, "Turning 30 this year, Barbie's ready to celebrate with a gala night on the town." She wears a golden gown with tulle overskirt for this occasion. She originally retailed for $45.00. **$60.00.**

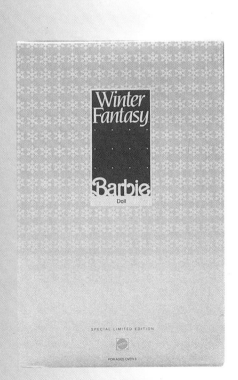

F.A.O. Schwarz 1990 **Winter Fantasy Barbie**, originally sold for $58.00, wears a blue velveteen gown with white faux fur trim, muff, and ornamental headpiece. In 1989 Mattel began changing Barbie doll's earrings from clear plastic with a "diamond" to painted metallic-looking earrings. Red and blue earrings stained some dolls' ears — known examples are the UNICEF dolls wearing blue earrings, the 1989 Happy Holidays Barbie with red earrings, and this Winter Fantasy Barbie with blue earrings. **$75.00.**

F.A.O. Schwarz 1990 **Winter Fantasy Barbie Replacement Head** was mailed to customers who complained about the earrings. The head has the hair ornament in her hair, but the replacement doll's earrings are silver. **$20.00.**

F.A.O. Schwarz 1991 **Night Sensation Barbie**, originally sold for $65.00, wears a black taffeta gown with pink ruffled bodice. She has a silver hangtag that reads, "Special Limited Edition F.A.O. Schwarz Fifth Avenue." Mattel used silver earrings on this doll. **$45.00.**

F.A.O. Schwarz 1992 **Madison Avenue Barbie** was created to commemorate the opening of the F.A.O. Schwarz Barbie Boutique on Madison Avenue in New York City. She has an upswept hairdo and wears a green swing coat over a hot pink crepe suit. She also has a pink teddy, sunglasses, and an F.A.O. Schwarz shopping bag. This doll originally sold for $65.00. **$90.00.**

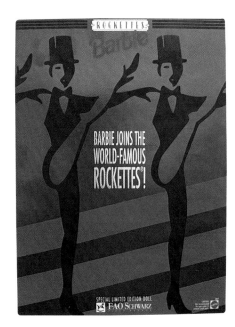

F.A.O. Schwarz 1992 **Barbie on Madison Deluxe Trunk** is a vinyl and plastic doll case with drawers and hangers. This trunk originally sold for $20.00, and all later cases sold for $25.00. **$17.00.**

F.A.O. Schwarz 1993 **Rockettes Barbie** portrays Barbie doll's premiere performance at New York's Radio City Music Hall on its 60th anniversary. Barbie has a bejeweled tux with tails, a top hat, and a cane, plus she has a dance skirt, gloves, and headpiece displayed on a paper doll. She originally sold for $65.00. **$65.00.**

F.A.O. Schwarz 1993 **Barbie Sea Holiday Cruise Ship** features a poolside area with smokestacks that convert to two plastic child-size cups, an umbrella that becomes a drinking straw, a working blender, a bedroom vanity, deck chairs, and accessories. This set sold for $140 in the 1993 F.A.O. Schwarz catalog. The same boat was repackaged as the Barbie Dream Boat in 1994 and retailed for $60.00 at most stores. **$45.00.**

F.A.O. Schwarz 1993 **Sea Holiday Ken** wears a white captain's uniform with golden lapels, a cap with golden brim, and a golden anchor necklace. He comes with blue swim trunks. **$20.00.**

F.A.O. Schwarz 1993 **Sea Holiday Midge** wears a yellow and pink two-piece swimsuit, long yellow skirt, yellow hat, and golden star and binoculars necklace. The Sea Holiday dolls and Cruise Ship were produced for the foreign market, but F.A.O. Schwarz and some doll shops carried the series exclusively in the U.S., although Sea Holiday Barbie was also shared with Toys "R" Us and in pictured in the Toys "R" Us section since she had greater distribution by that chain. **$22.00.**

F.A.O. Schwarz 1994 **Silver Screen Barbie** is advertised as a tribute to the legendary movie stars of the 1930s. Silver Screen Barbie doll has platinum blonde hair, a beauty mark, and rooted eyelashes, and she wears a silver lamé gown, gloves, and boa, which can be changed for her charmeuse teddy and robe. She originally sold for $70.00. **$77.00.**

F.A.O. Schwarz 1994 **Silver Screen Barbie Deluxe Trunk** is the same style as the Barbie on Madison Deluxe Trunk with a different handle design. **$18.00.**

F.A.O. Schwarz 1994 **Shopping Spree Barbie** wears a F.A.O. Schwarz Fifth Avenue logo sweatshirt, purple leggings, and a cap, and she carries an F.A.O. Schwarz shopping bag. Only the first edition has "F.A.O. Schwarz Souvenir Edition" printed on the box window. **$15.00.**

F.A.O. Schwarz 1995 **Shopping Spree Barbie** was sold through 1996. Later editions had no writing on the box window but had new warning information in the lower left box corner. These dolls sold for $24.99. **$15.00.**

F.A.O. Schwarz 1994 **Barbie's 3-in-1 House** transforms from a townhouse measuring 50" high x 22" wide to a traditional colonial or a modern ranch house. Even the furniture included with the house transforms — the sofa doubles as a working piano! This house sold for $189.00. **$75.00.**

F.A.O. Schwarz 1995 **Circus Star Barbie**, originally sold for $70.00, wears a colorful bodysuit, feathered headpiece, and a satin-lined black velvet cape. An umbrella is included to assist her on the high wire. **$55.00.**

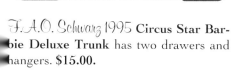

F.A.O. Schwarz 1995 **Circus Star Barbie Deluxe Trunk** has two drawers and hangers. **$15.00.**

F.A.O. Schwarz 1995 **Jeweled Splendor Barbie** is first in F.A.O. Schwarz's Signature Series Collection. She wears a black velvet gown with gold braid trim and jeweled bodice, and she has rooted eyelashes. She was released for $250.00. **$70.00.**

F.A.O. Schwarz 1995 **Barbie at FAO Take-Along** is listed as a travel caddie like the ones flight attendants use, with an extending handle and wheels. It holds six dolls and accessories and sold for $35.00. It features photos of Madison Avenue, Silver Screen, and Jeweled Splendor Barbie dolls on the case front. **$15.00.**

F.A.O. Schwarz 1996 **In-Line Skating Barbie** is a foreign-market doll sold in the U.S. primarily by F.A.O. Schwarz and JCPenney. She wears blue denim shorts, a white *B*-logo t-shirt, a multicolor shirt around her waist, elbow and knee pads, and skates. She carries a pink helmet. **$14.00.**

F.A.O. Schwarz 1996 **In-Line Skating Ken** is a foreign-market doll sold in the U.S. primarily by F.A.O. Schwarz and J.C. Penney. He has rooted brown hair and wears a yellow *K*-logo t-shirt, black denim shorts, a plaid shirt around his waist, elbow and knee pads, and skates. He has a red helmet. **$15.00.**

F.A.O. Schwarz 1996 **Statue of Liberty** Deluxe Trunk has the same construction as previous trunks. **$15.00.**

F.A.O. Schwarz 1996 **In-Line Skating Midge** is a foreign-market exclusive sold in the U.S. primarily by F.A.O. Schwarz for $24.99. She wears a purple *M*-logo t-shirt, striped shorts, a blue shirt around her waist, elbow and knee pads, and skates. She has a blue helmet. Note that all In-Line Skating dolls sold in the U.S. have a white warning label on the lower right box front; this warning was not required on dolls sold in other countries. **$18.00.**

F.A.O. Schwarz 1996 **Statue of Liberty Barbie**, originally sold for $75.00, is first in F.A.O. Schwarz's American Beauties Collection. This doll honors the 110th anniversary of the Statue of Liberty in her red, white, and blue gown with golden crown, torch, and book. The 1996 F.A.O. Schwarz Collectibles catalog incorrectly states that the doll's gown is sequined, although a child-size Statue of Liberty sequined costume was offered. **$65.00.**

F.A.O. Schwarz 1996 **Antique Rose Barbie**, originally sold for $250.00, is first in F.A.O. Schwarz's Floral Signature Collection and is an edition of 15,000. She wears an antique-tone satin ballgown embellished with fabric rosebuds and accented with rhinestones. She is scented with a floral bouquet. **$150.00.**

F.A.O. Schwarz 1997 **Lily Barbie**, second in the Floral Signature Collection and limited to 10,000 dolls, wears a white satin-faced silk organza gown featuring a silk lily with a golden beaded stamen. She originally sold for $199.00. **$130.00.**

F.A.O. Schwarz 1997 **Barbie at F.A.O.** wears an F.A.O. Schwarz sweatshirt, denim skirt, socks, and red shoes. She carries an F.A.O. Schwarz shopping bag. Her cap has a red brim, while the earlier Shopping Spree Barbie doll's cap has a blue brim. **$15.00.**

F.A.O. Schwarz 1997 **George Washington Barbie** is second in F.A.O. Schwarz's American Beauties Collection. She "honors the Father of our country in her own sartorial style," says the catalog. She wears a colonial coat and vest, ruffled jabot, and a plumed hat. Her hair is powder white. **$32.00.**

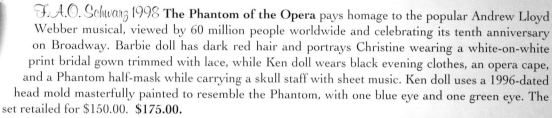

F.A.O. Schwarz 1998 **The Phantom of the Opera** pays homage to the popular Andrew Lloyd Webber musical, viewed by 60 million people worldwide and celebrating its tenth anniversary on Broadway. Barbie doll has dark red hair and portrays Christine wearing a white-on-white print bridal gown trimmed with lace, while Ken doll wears black evening clothes, an opera cape, and a Phantom half-mask while carrying a skull staff with sheet music. Ken doll uses a 1996-dated head mold masterfully painted to resemble the Phantom, with one blue eye and one green eye. The set retailed for $150.00. **$175.00.**

F.A.O. Schwarz 1998 **Summer in San Francisco Barbie**, blonde, is the premiere doll in the City Seasons Collection, a series featuring Barbie "in a fascinating city each season wearing a stunning outfit that epitomizes the beauty of that time of year." Summer in San Francisco Barbie was exclusive to F.A.O. Schwarz, but the remaining dolls in the collection were sold at most stores. She wears a crisp, yellow waffle pique suit and flower-trimmed straw hat, and she has short white gloves, sunglasses with blue lenses, and blue & white shoes. She carries a F.A.O. Schwarz shopping bag. The box reveals that, "after shopping and strolling past lovely Victorian houses, Barbie enjoys some seafood along with people-watching at Fisherman's Wharf." **$98.00.**

F.A.O. Schwarz 1998 **Summer in San Francisco Barbie**, redhead, is an edition of only 50 dolls raffled at F.A.O. Schwarz. The box window is signed by the designer, "All my Best/Robert Best/5/18/98." **$675.00.**

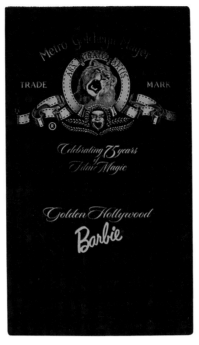

F.A.O. Schwarz 1999 **Golden Hollywood Barbie** (white or black) is first in this series which pays homage to the classic films of the Metro Goldwyn Mayer studio. The box front has the classic MGM tiger trademark with the caption, "Celebrating 75 years of Film Magic." Barbie doll wears a gold lamé gown that drapes in a classic style, and her upswept hairdo is accented by a black feathered ornament. Caucasian doll, **$50.00.** The black doll uses the Nichelle head mold; **$72.00.**

F.A.O. Schwarz 1999 **Le Papillon Barbie** is the first Bob Mackie Barbie doll sold as a retail store exclusive. Barbie wears a black gown with detailed butterfly wings and a headdress. She has pink hair. **$135.00.**

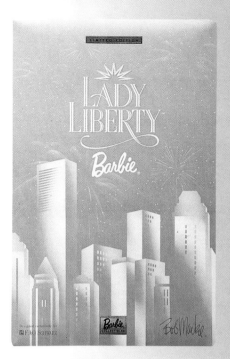

F.A.O. Schwarz 2000 **Lady Liberty Barbie**, an edition of 15,000 dolls, is called Bob Mackie's "millennium masterpiece" with her platinum hair, fitted metallic gown with embroidery, bugle beads, star sequin accents, and sweeping train. Her silver crown is attached to a full-length acrylic sweep of rhinestones and stars. **$195.00.**

F.A.O. Schwarz 2000 **F.A.O. Fun Barbie** (white or black) features Barbie doll with the block letters *F.A.O.* adorning her hair. She wears a blue corduroy jumper with striped shirt and is accompanied by the plush Patrick the Pup. **$22.00.**

F.A.O. Schwarz 2000 **Fashion Editor Barbie**, from the Barbie Fashion Model Collection, has a Silkstone body and wears a leopard-print skirt, a black turtleneck with a black wool boucle coat, black stockings, and high-heel Mary Janes. She has a black ribbon headband in her red hair and faux pearl stud earrings and a bracelet, and she carries a quilted bag and glasses. **$110.00.**

F.A.O. Schwarz 2000 **Mann's Chinese Theatre Barbie** (white or black) is wrapped in an elegant gown of black satin with a slim silhouette that sweeps into a sensational draped train. On the bodice, rhinestones mingle with elegant embroidery in Chinese red, fuchsia, and gold, reminiscent of the theatre's colors and design. A spectacular pouf of red satin on the side dramatically encircles her from the back, forming a tasseled stole that sweeps over one shoulder and under her arm. Golden jewelry set with Swarovski crystals, long black opera gloves, a bracelet, red shoes, and a red satin evening bag complete her ensemble. Mann's Chinese Theatre, completed in 1927, is a magnificent movie palace that attracts thousands of tourists to witness its astounding Chinese architecture and the famous celebrity footprints that cover the theatre's unique forecourt. Caucasian doll, **$48.00.** The black doll uses the Goddess of Africa head mold with light skin; **$60.00.**

84

F.A.O. Schwarz 2001 **Ravishing in Rouge Barbie**, from the Barbie Fashion Model Collection, has a Silkstone body and wears a crimson satin gown with a matching cape trimmed in faux sable, a black lace-trimmed petticoat, black gloves, pantyhose, golden and rhinestone jewelry, a floral brooch, and red shoes. She has brown hair and brown eyes. **$110.00.**

F.A.O. Schwarz 2002 **The Tango Barbie & Ken** features Barbie and Ken dolls as Latin dancers. Barbie wears a sultry red satin dress trimmed with red fringe and feathers, pink gloves, black fishnet pantyhose, a hair decoration, and black shoes. She has a new head mold, and the rose she holds in her mouth is removable. Ken wears black pinstriped pants with a matching vest, a red satin shirt with tie, and black shoes. He has rooted hair and debuts a new head mold. **$100.00.**

F.A.O. Schwarz 2002 **Chataine Barbie** is the F.A.O. exclusive brunette version of the Silkstone Barbie Fashion Model Collection blonde Capucine Barbie sold at most doll stores. She wears a taupe skirt with bustier, a jacket with golden accents, a faux fur stole, white pantyhose, and peach shoes. Only 600 brunettes were made. **$425.00.**

F.A.O. Schwarz 2002 **Fashion Designer Barbie** from the Barbie Fashion Model Collection has a Silkstone body and wears a red coat over a black tweed skirt and a red blouse with white buttons. She has a black scarf with white dots, black pantyhose, and black shoes, and a pair of golden scissors hangs on her chain necklace. Glasses and a sketch portfolio are included. **$95.00.**

F.A.O. Schwarz 2003 **Real Style Barbie** wears a blue floral dress with a pink boa. Glittery pants, a matching pink jacket, a lamé shirt, three purses, two pairs of shoes, two pairs of sunglasses, two hangers, and a shopping bag are included. **$18.00.**

F.A.O. Schwarz 2003 **Joyeux Barbie** is the first holiday doll from the Silkstone Barbie Fashion Model Collection. F.A.O. Schwarz offered 1,000 redheaded versions of the blonde Joyeux Barbie sold at most doll stores. She wears a white satin gown adorned with rhinestones, white gloves, white shoes, a flower hair ornament, and earrings. In Dec. 2003, F.A.O. Schwarz filed for chapter 11 bankruptcy, but flagship stores in New York and Las Vegas reopened in late 2004. **$320.00.**

FTD Florists 2000 **My Special Things Bouquet Barbie** has her blonde hair in pig tails, and she wears a short pink sundress with white floral designs. She was offered by FTD florists for $59.99 with a purple and pink resin purse container/vase holding a bouquet of flowers including a pale pink Gerbera Daisy, Alstromeria, lavender Daisy Poms, and white Larkspur. **$24.00.**

GAP 1996 **GAP Barbie** (white or black) wears GAP khakis, a denim jacket, and a GAP t-shirt. She carries a GAP cap, a GAP backpack, and a GAP shopping bag containing a pair of GAP jeans. Unique to her packaging is a carry cord on the box top. **$35.00.**

GAP 1997 **GAP Barbie & Kelly Giftset** (white or black) features Barbie doll with short hair and sister Kelly doll shopping at GAP KIDS for a size XX-small *GAP*-logo sweatshirt for Kelly (to match the larger one Barbie doll is wearing). Barbie doll also wears GAP jeans with white sneakers and carries black sunglasses. Kelly wears denim overalls, a red and white striped turtleneck, and sneakers. A GAP shopping bag and hanger are included. White set, **$38.00.** Black set, **$75.00.**

Gardaland 1996 **Gardaland Barbie** is exclusive to Italy's Gardaland amusement park. She wears a black top with satiny pink striped jacket with black cuffs, a matching skirt, golden star-shaped earrings, and pink gym shoes. She is packaged with a 4,000 lire coupon toward park admission. **$35.00.**

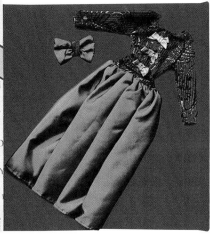

General Growth Management 1992 **Holiday Sensation Barbie Evening Gown Fashion** was a shopping mall promotional item. **$20.00.**

General Mills 1997 **Barbie Figurine** was available wearing either a pink party dress or a wedding dress in both Caucasian and African American versions. **$4.00 each.**

General Mills 1997 **Winter Dazzle Barbie** (white or black) wears a satiny pink coat-dress with faux fur collar and cuffs, white belt, white tights, and pink boots. A white faux-fur purse is included. She was available by mail for $9.99 plus three General Mills UPC symbols until January 31, 1998. Value City stores sold leftover dolls during the Christmas 1998 season for $8.99. **$14.00.**

Goldilocks Bakeshop 2001 **Goldilocks Kelly** has green eyes and wears a yellow and white gingham dress with a blue collar and cuffs and lacy white trim. She has a blue hairbow, white socks, and black shoes. She was created exclusively for the Goldilocks Bakeshop in the Philippines. **$24.00.**

Goldwin 1996 **Ellesse Barbie** is exclusive to the Goldwin stores of Japan. This series features the Ellesse Snow Wear Collection for Barbie — mix and match sportswear fashions that are comfortable and chic "with a splash of cheery color." Each doll in the collection comes with pink skis and ski poles, white ski boots, ski pants, and an Ellesse-logo hooded jacket in a variety of colors and styles. The dolls are re-dressed 1995 Winter Sports Barbie dolls. **$65.00 each.**

Grocery 1991 **Trail Blazin' Barbie** wears a white shirt with a red print skirt, matching hairbow and vest with fringe, and red boots. She is the first inexpensive exclusive shared by many U.S. grocery stores. **$14.00.**

Grocery 1992 **Pretty Hearts Barbie** uses the same fabrics as 1984's Loving You Barbie. There is no mention of Valentine's Day on her box, but that is the season in which she was marketed. **$15.00.**

Grocery 1992 **Sweet Spring Barbie** wears a multicolor spring dress with hot pink trim and a yellow straw hat. She carries a basket of flowers. **$12.00.**

Grocery 1992 **Party Premiere Barbie** wears a gold lamé and pink party dress. She was sold during the 1992 Christmas holiday season. **$15.00.**

Grocery 1993 **Spring Bouquet Barbie** wears a pastel gown with sheer sleeves. Her hair is very curly. **$12.00.**

Grocery 1993 **Red Romance Barbie** (left) wears a short pink dress with red trim and a red heart at the waist. Her box says, "For your own special sweetheart," but Valentine's Day is not mentioned. **$10.00.**

1993 **Sweetheart Barbie** (right) from Japan is Red Romance Barbie in Japanese packaging. The story on her box reveals Japanese attitudes about Barbie doll: "Sweetheart Barbie is wearing her favorite dress because she's going to spend the day with her best friends. They'll go shopping, have strawberry shortcake in a trendy café and then go to the beauty parlor to have their hair done for the party in the evening. Sweetheart Barbie is popular because she always knows of fun things to do!" **$16.00.**

Grocery 1993 **Back to School Barbie** wears a *B*-logo red, white, and blue sweater over a red plaid skirt, and she has a red hairbow. **$14.00.**

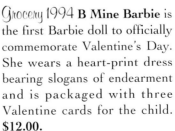

Grocery 1993 **Holiday Hostess Barbie** is dressed in traditional Santa's helper attire in "the happiest of holiday looks." She is the first in a series of annual holiday-themed grocery store dolls. **$18.00.**

Grocery 1994 **B Mine Barbie** is the first Barbie doll to officially commemorate Valentine's Day. She wears a heart-print dress bearing slogans of endearment and is packaged with three Valentine cards for the child. **$12.00.**

Barbie Fashion Greeting Card 1996 **I Love You!** uses the same material as B Mine Barbie doll. Collectors enjoy finding similarities like these among dolls and fashions. **$5.00.**

Barbie Fashion Greeting Card 1995 **Happy Easter!** uses the same egg-print dress material worn by Easter Fun Barbie. **$5.00.**

Grocery 1994 **Easter Fun Barbie** marks the first time the Easter holiday is used in a Barbie doll's name. She wears a white egg-print dress with pink trim and a hairbow, and she has stickers for decorating Easter eggs. **$11.00.**

Grocery 1994 **Holiday Dreams Barbie** is historically important since she is the first U.S. Barbie doll to specifically refer to the Christmas holiday; other dolls have used non-specific terms like "Happy Holidays," but this doll's box says, "Ready for Christmas morning!" She wears a red nightshirt and Santa cap and has a doll-size gift box. **$16.00.**

Grocery 1995 **Valentine Barbie** wears a red and white Cupid and heart-print dress with a choker and hair ribbon. She comes with a Barbie doll photo and frame. **$15.00.**

Barbie Fashion Greeting Card 1996 **I Love You!** uses the same material as Valentine Barbie doll's dress. **$5.00.**

Barbie Fashion Greeting Cards 1996 **Happy Easter!** in blue uses the same design as Easter Party Barbie. **$5.00.**

Grocery 1995 **Easter Party Barbie** wears a chick and egg-print dress. She comes with an Easter egg holder, dye, and stickers. **$10.00.**

Grocery 1995 **Easter Party Barbie** from Canada is the same as the U.S. doll except stickers in both English and French cover her box. **$14.00.**

Grocery 1995 **Caroling Fun Barbie** wears a red Christmas tree–print sweater, green leggings, and earmuffs, with white mittens hanging around her neck. **$14.00.**

Barbie Fashion Greeting Cards 1996 **Happy Easter!** in pink uses the same design as Easter Party Barbie. **$5.00.**

Grocery 1995 **Schooltime Fun Barbie** wears a blue school icons-print dress over a white shirt. She carries a red and yellow backpack. **$10.00.**

Grocery 1996 **Easter Basket Barbie** wears a blue bunny/Easter basket-print dress. She has a paper egg holder, cardboard basket, and painted white bunny. The bunny in this set was first used in a solid pink color with 1995's Kelly doll. **$12.00.**

Grocery 1996 **Valentine Sweetheart Barbie** wears a red and white heart pattern dress with white underskirt and cuffs. She comes with a picture frame and a photo of Ken. **$12.00.**

Grocery 1996 **Graduation Barbie** Store Display features Barbie doll's cap and diploma atop the Mattel logo, along with a "Class of '96" ribbon. The display is 59" tall. **$25.00.**

Grocery 1996 **Graduation Barbie** wears a dark blue graduation cap and gown and carries a blank diploma. She is historically important because she is the first Barbie doll sold as a graduate, and the year 1996 is featured on the box front. **$15.00.**

Grocery 1996 **Graduation Barbie Prototype/Sample** doll wears an *orange* gown with blue dots and a blue cap! **$75.00.**

Grocery 1996 **School Spirit Barbie** wears a trendy first day back-to-school outfit: a black shirt, an apple necklace, a red plaid double-belted miniskirt, red leggings, and a red headband. **$11.00.**

Grocery 1996 **Holiday Season Barbie** wears a Christmas tree–design knit sweater, a red skirt, a Santa cap, and black boots. She has white legs. **$14.00.**

Grocery 1996 **Holiday Season Barbie**, black, is the first African American grocery store exclusive doll. She uses the Christie head mold. **$15.00.**

Grocery 1997 **Birthday Surprise Barbie** (white or black) is the first birthday-themed grocery Barbie doll. She wears a bright pink gift-and-party-hat-print dress with a confetti bow. Surprise! The cardboard gift box at the doll's side contains...nothing! **$10.00.**

Grocery 1997 **Valentine Fun Barbie** (white or black) wears a pink heart-print miniskirt, a white top with heart designs, a matching cap, and a red belt with a silver heart-shaped buckle. Her heart-shaped purse opens, and she has Valentine stickers for the child. **$9.00.**

Grocery 1997 **Easter Barbie** (white or black) wears a pink and white print dress featuring bunnies, Easter eggs, flowers, and butterflies, and she has a pink hairbow. She carries a white plastic basket containing cloth flowers. **$9.00.**

Grocery 1997 **Graduation Barbie** (white or black) wears a purple cap and gown and a "CLASS OF 1997" banner. She carries a cardboard bouquet of flowers and a blank diploma. Notice the year is not printed on this year's Graduation Barbie doll's box front. **$12.00.**

Grocery 1997 **Back-to-School Barbie** (white or black) wears a denim skirt with a matching vest, a red belt with silver buckle, and a red apple-print t-shirt. She carries a book with seven lined pages. Two Barbie cut-out bookmarks are on the box back. **$9.00.**

Grocery 1997 **Holiday Treats Barbie** (white or black) wears a red dress with a white gingerbread man apron with green trim and a green hairband. **$10.00.**

 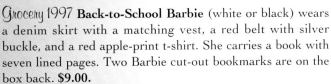  

Grocery 1997 **Holiday Treats Fiesta Barbie**, brunette, is supposed to be the Hispanic version of Holiday Treats Barbie, but instead of using an ethnic head mold, the doll has the SuperStar Barbie head mold with brown hair and green eyes, making her technically more a brunette version of Barbie than Hispanic. She had limited distribution. **$14.00.**

Grocery 1998 **Birthday Party Barbie** (white or black) wears a balloon-print white party dress with pink ribbons and a hairbow. **$9.00.**

Grocery 1998 **Birthday Party Barbie Store Display** has a sign that says, "Special Edition Birthday Barbie" with the Mattel logo on a gift box. **$22.00.**

Grocery 1998 **Coca-Cola Picnic Barbie** (white or black) wears red and white checked pants and a red T-shirt under a blue denim Coca-Cola logo vest. She comes with a Coca-Cola flying disc, a cardboard Coca-Cola cooler, and a Coca-Cola bottle. **$12.00.**

Grocery 1998 **Coca-Cola Picnic Barbie Store Display** features three large Coca-Cola bottles and the Mattel logo amidst bubbles. The display is 55" tall. **$25.00.**

Grocery 1998 **Valentine Barbie** (white or black) wears a satiny pink heart-print dress with a purple bow and a purple headband. She carries a red plastic heart-shaped candy box with a lift-off lid; this heart box was first used in gold tone with 1994's Locket Surprise Ken. Two cut-out Valentines are on the box back. **$10.00.**

Grocery 1998 **Color with Me Barbie** wears a pink sun-logo T-shirt, a matching skirt, a white vest, a yellow belt, and pink shoes. She carries a Barbie coloring book and has a fold-out box liner for the child to color. She comes with a sun ring for the child. **$10.00.**

Grocery 1998 **Easter Style Barbie** (white or black) wears a white dress featuring Easter eggs, hearts, and flowers, and she has a pink hat with a yellow flower on the brim. She carries a cardboard basket of flowers. Two cardboard egg holder cut-outs are on the box back. **$8.00.**

Grocery 1998 **Graduation Barbie** (white or black) wears a light blue cap and gown and a "CLASS OF 1998" banner. She carries a blank diploma and a cardboard bouquet of flowers. Besides the usual grocery and specialty outlets, Target stores sold the 1998 Graduation Barbie dolls. **$12.00.**

Grocery 1998 **Schooltime Fun Barbie** has brown eyes and wears a red corduroy top with an "ABC" logo, striped tights, and a red headband. She comes with an opening yellow plastic lunchbox. **$10.00.**

Grocery 1998 **Festive Season Barbie** wears a silver snowflake–design green dress with white faux fur collar and red pumps. She comes with a red cloth "Barbie" stocking. **$12.00.**

Grocery 1998 **Festive Season Barbie**, black, uses the Christie head mold with light skin, causing some collectors to refer to her as Hispanic or ethnic. **$14.00.**

Grocery 1999 **Make-A-Valentine Barbie** wears a pink and yellow heart-print skirt and a shiny pink top. She is the first grocery store doll to use the Mackie head mold. A "groovy" ring is included for the child. **$9.00.**

Grocery 1999 **Make-A-Valentine Barbie**, black, uses the Nichelle head mold with dark skin and pink lips. The doll's box liner folds out to become stencils for the child, with such phrases as "I Love You," "be mine," and "friends 4 ever," along with heart, flower, and lips stencils. **$10.00.**

Grocery 1999 **Easter Surprise Barbie** wears a satiny blue top with a bunny, egg, and flower-print purple skirt and purple shoes. The blue plastic egg contains cardboard candy, an egg, flowers, a bunny, and a chick. **$8.00.**

Grocery 1999 **Easter Surprise Barbie**, black, uses the Nichelle head mold. The doll's box liner contains punch-outs of Mr. Bunny and Ms. Chick and their wardrobes. **$10.00.**

Grocery 1999 **Barbie Exclusive Easter Doll** was packaged for Harmony Foods in Australia with four milk chocolate eggs. The doll is otherwise identical to Easter Surprise Barbie. The box design obstructs the doll's face. **$25.00.**

Grocery 1999 **Ballerina Dreams Barbie** wears an iridescent blue ballet costume with sparkly tulle skirt, sheer pantyhose, and blue ballet slippers. She has reddish-blonde hair tied with a ribbon and uses the Mackie head mold. Her box liner folds out to become a stage. **$14.00.**

Grocery 1999 **Breakfast with Barbie** is a soft-bodied doll wearing blue pajamas and pink slippers. She comes with a bowl, spoon, and cardboard box of Honey Nut Cheerios and a milk carton. Her box refers to the Got Milk? ad campaign. The first soft-bodied Barbie doll was 1994's Bedtime Barbie. **$15.00.**

Grocery 1999 **Breakfast with Barbie Got Milk? Poster** was a mail-away premium offered on the Breakfast with Barbie doll's box. **$8.00.**

Grocery 1999 **Coca-Cola Party Barbie** wears a red Coca-Cola outfit with white sleeves, white socks, and red sneakers with white laces. She carries a plush Coca-Cola polar bear. The package liner folds out into a play scene. The doll is pictured on the box back with short, chin-length hair. She was also sold at K-Mart. **$10.00.**

Grocery 1999 **Pearl Beach Barbie, Christie, and Teresa** Easter Baskets packaged these playine 1998 Pearl Beach dolls with a basket of candy. Walgreen's and Target also sold these dolls. **$15.00 each.**

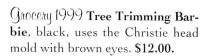

Grocery 1999 **Tree Trimming Barbie**, black, uses the Christie head mold with brown eyes. **$12.00.**

Grocery 1999 **Tree Trimming Barbie** has green eyes and wears green leggings and a sweater with a red headband. A cardboard Christmas tree with cardboard decorations is included. **$12.00.**

Grocery 2000 **Campbell's Alphabet Soup Barbie** wears a red and black Campbell's sweater and khaki pants. She carries a bottle of Campbell's tomato soup and a red bowl. She is the first grocery store doll to use the Generation Girl head mold. **$15.00.**

Grocery 2000 **Coca-Cola Splash Barbie** wears a red and white Coca-Cola top with floral-print red shorts, black sunglasses, and black sandals. An inflatable blue Coca-Cola inner tube, a white Coca-Cola t-shirt, a Coca-Cola bottle, and a Coca-Cola cooler are included. **$18.00.**

Grocery 2000 **Coca-Cola Splash Barbie**, black, uses the Christie head mold. **$24.00.**

Grocery 2000 **XXXOOO Barbie** wears a sparkly silver top covered with mirror-finish circles, a red ribbon belt with silver circle buckle, a satiny red skirt, white panty-hose, and red pumps. She has holographic strands in her hair. Her inner package backing has Valentine's punch outs. **$14.00.**

Grocery 2000 **XXXOOO Barbie,** black, uses the Asha head mold and has holographic strands in her black hair. **$12.00.**

Grocery 2000 **Easter Treats Barbie** from Japan uses the Mackie head mold with brown eyes and bangs, while the U.S. Caucasian Easter Treats Barbie uses the Mackie head mold with blue eyes. She carries a milk bottle and a yellow Easter basket holding two "live" bunnies! **$24.00.**

Grocery 2000 **Easter Treats Barbie,** black, uses the Nichelle head mold. **$14.00.**

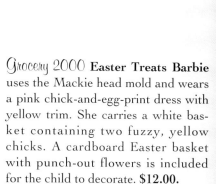

Grocery 2000 **Easter Treats Barbie** uses the Mackie head mold and wears a pink chick-and-egg-print dress with yellow trim. She carries a white basket containing two fuzzy, yellow chicks. A cardboard Easter basket with punch-out flowers is included for the child to decorate. **$12.00.**

Grocery 2000 **Millennium Grad Barbie** (white or black) was available in a black gown with a white collar or a blue gown with a white collar. A "2000 GRADUATE" banner is draped over their left shoulders, and each carries a diploma tied with a yellow ribbon. An illustrated eight-page cardboard yearbook featuring an illustrated tiger on the cover is also included. **$18.00 each.**

Grocery 2000 **Holiday Surprise Barbie** (white or black) has green eyes and wears a long green dress decorated with silver and red glitter ornament designs, and she has a glittery silver snowflake necklace. She carries a cardboard gift box containing a heart, teardrop, or oval charm necklace for the child. **$12.00.**

Grocery 2001 **Very Valentine Barbie** (white or black) wears a long, pink heart-print dress with a red jacket and a heart-design choker. **$10.00.**

Grocery 2001 **Flower Mania Barbie** (white or black) wears a satiny pink spring dress with net overskirt and net wrap. Her net overskirt holds plastic flowers and butterflies. A flower and butterfly charm necklace is included for the child. **$10.00.**

Grocery 2001 **Life Savers Barbie** (white or black) wears a colorful yellow, orange, green, and red Life Savers–print dress with lime green "plastic fantastic" jacket, earrings, and shoes. Three bracelets are included for the child. The standard Five Flavor Roll of Life Savers was introduced in 1935. **$15.00.**

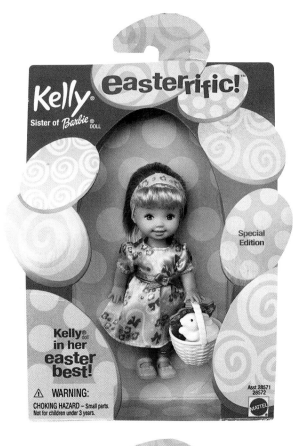

Grocery 2001 **Easterrific Kelly** is a grocery store series of Kelly dolls dressed in Easter-themed costumes, featuring Kelly as a Cheery Chick! Kelly as a Funny Bunny! (white or black), and Kelly in her Easter Best! **$9.00.**

Grocery 2001 **School Cool Barbie**, Christie, and Teresa dolls are packaged in vinyl carry cases. Each doll wears a floral-themed fashion with a scarf and striped hat. A plastic lunch box, two pencils, and a notepad are included. **$12.00.**

Grocery 2001 **Enchanted Halloween Barbie** (white or black) wears a long black dress with metallic orange glitter and dramatic flames, black boots, and a satiny black hat with orange brim. She has an orange streak in her hair. A cardboard Halloween treat bag is included. **$15.00.**

Grocery 2001 **Holiday Excitement Barbie** (white or black) wears a slim white dress covered with silver dots, sheer white sleeves with glitter and faux fur cuffs, a hat with faux fur trim, and silver boots. A holographic snowflake-design bracelet is included for the child. **$15.00.**

Grocery 2001 **Elf Kelly** (white or black) is the first grocery store Christmas-themed Kelly. The dolls may also be used as Christmas tree ornaments. An African American counterpart exists for each doll in this series. **$10.00.**

Grocery 2001 **Angel Desiree** or **Angel Lorena.** **$12.00.**

Grocery 2001 **Reindeer Chelsie** or **Reindeer Keeya.** **$15.00.**

111

Grocery 2001 **Angel Lorena/Elf Kelly/Snowman Tommy** 3-pack was sold at select stores. **$32.00.**

Grocery 2001 **Snowman Tommy** (white or black). **$15.00.**

Grocery 2002 **Oreo School Time Fun Barbie** wears a blue and white turtleneck shirt decorated with Oreo cookie designs, a blue vinyl vest, and a blue corduroy skirt with an Oreo pocket. She carries an Oreo purse. **$12.00.**

Grocery 2002 **Oreo School Time Fun Barbie** (black) is very hard to find. Her price has escalated due to sellers claiming that she was recalled because the term *Oreo* has been used as a racial epithet. **$25.00.**

Grocery 2002 **Easter Charm Barbie** wears a satiny blue dress with sheer lavender overskirt and shoes. She has very pale skin, and her lavender headband matches her earrings and striking lavender eyes. A plastic egg and a cardboard and ribbon bracelet is included for the child. **$11.00.**

Grocery 2002 **Valentine Wishes Barbie** (white or black) wears a pink heart-and-floral-design dress with glitter. Her cardboard heart-shaped purse is for carrying her doll-sized Valentine cards. **$10.00.**

Grocery 2002 **Fluffy Tail Kelly**, white, wears a purple and white plush bunny suit. Fluffy Tail brunette Kelly wears a yellow and white plush bunny suit. Fluffy Tail redhead Kelly wears a pink and white plush bunny suit. Each doll has a fluffy white tail that can be touched through the box back, and each doll carries an Easter basket containing a bunny. **$10.00** each. Fluffy Tail Kelly, black, wears a purple and white plush bunny suit. **$18.00.**

Grocery 2002 **Easter Charm Barbie**, black, has lavender eyes. **$11.00.**

113

Grocery 2002 **Class of 2002 Graduation Barbie** (white or black) was available in either a black or a white graduation gown. The dolls wear pink "CLASS OF 2002" banners over their right shoulders, and their hats have pink tassels. The same eight-page yearbook used with the Millennium Grad Barbie dolls is included with these Class of 2002 dolls. **$15.00 each.**

Grocery 2002 **Jell-O Fun Barbie** (white or black) wears a sleeveless white JELL-O tank top, pink JELL-O cube-design pants with silver buckle, and clear pink boots. A real box of Very Berry Barbie JELL-O and a *B* gelatin mold are included, along with a miniature measuring cup, bowl, spoon, and box of JELL-O for Barbie doll. **$14.00.**

Grocery 2002 **School Style Barbie, Christie, or Teresa** wears a plaid skirt with a turtleneck shirt and boots. She is packaged in a vinyl lunch box-style tote and comes with eyeglasses, two pencils, a purse, a doll-size pencil, note paper, scissors, a glue bottle, a folder, and a crayon box. **$12.00.**

Grocery 2002 **Halloween Glow Barbie** (white or black) wears a long purple gown with black swirl designs and black lace-up bodice adorned with glitter. She has a witch's hat, a Halloween treat bag, and a glow-in-the-dark hair extension. **$16.00.**

Grocery 2002 **Season's Sparkle Barbie** (white or black) wears a red holiday dress decorated with white and holographic snowflakes and a sheer red shawl. The child-size red ring with three interchangeable holographic snowflake sequins doubles as the doll's necklace. **$14.00.**

Grocery 2002 **Peppermint Kelly** (white or black) wears a satiny white gown with red peppermint stripes. Her hair has red streaks. **$8.00.**

Grocery 2002 **Caroling Lorena** carries a candle and wears a charming red Victorian caroling fashion with faux fur–trimmed cape. **$8.00.**

Grocery 2002 **Maura doll** is the Canadian version of Caroling Lorena doll. **$14.00.**

Grocery 2002 **Christmas Tree Chelsie or Deidre** is dressed like a Christmas tree, with a green cone-shaped hat with a star on top. **$10.00.**

Grocery 2002 **Poinsettia Jenny** is dressed like a Poinsettia, with her collar simulating the red petals of the flower. $10.00.

Grocery 2002 **Coca-Cola Noel Barbie**, exclusive to Canada, wears a sparkly red shirt featuring a large silver snowflake, white pants with the Coca-Cola logo and red bubble designs, and red boots. She holds a Coca-Cola bottle tied with a red ribbon and comes with three cardboard holiday ornaments. $25.00.

Grocery 2003 **Barnum's Animals Crackers Kelly and Friends** are dressed as animals representing the famous cookies. Each doll carries a tiny box of Barnum's Animals Crackers cookies. Kelly doll is an elephant, Jenny doll is a tiger, and Kayla doll is a lion. **$8.00 each**. Deidre doll is a lion; **$12.00**.

Grocery 2003 **X-O Valentine Barbie** (white or black) wears a pink and red dress with a red bodice featuring pink *X* and *O* letters and a pink and red striped skirt with glitter. A cardboard tic-tac-toe game is included. Her box back states that *X* stands for *kiss* and *O* stands for *hug*. **$10.00.**

Grocery 2003 **Easter Magic Barbie** (white or black) wears a knit pink top with a floral-print skirt, net over-skirt with glitter, and a satiny pink waist band. She comes with an empty pink plastic egg for the child. **$9.00.**

Grocery 2003 **Cute as a Bunny Kelly** wears a pink and white bunny suit, Cute as a Bunny Marisa wears a purple and yellow bunny suit, and Cute as a Bunny Melody wears a blue and white bunny suit. Each doll carries a plastic bunch of carrots. **$10.00 each.**

Grocery 2003 **My Graduation 2003 Barbie** (white or black) was available in either a black gown with a white collar or a purple gown with a white collar. A pink "GRADUATION 2003" banner drapes around her neck, and she carries a new eight-page yearbook with real photos and a miniature diploma in a cardboard folder. A cardboard "2003" charm is included for the child. **$12.00 each.**

Grocery 2003 **School Cool Barbie** (white or black) wears sparkly blue jeans and a *B* logo shirt. She is packaged inside a vinyl backpack and comes with a chalkboard key chain, chalk, a wipe-off sponge, and cardboard school accessories. **$14.00.**

Grocery 2003 **MASKerade Party Barbie** (white or black) has brown eyes and wears a cat costume with orange faux fur collar, cuffs, and hem, an attached cat tail, a cat ears' headband, and black boots. She carries a cardboard cat mask, and a matching child-size mask can be cut out of the box back. **$14.00.**

121

Grocery 2003 **Holiday Joy Barbie** (white or black) wears a lovely metallic green dress with sheer coat adorned with red and green glittery holly and berry designs. A snowflake holiday ornament is included for the child. **$14.00.**

Grocery 2003 **Santa Claus Kelly, Holiday Cheer Kerstie, Snow Sparkle Nia, or Nutcracker Tommy. $9.00 each.**

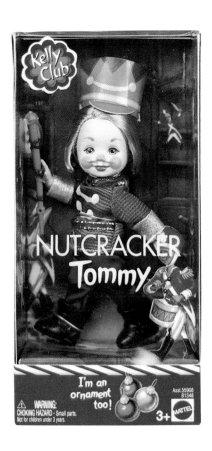

Grocery 2004 **My Scene Barbie**, exclusive to Canada, was released for Valentine's Day and is often called "Heartbreaker" Barbie, although that term is not on her box. Note the large heart design on her box window. She wears a pink top with a matching headband, navy blue pin-striped flared white pants, and boots. Her extra fashion is a white miniskirt with a pink and red floral top. A white "My Scene 33" purse and a cell phone are included. **$25.00.**

Grocery 2004 **My Scene Madison**, exclusive to Canada, was also released for Valentine's Day 2004. She wears jeans and a red, white, and black top with red floral headband. Her extra fashion is a red skirt with a white and black Chic tank shirt with pink mesh, and a purse and cell phone are included. **$25.00.**

Grocery 2004 **Valentine Romance Barbie** (white or black) wears a satiny pink dress with rose-print skirt. A golden locket containing the photos of Valentine Romance Barbie and 40th Anniversary Ken is included. **$12.00.**

Grocery 2004 **Easter Delights Barbie** (white or black) wears a lavender egg-print spring dress and carries a yellow Easter basket. An applicator is included to "paint" her bunny, chick, and jelly beans with cool water. **$10.00.**

123

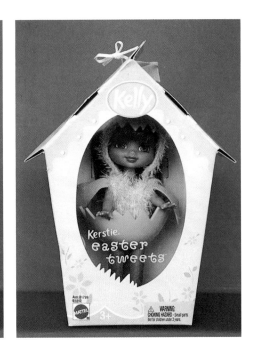

Grocery 2004 **Easter Tweets Kelly, Deidre, Kerstie, and Maria** have large heads and are dressed as chicks emerging from broken eggshells. **$9.00 each.**

Grocery 2004 **Easter Tweets Kelly Store Display** is designed to look like a giant bird house holding 16 rows of Easter Tweets Kelly and friends dolls on four levels. **$20.00.**

Grocery 2004 **My Graduation Barbie** was available in either a black or a pink graduation gown with a white collar and a "GRADUATE OF 2004" sash with tassels. She carries a "Class of 2004" graduation program and a single flower. Her box back reveals that the class colors are pink and black, and the class speaker is Barbie, who begins her speech, "Welcome, family and friends. Today is the beginning of our new dreams…" **$12.00.**

Grocery 2004 **My Graduation Barbie**, brunette, uses the Lea head mold with brown hair and green eyes. She wears the black graduation gown. **$18.00.**

Grocery 2004 **My Graduation Barbie**, black, wears the pink graduation gown. **$12.00.**

Grocery 2004 **My Graduation Barbie** Store Display features an illustration of graduation caps tossed in the air surrounding the pink "Barbie My Graduation 2004" banner. **$20.00.**

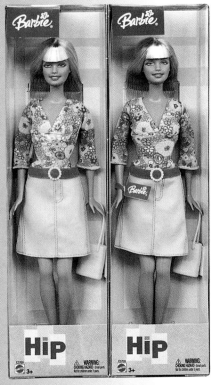

Grocery 2004 **Hip Barbie**, black, is the first retail store exclusive African American Barbie doll to use the Generation Girl Barbie head mold. **$16.00.**

Grocery 2004 **Hip Barbie**, blonde or brunette, wears a floral blouse with a belted skirt. The earliest dolls sold do not have the "Barbie" wrist tag. Wrist tags, used on most Barbie-family dolls sold from 1961 to 1972, were re-introduced on Barbie and friends dolls in 2004. **$10.00.**

Grocery 2004 **Rock Star Barbie** wears a pink "ROCK 'N ROLL" shirt with black net sleeves, jeans covered with "Barbie," a black belt with studs, and boots, and she comes with an extra fashion with plaid skirt, black shirt, red tights, and pink and black striped socks. Also included is a child-size CD case, two doll-size CDs with cases, a microphone, and a boom box. She debuts a noticeably-enlarged version of the Generation Girl Barbie head mold. **$18.00.**

Grocery 2004 **Special Wishes Barbie** wears a pink and purple dress decorated with flowers, butterflies, hearts, and the ponytail Barbie silhouette. She carries a cardboard gift box. A mini recording unit allows the purchaser to record a six-second message for the recipient of the doll. **$12.00.**

Grocery 2004 **Halloween Enchantress Barbie**, white or black, wears a black dress with silver star accents, a matching hat with orange brim, boots, and a star choker. **$14.00.**

Grocery 2004 **Holiday Party Kelly** holds a metallic gift box, **Winter Treat Becky** has a cup of cocoa, **Holiday Angel Deidre** has glittery wings and a halo, and **Mistletoe Kisses Tommy** holds mistletoe and has three kiss prints on his cheek. **$9.00 each.**

127

Grolier 1999 **Secret of the Three Teardrops Barbie** was available through Grolier's Barbie & Friends Book Club. She is dressed for a Venetian masquerade ball in a cream, gold, and blue gown with a gold-and-white teardrop pattern and three "sapphire" teardrop jewels on the bodice. She has powder-white hair, a beauty mark by her eye, and a blue mask with a feather. **$45.00.**

Grolier 2001 **The Front Window Barbie** wears an early 20th century satiny striped ivory and green gown with floral designs, purple cuffs, a purple collar with a "jewel," and a purple hat with a flower decoration. She carries a Susan B. Anthony lecture poster. According to her box story, Barbie doll began publishing her own newspaper, called *The Front Window*, that dealt with suffrage and the issues of the day. **$35.00.**

128

Hallmark 1994 **Victorian Elegance Barbie** was inspired by an antique London greeting card of 1872. She wears a skating costume with faux fur collar, cuffs, muff, and hat. She comes with ice skates and two miniature greeting cards. She originally cost $40.00. **$22.00.**

Hallmark 1995 **Holiday Memories Barbie** commemorates the 85th anniversary of Hallmark Cards. She was inspired by an antique greeting card and was originally designed as a brunette, but only blondes reached mass production since the brunette doll's dark hair blended with the faux fur collar on her white flocked coat. She has two miniature cards. **$20.00.**

Hallmark 1996 **Sweet Valentine Barbie** is first in Hallmark's Be My Valentine Collector Series. She wears an 1830s-style satiny pink gown with ribbon roses (reflecting the importance of the rose as a symbol of love) and has a nineteenth century Valentine card. **$20.00.**

Hallmark 1996 **Yuletide Romance Barbie** is dressed in an emerald green satiny gown with fitted velvet gold-trim jacket, as depicted in an early 1900s greeting card. She has red hair and green eyes and comes with two miniature greeting cards. **$20.00.**

Hallmark 1997 **Sentimental Valentine Barbie**, second in the Be My Valentine Collector Series, wears a crimson velvet lace-trimmed gown and drop-pearl headpiece, inspired by an 1830s Valentine card. **$22.00.**

Hallmark 1997 **Holiday Traditions Barbie** is first in Hallmark's Holiday Homecoming Collector Series. She wears a plum jacket with white faux fur cuffs and collar, a full skirt, and a velvety hat with feather. She wears a golden heart pin on her jacket and comes with a reproduction of an early 1900s greeting card. **$20.00.**

Hallmark 1998 **Fair Valentine Barbie** wears 1830s pink and blue daytime attire with a lacy white apron for strolling in the garden. This fashion is based on the painting *Portrait of a Woman* by Jacques-Louis David/Jean H. Fragonard. She is the third and final doll in the Be My Valentine series. **$22.00.**

Hallmark 1998 **Holiday Voyage Barbie**, second in the Holiday Homecoming Collector Series, is dressed for her 1920s luxury liner cruise as she returns from a Grand Tour of Europe. She wears a red and black dolman coat with faux fur trim, a red dropped-waist dress, a long strand of pearls, and a black cloche hat. She comes with a miniature "Greetings" card from the 1920s. Many collectors consider her the Titanic Barbie doll. **$30.00.**

Hallmark 1999 **Holiday Sensation Barbie** wears a lovely late 1940s green evening gown with a matching bolero jacket, and her hair is worn in a snood. A miniature Hallmark greeting card from the 1940s is included. She is the third and final doll in the Holiday Homecoming Collector Series. **$35.00.**

Hamleys 1996 **West End Barbie** from London features Barbie doll wearing a white sweatshirt with the Hamleys logo, red leggings, black boots, and a baseball cap. She carries a Hamleys shopping bag and was sold at Hamleys toy stores in England. Founded in 1760, Hamleys calls itself "the Finest Toyshop in the World." There were 20,000 dolls produced, retailing for $30.00 each U.S. **$18.00.**

Hard Rock Café 2003 **Hard Rock Café Barbie** was sold at Hard Rock Cafes for $69.99, and the price tag on her box identifies the doll as "Rock Star Barbie." Hard Rock Café Barbie wears a camisole, black "leather" pants, boots, a leopard-print coat with red trim, and blue sunglasses. She uses the Lara head mold and has a navel stud and belly tattoos. The Hard Rock Café first opened its doors in London, England, on June 14, 1971, with one guiding philosophy: "Love all — serve all!" Hard Rock Café now operates 100 cafes in over 30 countries. The box calls Barbie, "an international phenomenon headlining the hottest musical venue! A hip habitue with her own Hard Rock Café electric guitar, she always plays hard and shows her free spirit." **$200.00.**

Harley-Davidson 1997 **Harley-Davidson Barbie**, shared by Harley-Davidson dealerships and Toys "R" Us, was the most sought-after doll of 1997. Her box back says, "At last, two American icons meet: Barbie and Harley-Davidson. A vision of black faux leather, blonde hair and 'silver studs,' she's today's free-spirited woman." She wears a leather-look black motorcycle jacket with a working zipper and the H-D logo on back, matching pants with silvertone studs, a red leather-look vest with attached blue dickey, a black belt with a silver "H-D" buckle and chain, a black motorcycle cap, and biker boots; a helmet, sunglasses, and an "H-D" backpack are included. She has a beauty mark above her lips. **$265.00.**

Harley-Davidson 1998 **Harley-Davidson 95th Anniversary Barbie** is a one-of-a-kind doll with motorcycle, auctioned for $26,500 at an MDA benefit on June 13, 1998, in Milwaukee, Wisconsin. Barbie doll has genuine leather cap, jacket, vest, pants, and backpack, with sterling silver rivets and pins.

Harley-Davidson 1998 **Harley-Davidson Barbie** second edition has red hair and a beauty mark by her eye. She wears a distressed faux leather jacket with golden studs, denim jean shorts with chaps, a white t-shirt with the Harley-Davidson logo, a scarf, a hat with sunglasses, and boots. A Harley-Davidson satchel and helmet are included. **$75.00.**

Harley-Davidson 1999 **Harley-Davidson Barbie** third edition wears a white Harley-Davidson t-shirt, black pants, a black "leather" coat with working zipper, a red scarf, a back "leather" hat, and boots. A riding helmet and a "leather" backpack are included. **$68.00.**

Harley-Davidson 1999 **Harley-Davidson Ken** debuts a new closed-mouth head mold dated 1999. He has blue eyes, rooted brown hair in a ponytail, and a painted goatee. He wears a white "Harley-Davidson Motor Cycles" t-shirt, jeans, a black belt with a "Harley-Davidson" buckle, a black "leather" jacket with working zipper, and boots. A riding helmet and black sunglasses are included. **$85.00.**

Harley-Davidson 2000 **Harley-Davidson Barbie** fourth edition wears a "Harley-Davidson Motor Cycles" black and brown "leather" jacket with working zipper, a sleeveless "Harley-Davidson Motor Cycles" t-shirt, black "leather" pants with a chain belt, a scarf, boots, and sunglasses. A backpack and helmet are included. **$60.00.**

Harley-Daivdson 2000 **Harley-Davidson Ken** second edition has the 1999-dated Ken head with brown eyes and a painted beard. He is the only Ken to have painted chest hair. He wears a blue denim shirt with a black leatherette vest, a white "Harley-Davidson Motor Cycles" t-shirt, jeans, chaps, a key fob, boots, a bandanna, and goggles. A helmet is included. **$45.00.**

Harley-Davidson 2000 **Harley-Davidson Motor Cycle** is an authentic Harley-Davidson Fat Boy replica with stylish floorboards and die-cast chrome-look accents. **$50.00.**

Harley-Davidson 2001 **Harley-Davidson Barbie** fifth edition wears a black top with the Harley-Davidson Motor Cycles logo, black "leather" pants with flame designs on the legs; a black "leather" jacket with a working zipper, the Harley-Davidson name, and flames designs on the sleeves; boots, and motorcycle glasses. She comes with a helmet and a "leather" backpack. White, **$70.00**; black, **$100.00**.

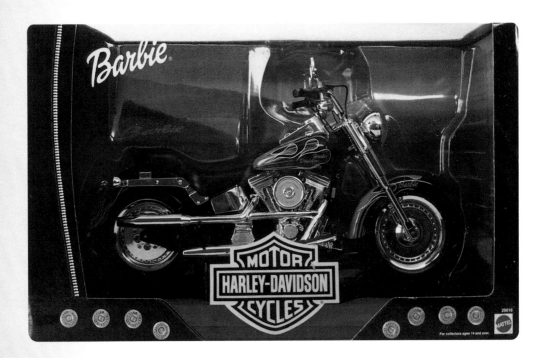

Harley-Davidson 2001 **Harley-Davidson Motor Cycle** is an authentic Harley-Davidson Fat Boy replica with a custom-painted Black Flames design, stylish floorboards, and die-cast chrome-look accents. The box states that Barbie doll makes her way along the curvy California coastline on this motorcycle. Unlike the previous Harley-Davidson Barbie releases, this motorcycle was not sold at Toys "R" Us and could only be purchased at Harley-Davidson dealerships. It is very hard to find. **$175.00**.

Harrods 1996 **Easy Chic Barbie,** from London, was designed by Luigi Avenoso, winner of the 1996 Barbie Fashion Awards Business/Professional category; his winning design is modeled by this doll. Easy Chic Barbie wears a black two-piece suit with white lining, short white gloves, black pumps, and a black and white marabou feather hat. A black handbag and sunglasses are included. Only 250 dolls were produced. **$395.00.**

Harvey Nichols 1995 **Barbie at Harvey Nichols** is an extremely-limited edition of only 250 dolls for the Harvey Nichols store in London. The doll is a blonde 35th Anniversary Barbie doll re-dressed in a black dress, pink silk shantung jacket, marabou-trimmed scarf, and patent leather belt. A purse, sunglasses, and shoes are included. The story on the box states that Barbie spent her 36th birthday in London. **$400.00.**

Hills 1990 **Evening Sparkle Barbie** wears an iridescent white minidress with a long sheer blue skirt/cape and boa. **$12.00.**

Hills 1989 **Party Lace Barbie** wears a short lavender gown with lace trim, and she has a tiny cloth purse. **$14.00.**

Hills 1991 **Midnight Rose Barbie** doll's gown becomes a short silver lamé minidress when the long pink tulle skirt is removed. **$14.00.**

Hills 1992 **Blue Elegance Barbie** doll's dress is versatile; it can be a blue lamé minidress or a full-length ballgown with dotted net overlay, and the long skirt can be worn as a cape. **$18.00.**

Hills 1994 **Polly Pocket Barbie** ties in with Mattel's popular tiny Polly Pocket dolls. Polly Pocket Barbie doll's floral-print dress has pockets in which to carry the two tiny dolls included in the package. **$12.00.**

Hills 1995 **Barbie & Champion** is a foreign-market set that was sold as an exclusive by several U.S. retailers. F.A.O. Schwarz listed her as Royal Rider Barbie in its catalog. The doll was sold individually in Europe as Horse Riding Barbie. **$25.00.**

Hills 1995 **Sea Pearl Mermaid Barbie** features Barbie doll wearing an iridescent top and a mermaid fish tail! She is one of the earliest Barbie dolls to use the popular Shani-mold arms. **$15.00.**

Hills 1996 **Teddy Fun Barbie** wears a teddy bear–print skirt, a white teddy bear–face t-shirt, a denim vest, and pink gymshoes. She carries a stuffed pink bear named Teddy. **$12.00.**

Hills 1997 **Hula Hoop Barbie** wears a pink and white striped skirt, a white Hula Hoop t-shirt, a satiny pink jacket, socks, and pink gym shoes. She holds a blue Hula Hoop around her waist. Hula Hoops were introduced one year before Barbie doll debuted. **$15.00.**

Hills 1998 **Sidewalk Chalk Barbie** wears a white t-shirt under short crayon-stripe print overalls with yellow pockets. Pink sidewalk chalk is included for the child. **$10.00.**

Home Shopping Club 1991 **Evening Flame Barbie** is the first U.S. vinyl Barbie doll to be individually numbered. She wears a bra, half slip, and pantyhose under her stunning red gown, and she has a gold foil wrist tag. **$45.00.**

Home Shopping Network 1999 **Golden Allure Barbie** wears a white dress with golden highlights and faux fur cuffs, shimmery pantyhose, a golden necklace, and metallic gold shoes. **$20.00.**

Home Shopping Network 2000 **Premiere Night Barbie** is ready for her solo performance in a theater production by Ken. She wears a dramatic purple gown with silver accents and a matching cape, with stunning silver and purple jewelry. She uses the Mackie head mold with platinum hair, violet eyes, and red lips. **$35.00.**

Hudson's Bay Company 1995 **City Style Barbie** commemorates the 325th anniversary of the Hudson's Bay Company in Canada, which was founded in 1670. She wears the same white suit used on the Classique City Style Barbie, but this doll has both the City Style shopping bag as well as a striped Hudson's Bay store bag. Only 3,000 dolls were produced by Mattel Canada and sold for $39.99, the same issue price for every Hudson's Bay exclusive. **$55.00.**

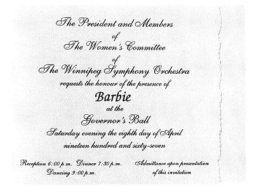

Hudson's Bay Company 1995 **Governor's Ball Barbie** is identical to JCPenney's Royal Enchantment Barbie, except Governor's Ball Barbie doll also comes with a replica invitation to the 1967 Governor's Ball held during Canada's centennial celebration. **$40.00.**

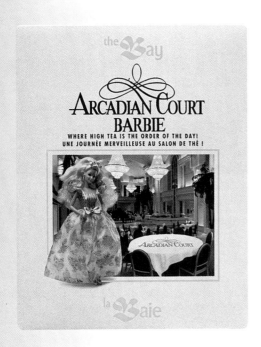

Hudson's Bay Company 1996 **Arcadian Court Barbie**, an edition of 2,900, is packaged with a doll-size Arcadian Court tablecloth, napkins, and a high tea menu. Arcadian Court Barbie doll lacks the golden necklace and long gold lamé waist bow ribbons of the Sears Ribbons & Roses Barbie doll, but she is otherwise identical. **$48.00.**

Hudson's Bay Company 1996 **School Spirit Barbie** repackages the U.S. grocery store School Spirit Barbie with an extra Hudson's Bay striped Point Blanket coat and hat. **$38.00.**

Hudson's Bay Company 1996 **Calvin Klein Jeans Barbie**, a Bloomingdale's exclusive in the U.S., was sold by the Hudson's Bay Company as their Canadian exclusive. A sticker on the box front covering the "Bloomingdale's Limited Edition" phrase is the only difference between the Hudson's Bay doll and the Bloomingdale's doll. **$30.00.**

Hudson's Bay Company 1997 **Barbie On Bay** repackages the Sam's Club Sweet Moments Barbie with an extra white sweater with pink trim; the sweater has the Barbie logo on the front and "Barbie on Bay" on the back. **$30.00.**

Hudson's Bay Company 1997 **Toyland Barbie** is a Hills Hula Hoop Barbie repackaged with a Hudson's Bay shopping bag and a pink teddy bear borrowed from Hills Teddy Fun Barbie. **$32.00.**

JCPenney 1988 **The Heart Family Baby Cousins Janet & Potty Chair and Nellie & Rocking Horse** was a set packaged exclusively for JCPenney. The Heart Family are Barbie doll's friends, and the Baby Cousins were sold individually in blue boxes at most stores. **$45.00.**

JCPenney 1988 **The Heart Family Baby Cousins Kenny & Tricycle and Honey & Highchair** was a set packaged exclusively for JCPenney. **$45.00.**

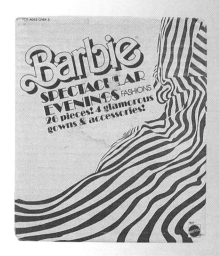

JCPenney 1988 **Barbie Spectacular Evenings Fashions** contains four glamorous gowns packaged in a white catalog box. The pink and silver gown uses 1987's Jewel Secrets Barbie doll's dress material in the style of 1983's Dream Date Barbie doll's gown. The white gown with silver dots is in the style of the Oscar de la Renta Collector Series IV fashion. **$28.00.**

JCPenney 1988 **Barbie Vacation Fun Fashions** contains eight different outfits made from past children's line materials including the Rockers, Jewel Secrets, California, and Magic Moves lines. **$24.00.**

145

JCPenney 1989 **Barbie Evening Fashions** is a 28-piece wardrobe set that makes five outfits. The four outfits from the 1988 Spectacular Evenings set were revamped for this 1989 edition. The purple and gray fashion is in the style of 1983's Dream Date Barbie doll's costume. The blue and silver dress appears to be a knee-length version of Oscar de la Renta's Series IV fashion. The red and white fashion is nearly identical to Target's 1989 Gold & Lace Barbie doll's ensemble. **$25.00.**

JCPenney 1989 **Barbie Casual Fashions** contains eight fashions (with an emphasis on denim and pastels) along with play accessories. **$20.00.**

JCPenney 1990 **Barbie Casual Wear Fashions** contains 23 pieces that can be used to make seven different outfits. **$20.00.**

JCPenney 1990 **Barbie Evening Fashions** contains a 14-piece wardrobe for five party looks. Notice the blue dress in the style of Sweet Roses Barbie doll's short pink dress and the iridescent dress with hat in the style of Brazilian Barbie doll's costume. **$22.00.**

JCPenney 1990 **Evening Elegance Barbie** begins the Evening Elegance Series of Barbie dolls. Packaged for the JCPenney catalog in sealed white mailing cartons, the doll wears a pink dress with silver lamé midriff and overskirt with either a silver dot pattern (left) or butterfly lace pattern (right). She cost $20.00 in the JCPenney catalog. **$26.00.**

JCPenney 1991 **Enchanted Evening Barbie**, second in the Evening Elegance Series, wears a multicolor metallic diamond-design coat with faux fur trim over a lavender gown with a faux fur hat with simulated amethyst. This is the most desirable of all the JCPenney Barbie dolls. JCPenney's Evening Elegance series of dolls retailed for $25.00 each from 1991 through 1995. **$36.00.**

JCPenney 1991 **Barbie Costume Ball Fashion 2-Pack** includes two transforming costumes with cardboard masks that allow Barbie doll to be a genie or a mermaid. Both fashions were sold separately at most stores. **$20.00.**

JCPenney 1991 **Barbie Private Collection Fashion 2-Pack** contains two foreign-market fashions sold exclusively in the U.S. by JCPenney. **$28.00.**

JCPenney 1992 **Evening Sensation Barbie**, third in the Evening Elegance Series, wears a velvety blue gown with a jewel-tone cape and matching hair decoration. **$27.00.**

JCPenney 1992 **Barbie & Ken United Colors of Benetton Fashion 2-Pack** contains a floral-design skirt and jacket fashion with shirt, leggings, and a scarf for Barbie, and a racing fashion for Ken. **$20.00.**

JCPenney 1992 **Snap 'N Play Barbie Deluxe Gift Set** uses Teen Talk Barbie doll's fuller face mold designed to make Barbie doll look like a teenager. This set was also sold by Sears and Toys "R" Us. She is the first Barbie doll to have plastic snap-on clothing, which combines in five complete outfit combinations. **$22.00.**

JCPenney 1993 **Barbie Café** from Italy was sold exclusively in the U.S. by JCPenney for $29.99. The café includes a cappuccino machine and color-change dishes. **$30.00.**

JCPenney 1993 **Caboodles Barbie** with Child-Size Caboodles Case uses a children's line Caboodles Barbie, packaged in a brown shipping box, with a children's pink exclusive Caboodles carry case. The doll has real lipstick, blush, fragrance, and her own doll-size Caboodles case. **$20.00.**

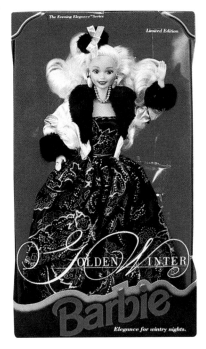

JCPenney 1993 **Golden Winter Barbie**, fourth in the Evening Elegance Series, wears a dramatic black dress with a gold, blue and red pattern, a gold lamé jacket with black faux fur trim, and a hair decoration. **$25.00.**

JCPenney 1994 **Happy Meal Stacie and Whitney Gift Set** contains the children's line Happy Meal Stacie and her friend Happy Meal Whitney, repackaged in a white shipping box. Their Happy Meal boxes contain real jewelry for the child. **$24.00.**

JCPenney 1995 **Barbie Deluxe Fashion Doll Trunk** carry case has quilted sides and holds six dolls. **$15.00.**

JCPenney 1994 **Night Dazzle Barbie,** fifth in the Evening Elegance Series, wears a red satin dress with a white and black flocked overskirt and red hairbow. She is one of a very few exclusive Barbie dolls to be made in two different countries, China and Malaysia, and there are slight differences between the dolls from each country. **$24.00.**

JCPenney 1993 **Paint 'N Dazzle Barbie Fashion Pak** includes four Paint 'N Dazzle fashions with Tulip fabric paint and dress decorations. These four fashions were sold separately in most stores. **$35.00.**

JCPenney 1995 **Polly Pocket Stacie & Polly Pocket Locket Giftset** consists of the children's line Polly Pocket Stacie repackaged with a Polly Pocket Locket set on a blister card. The extra locket set included varies from set to set, even though the box says a Baby and Blanket Locket is included. **$15.00.**

JCPenney 1995 **Royal Enchantment Barbie**, sixth in the Evening Elegance Series, is called Royal Elegance Barbie in the JCPenney catalog. She wears a woven metallic green overskirt and bodice with golden bows, a gold floral print on cream satin underskirt, and green opera gloves. **$20.00.**

JCPenney 1995 **Solo in the Spotlight Display Case** was shown in the Penney's catalog with a silver top and bottom with red stickers, but early cases were black with red stickers. **$10.00.**

JCPenney 1995 **Solo in the Spotlight Display Case** appeared later with a silver top and bottom with red stickers as featured in the Penney's catalog photo. **$10.00.**

JCPenney 1996 **Barbie Foam 'n Color Doll & Hair Color Gift Set** is a repackaged children's line Foam 'n Color Barbie in a pink swimsuit with extra hair coloring solution. **$15.00.**

JCPenney 1996 **The Original Arizona Jean Company Barbie** is dressed in an Arizona Jean Co. outfit with blue denim jeans, a white t-shirt, and red denim jacket, all adorned with the Arizona Jean Co. logo. She carries an Original Arizona Jean Company backpack. **$14.00.**

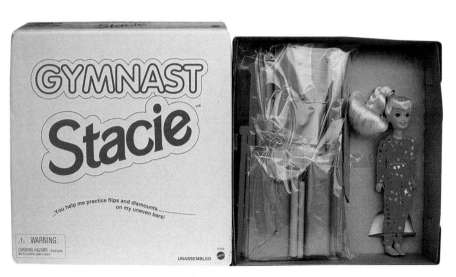

JCPenney 1996 **Gymnast Stacie** was sold in a white mailing box and comes with extra gymnastics equipment taken from the children's line Gymnast series — she has Gymnast Janet's vault, Gymnast Whitney's balance beam, and her own uneven bars. Gymnast Stacie has a new, more poseable body. **$18.00.**

JCPenney 1996 **Winter Renaissance Barbie**, seventh in the Evening Elegance Series, wears a blue bodice and skirt flocked with a classic snowflake design and complemented with a light blue jacket trimmed with imitation fur. The issue price of $35.00 is $10.00 higher than the previous seven Evening Elegance Series dolls. **$20.00.**

JCPenney 1997 **Evening Majesty Barbie,** eighth in the Evening Elegance Series, wears a golden satin bodice trimmed with black imitation fur and a royal lavender satin skirt with golden inset. The JCPenney catalog states, "The music will stop when she enters the ball." **$25.00.**

JCPenney 1997 **The Original Arizona Jean Company Barbie** wears a plaid shirt, a red skirt, an Arizona Jean Company blue denim vest, black tights, and black shoes. She carries an Arizona Jean Company denim backpack. Surplus 1996 and 1997 Arizona Jean Company Barbie dolls were found for $9.99 at the Hills and Meijer stores in early 1999, a surprising fact since neither store sold Arizona Jean Company clothing. **$18.00.**

JCPenney 1998 **Evening Enchantment Barbie,** ninth and last in the Evening Elegance Series, is the only doll in that series to use the Mackie head mold. She wears a glittery red and orange chiffon gown with feathers on the bodice and a train-length skirt. **$26.00.**

154

JCPenney 1998 **The Original Arizona Jean Company Barbie** wears khaki shortalls with a striped V-neck t-shirt and socks. "The Original Arizona Jean Company" logo is on her extra red sweatshirt and backpack. **$20.00.**

JCPenney 1998 **Barbie & Walking Beauty Gift Set** packages the playline Horse Riding Barbie with her horse, Walking Beauty, which makes kissing and neighing sounds. **$35.00.**

JCPenney 1999 **My Wardrobe Barbie** is an exclusive shared with Sears and Service Merchandise. She uses the Mackie head mold and has a pink, silver, and white mix-and-match wardrobe. **$20.00.**

JCPenney 2000 **Glamorama Barbie** uses the Generation Girl Barbie head mold. Barbie doll's boutique with counter, cash register, and mix and match clothing and accessories are included. This set was shared with Sears and several other retailers. **$22.00.**

Japan Air Lines 1997 **JAL Barbie** was sold aboard domestic Japanese Air Lines flights only and is limited to 30,000 dolls. JAL Barbie wears a navy blue stewardess fashion with golden buttons, a white shirt with bowtie, sheer black stockings, and a blue hairbow. She comes with a suit vest, a map-print apron, a leather-look flight bag, a Japanese passport, and a plastic serving cart with food and beverages. **$150.00.**

JCPenney 2003 **Style Barbie**, blonde or brunette, is the first Barbie doll truly exclusive to JCPenney since 1998, although she is merely a foreign-market Style Barbie with the addition of a JCPenney exclusive sticker on her box window. She uses the Generation Girl Barbie head mold, and she wears a blue floral-print dress and blue shoes. A necklace matching Barbie doll's dress is included for the child. **$15.00.**

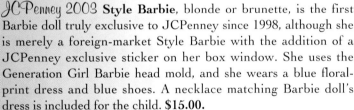

Jollibee 1995 **Jollibee Barbie** #62123 is one of four dolls created for the Jollibee restaurants in the Philippines. The box front shows Jollibee's mascots, and the box sides illustrate Jollibee's fare: the Yum-burger, french fries, peach-mango pie, the Jolly Twirl (ice cream cone), and Coca-Cola. This doll has blonde hair pulled to the top of her head. She wears a hot pink shirt and a blue denim skirt. **$45.00.**

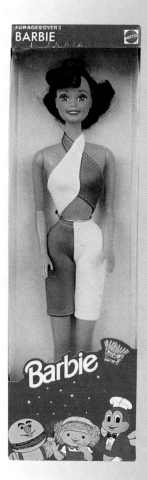

Jollibee 1995 **Jollibee Barbie** #62124 wears a red and white striped top and a white skirt with red dots. **$45.00.**

Jollibee 1995 **Jollibee Barbie** #62125 is the only brown-eyed brunette in the series. She wears a blue and yellow playsuit. **$45.00.**

Jollibee 1995 **Jollibee Barbie** #62126 wears a satiny blue bodice with a lacy floral-design white skirt. **$45.00.**

Kastner & Ohler 1998 **Kastner & Ohler Barbie** cele-brates the 125th anniversary of the Kastner & Ohler store of Austria in a lovely 19th century fashion with matching hat adorned with flowers. Barbie doll carries a parasol and has a hang tag that read, "Fashion Dreams by E. Stelzer Vienna" on the front, with the doll's individual number on the reverse. She is a re-dressed Chilean Barbie. **$275.00.**

Kay-Bee 1994 **3 Looks Barbie** is an international-market doll sold exclu-sively in the U.S. by Kay Bee. Her silver lamé and pink ensemble transforms from a bathing suit to a ballerina costume to a ball gown. **$12.00.**

Kay-Bee 1995 **The Flintstones Funwear** Fashions are four casual ensembles featuring Dino, Fred, Pebbles, and "Yabba-Dabba-Doo!" **$8.00 each.**

Kay-Bee 1994 **The Flintstones Funwear Gift Set,** available in two assortments, includes four casual ensembles for Barbie with only two pairs of pumps. Notice that one of the gift sets includes three of the four separately-carded Flintstones Funwear Fashions. **$12.00 each.**

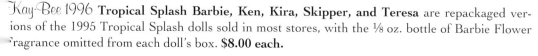

Kay-Bee 1996 **Tropical Splash Barbie, Ken, Kira, Skipper, and Teresa** are repackaged versions of the 1995 Tropical Splash dolls sold in most stores, with the ⅛ oz. bottle of Barbie Flower Fragrance omitted from each doll's box. **$8.00 each.**

Kay-Bee 1997 **Chic Barbie** is a foreign-market doll sold exclusively in the U.S. by Kay-Bee. She wears a blue sundress with white floral designs and a satiny pink jacket. **$10.00.**

Kay-Bee 1997 **Fantasy Ball Barbie** is attired for the ball in a gown of metallic burgundy, turquoise, and pink, with golden accents and pink satin ribbons and a sheer pink wrap. She has a lovely pale skin tone with violet eyes. **$15.00.**

Kay-Bee 1997 **Fantasy Ball Barbie**, black, had limited distribution. She uses the Christie head mold with light skin tone. **$18.00.**

Kay-Bee 1997 **Fantasy Ball Barbie Stamper** was a free gift to customers who pre-ordered the Nascar Barbie doll at Kay-Bee stores. The figurine is a miniature plastic version of Fantasy Ball Barbie doll and stamps the doll's portrait. **$5.00.**

Kay-Bee 1997 **My First Barbie** (white or Hispanic) is a repackaged 1996 My First Tea Party Barbie with her tea service omitted. **$10.00.**

Kay-Bee 1997 **Barbie Style** is a foreign-market doll sold exclusively in the U.S. by Kay-Bee. She wears a white turtleneck with red stripes on the sleeves and a denim overalls-style dress. **$10.00.**

Kay-Bee 1998 **Barbie Style** is a foreign-market doll sold exclusively in the U.S. by Kay-Bee. She wears a denim dress with red, silver, and black heart-shaped pockets and matching lapels. **$10.00.**

Kay-Bee 1998 **Chic Barbie** is a foreign-market doll sold exclusively in the U.S. by Kay-Bee. Her dress has a blue bodice and her skirt has pink and white squares intersected with yellow crosses. **$9.00.**

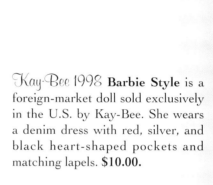

Kay-Bee 1998 **Children's Day Barbie** is a European-market doll celebrating the Children's Day holiday. Kay-Bee acquired surplus dolls and sold them in the U.S., with the addition of "WARNING" stickers on their box windows. **$10.00.**

161

Kay-Bee 1998 **Fashion Avenue Barbie** wears a turquoise blue floral-print gown with gloves, a ribbon choker, and black shoes. She comes with a miniature party invitation. **$15.00.**

Kay-Bee 1998 **Starlight Carousel Barbie** wears a fanciful gown with shimmering blue bodice and metallic-look silver gown with pastel stripes. **$15.00.**

Kay-Bee 1998 **Winter Rhapsody Barbie**, the 1997 Avon exclusive, was found at Kay-Bee Toys with a "Winter Rhapsody Barbie" sticker with snowflake designs adhered to the box lid to cover the words, "AN AVON EXCLUSIVE…AVON." **$20.00.**

KB 1999 **Barbie Style** (blonde) is a foreign-market doll sold exclusively in the U.S. by KB. She wears a red floral-design skirt and matching vest with black collar. The KB version uses the SuperStar Barbie head mold, while the European version has the Mackie head mold. **$12.00.**

KB 1999 **Barbie Style** (brunette or redhead) is among the last Barbie dolls sold in the U.S. with the SuperStar Barbie head mold. The brunette has brown eyes and wears a yellow floral top with a black skirt. The redhead has green eyes and wears a green floral top with black slacks. **$12.00.**

KB 1999 **Bath Boutique Barbie** (white or black) is a repackaged version of the 1998 Bath Boutique Barbie sold at most stores, except the KB dolls have slimmer, cardboard boxes instead of the plastic carry case boxes the earlier dolls were sold inside, and the KB dolls omit Barbie doll's slippers, bath accessories, and washcloth. **$10.00.**

KB 1999 **Cool Sitter Teen Skipper** was shrink-wrapped with two Li'l Friends of Shelly for sale in the U.K., but excess sets were sold in U.S. KB Toys stores. **$20.00.**

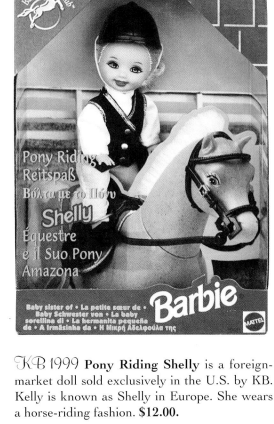

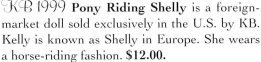

𝒦ℬ 1999 **Hot Wheels Racing KB Toys Barbie Hot Wheels Car**, an edition of 50,000, is a special KB premium sent by mail in spring 1999 to purchasers of the NASCAR 50th Anniversary Barbie. "Barbie Collectibles" is on the car's trunk, and the number "44" is on the hood. **$10.00.**

𝒦ℬ 1999 **Pony Riding Shelly** is a foreign-market doll sold exclusively in the U.S. by KB. Kelly is known as Shelly in Europe. She wears a horse-riding fashion. **$12.00.**

𝒦ℬ 1999 **Riviera Barbie** is a foreign-market doll sold exclusively in the U.S. by KB. She has the SuperStar Barbie head with short hair, and she wears a blue sundress with white daisy designs. **$9.00.**

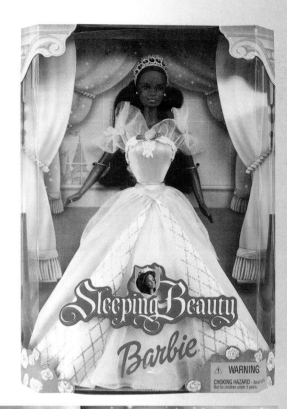

KB 1999 **Sleeping Beauty Barbie** is a less elaborate version of the 1998 Sleeping Beauty Barbie sold at most stores. She uses the Mackie head mold, with the closing-eyes feature eliminated and her musical pillow omitted. **$20.00.**

Her eyes magically open and close!

KB 1999 **Sleeping Beauty Barbie**, black, was sold at KB with the Asha head mold. The 1998 Sleeping Beauty black Barbie with the sleep-eyes feature and the musical pillow is shown for comparison. **$20.00.**

KB 1999 **Weekend Barbie** is a foreign-market doll sold exclusively in the U.S. by KB. She has the Superstar Barbie head with golden blonde hair, and she wears a pink shirt with floral-design white bib shortalls. **$9.00.**

KB 1999 Barbie Deluxe Trunk Carry Case features a photo of a blonde Starlight Carousel Barbie on the case front. No blonde Starlight Carousel Barbie dolls were ever sold in stores. **$15.00.**

KB 1999 KB Toys Toy Store is similar to the Barbie Toy Store sold at most stores, but this set is customized for KB with a KB Toys sign, a KB shopping cart, and KB shopping bags. Notice that Kay-Bee abbreviated its name to KB. **$15.00.**

KB 2000 Butterfly Art Barbie was repackaged for KB in a slimmer box than used for the 1999 Butterfly Art Barbie sold in most stores. The KB version has straight hair and a longer denim skirt, while the original has crimped hair and a shorter denim skirt with fringe. **$10.00.**

166

    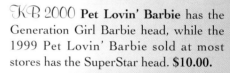

$\mathcal{KB}$ 2000 **Flower Shop Barbie** wears a ribbed pink top with a floral skirt and a green vinyl apron. $12.00. The U.S. doll sold at KB uses the Generation Girl Barbie head mold with blue eyes, while the Japanese version has the SuperStar Barbie head mold with brown eyes. $24.00.

$\mathcal{KB}$ 2000 **Pet Lovin' Barbie** has the Generation Girl Barbie head, while the 1999 Pet Lovin' Barbie sold at most stores has the SuperStar head. $10.00.

$\mathcal{KB}$ 2000 **Rapunzel Barbie** (white or black) is a revamped version of the popular 1998 Rapunzel Barbie sold at most stores. The KB version has shorter hair, a less-elaborate gown featuring a dark pink dress with gold-speckled sheer pink overskirt, and a pink tiara, while the 1998 doll sold elsewhere has a pale pink satiny gown with golden criss-cross bodice and golden collar, and a magnificent golden crown with "jewels" rests atop her head. **$18.00.**

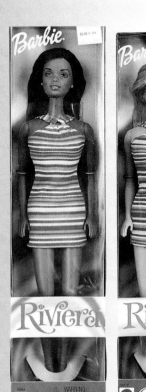

KB 2000 **Riviera Barbie** (white or black) wears a purple-striped dress. **$9.00.**

KB 2001 **Happenin' Hair Barbie, Christie, and Teresa** were repackaged for KB in slimmer boxes with simplified hairstyles lacking the bangs and pigtails of the 2000 Happenin' Hair dolls and using straight arms instead of the bending arms of the originals. The KB dolls' jeans also lack the pockets found on the earlier dolls' jeans, and the dolls do not have necklaces. **$10.00 each.**

$\mathcal{KB}$ 2001 **Hollywood Nails Barbie or Christie** is a repackaged version of the 2000 Hollywood Nails doll. The KB versions have simplified hairstyles lacking the streaks of the originals, and the scarf, fuzzy skirt, purse, nail glitter, and shaker were omitted. **$11.00.**

$\mathcal{KB}$ 2001 **Horse Riding Barbie** wears cream-colored ribbed pants with a matching turtleneck, brown boots, a blue jacket, and a black riding hat. She was also sold at several other retailers. **$11.00.**

𝒦ℬ 2001 **Pajama Fun Skipper and Nikki** are repackaged versions of the 2000 Pajama Fun dolls sold at most stores, except their boxes are slimmer and their tote bags/sleeping bags and inflatable pillows have been omitted. Nikki uses the Teen Skipper head mold. **$12.00 each.**

𝒦ℬ 2001 **Pet Doctor On The Go!** vehicle is an SUV with an examination table with shower head and hose that pops out of the back of the vehicle. A puppy, milk bottle, dog food dish, and medical supplies are included. **$15.00.**

𝒦ℬ 2001 **Pet Doctor Barbie** has green eyes and wears a red shirt, black Capri pants, a white doctor's coat with a "Barbie Pet Doctor" badge, black shoes, and a stethoscope. A dog, an ear checker, a watch, a clipboard, a bowl, Beggin' Strips, and a brush are included. The Veterinarian Barbie magazine cover included promotes the story "The Barking Blues." **$15.00.**

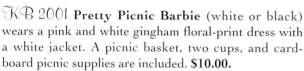

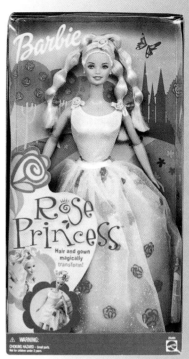

$\mathcal{KB}$ 2001 **Pretty Picnic Barbie** (white or black) wears a pink and white gingham floral-print dress with a white jacket. A picnic basket, two cups, and cardboard picnic supplies are included. **$10.00.**

$\mathcal{KB}$ 2001 **Rose Princess Barbie** is a repackaged version of the Rose Princess Barbie sold in most stores. The KB version's costume was altered to omit the rosettes on Barbie doll's headband and shoulder straps, replacing them with a single rosette on her bodice; this version's sheer floral overskirt lacks the glitter of the earlier doll. The *Rose Princess* name on the doll's box window is pink on the regular version and white on the KB version, and the inset box photo was altered for KB. **$12.00.**

$\mathcal{KB}$ 2001 **Teacher Barbie** (white or black) wears a blue dress with white collar and cuffs, a school-themed print black vest, blue eyeglasses, and black shoes. A school room backdrop, chalkboard, chalk, books, pencils, and an eraser are included. **$15.00.**

KB 2001 **Time For Tea Barbie** (white or black) wears a satiny red dress and comes with a pink tea set. The black doll uses the Christie head mold. **$10.00.**

KB 2002 **Baking Fun Barbie** wears a pink apron over her floral dress and comes with a mixer that really spins, a measuring cup, a mixing bowl, a cookie sheet, a whisk, and tiny recipe cards for Barbie. **$12.00.**

KB 2002 **Cool Clips Barbie, Christie, and Teresa** were repackaged for KB in slimmer boxes than the 2000 Cool Clips dolls sold in most stores, and their dresses lack the holographic dots covering the original dolls' dresses. They also each have shorter hair, three fewer flowers on their dresses, two fewer color-change hair extensions, no necklace, and three fewer hair gems. **$12.00 each.**

𝒦𝐵 2002 **Hot Spot Barbie** (white or black) wears a short white dress covered with pink and blue dots. **$9.00.**

𝒦𝐵 2002 **New York Barbie** is the original name for Hot Spot Barbie, but the *New York* name was changed to *Hot Spot* on dolls produced after 9/11. New York Barbie is very hard to find. **$35.00.**

𝒦𝐵 2002 **Love 'n Care Kelly** wears a pink nightgown with striped sleeves that match her pillow. Cold water makes her chicken pox appear, and they disappear with warm water. This is a repackaged set for KB; the original version sold in most stores comes with an extra dress hanging in the box in the place where this set has added a window to the box liner. The pink teddy bear from the earlier set was also omitted. **$12.00.**

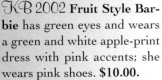

2002 **Fruit Style Barbie**, red-head, was not available in the U.S. She wears the grape-print dress found on the black KB Fruit Style Barbie. **$18.00.**

KB 2002 **Fruit Style Barbie** has green eyes and wears a green and white apple-print dress with pink accents; she wears pink shoes. **$10.00.**

KB 2002 **Fruit Style Barbie**, black, wears a purple & white grape-print dress and green shoes. **$10.00.**

KB 2002 **Lunch Date Barbie** (white or black) wears a white floral print shirt with pink Capri pants and molded-on pink slippers. **$8.00.**

KB 2002 **Nutcracker Kelly Special Collectible Set!** (white or black) repackages Kelly as Snow Fairy, Jenny as Flower Fairy, and Kelly as Peppermint Girl in a three-doll boxed set with a carry handle. **$16.00.**

174

KB 2002 **Photo Student Ken** wears a red shirt with khaki shorts. The box back reveals that Ken is taking Photography 101 at his school. A dog, a camera with two interchangeable lenses, a tray, tongs, and three color-change photographs are included. **$18.00.**

KB 2002 **Shoes Galore Barbie** wears a pink dress decorated with shoes, sunglasses, and purses. Seven pairs of shoes are included. **$10.00.**

KB 2002 **Princess Bride Barbie** wears a white wedding gown with a pink tiara, and she holds a pink mirror with a lenticular (changing) portrait. This KB doll is a simplified version of the 2001 Princess Bride Barbie sold at most stores with a silver tiara, a silver mirror, a pearl necklace, and a blue bodice. **$18.00.**

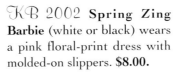

KB 2002 **Spring Zing Barbie** (white or black) wears a pink floral-print dress with molded-on slippers. **$8.00.**

KB 2002 **Weekend Style Barbie** includes Barbie doll wearing a pink floral-print dress, and she comes with a plaid skirt, an orange top, a bathing suit, three pairs of shoes, two pairs of sunglasses, a purse, a radio, a shopping bag containing four Barbie magazines, and a towel. **$12.00.**

KB 2003 **City Pretty Barbie** (white or black) wears a pink, orange, and white ziz-zag-print dress, orange boots, and an orange headband. She is very similar to Big Lots' Weekend Style Barbie dolls. **$8.00.**

KB 2003 **Bead Party Barbie** wears a purple vinyl skirt, a white shirt decorated with purple and yellow circles, a purple headband, and a purple and yellow bead belt. Purple and yellow pop beads make jewelry for the doll or the child, and purple sunglasses for Barbie doll are included. **$9.00.**

KB 2003 **Dream Princess Barbie** wears a pink dress with a sparkly purple bodice, glittery pink overskirt, and a pink crown, and she holds a pink mirror with a lenticular portrait that inexplicably shows the old Princess Barbie with a white bodice, pearl necklace, and a silver crown, as well as a blonde Prince Ken. **$16.00.**

KB 2003 **Flower Surprise Barbie** wears a long pink gown decorated with a garden scene. The large flowers on her dress are actually secret pockets for holding her purse or beauty accessories. Except for the pink dress color, this doll is almost identical to the Big Lots Garden Surprise Barbie dolls. **$16.00.**

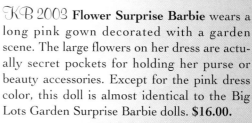

KB 2003 **Garden Party Barbie** wears a satiny pink floral design dress with a lavender handbag. **$8.00.**

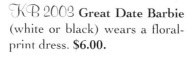

KB 2003 **Great Date Barbie** (white or black) wears a floral-print dress. **$6.00.**

KB 2003 **Hair Magic Barbie** wears a purple, blue, and pink dress with a blue belt and blue boots. Her three hair extensions change color with water. Four flower hair clips, four hair swirls, and a water spray bottle are included. This doll is very similar to the Big Lots Stylin' Hair dolls. **$10.00.**

KB 2003 **Happy Family Photo Album** is a child-size spiral-bound photo album offered free with any $15.00 Happy Family purchase in early 2003. **$10.00.**

KB 2003 **Tiny Steps Kelly** can walk along when her doll carriage is pulled. A rag doll and plastic blue bear are included. The 1999 Tiny Steps Kelly sold at most stores includes more toys. **$10.00.**

KB 2003 **Wedding Day Barbie** wears a satiny white wedding gown with a sheer white jacket, a tulle veil, and white pumps. She holds three pink flowers, and her box back says, "Imagine Barbie on her special day." The wedding invitation states that her wedding is on Sunday, the 31st. **$15.00.**

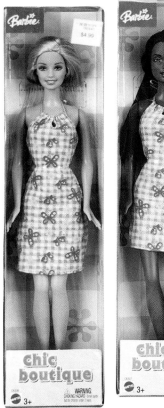

KB 2004 **Chic Boutique Barbie** (white or black) wears a purple and white gingham dress with butterfly and flower designs. **$6.00.**

KB 2004 **City Style Barbie** features an assortment of Barbie dolls wearing trendy fashions, including a blue stewardess-look dress with pink scarf "for the museum," a "58" baseball shirt with blue skirt "to check out the new spot in town," Capri pants and a floral-print shirt "for a lunch date," or a brown suede skirt with top "to go downtown." The Caucasian dolls have been found with fabric variations. **$6.00.**

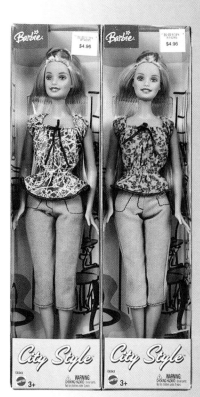

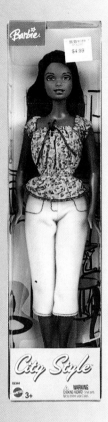

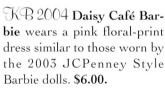

KB 2004 **Daisy Café Barbie** wears a pink floral-print dress similar to those worn by the 2003 JCPenney Style Barbie dolls. **$6.00.**

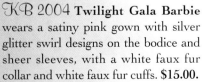

KB 2004 **Twilight Gala Barbie** wears a satiny pink gown with silver glitter swirl designs on the bodice and sheer sleeves, with a white faux fur collar and white faux fur cuffs. **$15.00.**

Kellogg's 1972 **Forget-Me-Nots Barbie** is a Kellogg's promotional doll packaging the Sun Set Malibu Barbie with wrist tag as a "baggie" doll with a colorful yellow header card featuring illustrations of a girl and a boy with a string tied around his index finger. The suggested retail of $3.49 is printed on the card, partially covered by the Mattel logo. **$295.00.**

Kellogg's 1972 **Miss America special mail-away offer** from the Kellogg's Company. For $3.00 plus two box tops from Kellogg's Corn Flakes or Kellogg's Pop Tarts, Kellogg's sent out a Mattel Walking Miss America doll. The cereal box offer is shown here.

Kellogg's 1972 **Miss America** is a Mattel Walking Miss America doll. This is the same doll sold in the Walk Lively Barbie line as Walking Miss America, but no walking stands were included with the Kellogg's dolls. This first Miss America has brown hair and rooted eyelashes. Laurie Lea Schaefer, Miss America of 1972, helped Kellogg's promote this doll. $150.00.

Kellogg's 1973 **Miss America** is from Mattel's Quick Curl Barbie series. The doll has painted eyelashes and brunette Quick Curl hair. 1973 Miss America Terry Ann Meeuwsen helped promote this doll. The brunette Quick Curl dolls were sent when the walking dolls were depleted. $125.00.

Kellogg's 1974 **Miss America** is now blonde, taken from Mattel's 1974 Quick Curl Barbie series but sent in a mailing box like the earlier two Miss America dolls. This offer expired Jan. 31, 1975. $100.00.

181

K-Mart/Kresge 1977 **Barbie and Her Super Fashion Fireworks** is the earliest Barbie doll exclusive for the Kresge stores, now called K-Mart. The doll uses the Stacey head mold and wears an orange swimsuit. She is packaged with four extra fashions. Notice how the hands differ on each of these sets. They originally sold for $2.97. These sets are very hard to find. **$75.00.**

K-Mart/Kresge 1977 **Barbie and Her Super Fashion Fireworks** is shown here with different sculpted hands and four different fashions. **$75.00.**

K-Mart/Kresge 1977 **Barbie and Her Super Fashion Fireworks** is shown here with slightly different sculpted hands and four different fashions. **$75.00.**

K-Mart/Kresge 1977 **Barbie and Her Super Fashion Fireworks** artwork depicts Barbie doll with the Stacey head mold amidst fireworks.

K-Mart

K-Mart 1979 **Barbie Bargain Fashions** are exclusive fashions with quality equivalent to the Barbie Best Buy fashions sold at most stores. Kay-Bee sold excess stock of these fashions. **$15.00 each.**

#1024

#1025

#1026

#1027

#1028

#1029

#1439

#1440

#1441

#3439

#3440

#3441

#3442

#3443

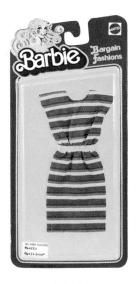

#3444

#5195

#5196

#5197

#5198

#5200

#5201

K-Mart 1980 **Barbie Fashion Favorites and Ken Fashion Favorites** exclusive to K-Mart are shown here. A second series was released in 1981. **$20.00 each.**

#3445

#3446

#3447

#3448

#3449

#3450

#3451

#3452

#5203

#5205

#5206

#5208

#5209

#4290

#4291

#4292

#4293

K-Mart 1983 **Barbie Fashion Classics** outfits feature Fashion Jeans Barbie on the packaging. K-Mart's exclusive Barbie and Ken fashions have many fabric variations. **$12.00 each.**

K·Mart

#4295

#4296

#5819

#4297

#4298

#5820

K·Mart 1983 **Ken Fashion Classics** feature Fashion Jeans Ken on the packages. **$15.00 each.**

K·Mart 1984 **Ken Fashion Classics** feature Dream Date Ken on each package. The fashions are repackaged 1983 Ken Fashion Classics. **$15.00 each.**

#5822

187

K-Mart 1984 **Barbie Fashion Classics** feature Angel Face Barbie on each package. The outfits in this 1984 series are repackaged children's line 1983 Barbie Fashion Classics, although #5701 uses a different color than the gray and pink original. **$15.00 each.**

#5701	#5703	#5703	#5705
#5707	#5708	#4283	#4284
#4285	#4286	#4287	#4288

K-Mart 1983 **Barbie Fashion Fantasy** outfits feature Fashion Jeans Barbie on the packaging. K-Mart's exclusive Barbie and Ken fashions have many fabric variations. **$12.00 each.**

#7497
#7498
#7499
#7500

#7501
#7502
#7503
#7504

#2860
#2861
#2862
#2863

#2864
#2865
#2866
#2867

K-Mart 1984 **Barbie Fashion Fun outfits** feature Sun Gold Barbie on the packaging. Barbie Fashion Fun 1986 outfits feature Tropical Barbie on the packaging. **$10.00 each.**

#7505

#7506

#7507

#7508

#7509
#7510
#7511
#7512

#2868
#2869
#2871
#2873

#2874
#2875

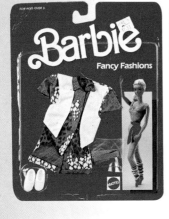

K-Mart 1984 **Barbie Fancy Fashions** feature Great Shape Barbie with her arms at her sides on all packaging. In 1985 K-Mart released a second series of Barbie Fancy Fashions that uses a new photo of Great Shape Barbie with one arm up. **$12.00 each.**

*My thanks to Christine Johnson for loaning me five of her K-Mart fashions.

#2876

#2883

#2884

#2885

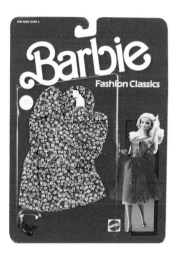

#2887

#2888

#2889

#2890

K·Mart 1986 **Barbie Fashion Classics** feature Day to Night Barbie on each package, and the K·Mart 1986 **Ken Fashion Classics** feature Day to Night Ken on each package. These fashions were shared with Toys "R" Us. $15.00 each.

#2892

#2893

#2894

#2895

#2896

#2897

K-Mart 1991 **Fashion Friends Fashions** include both Casual Wear and Dress Collection Fashions. All Fashion Friends outfits come with shoes. **$14.00 each.**

#7480
#7481
#7484
#7485

#7486
#7488
#7489
#7490

#7491

#7492

K-Mart 1989 **Peach Pretty Barbie** doll's peach gown with iridescent bodice and silver-speckled over-skirt switches from a mini to a midi or a full-length gown. A pleated silvery boa and two peach rosettes are included. **$20.00.**

K-Mart 1991 **Fashion Friends Party Dress** doll is one of three inexpensive Fashion Friends dolls by Mattel that use the Barbie and Skipper doll bodies. The doll has no real name other than Party Dress to give her personality. The box states, "Wears all Barbie Fashions." Fashion Friends Party Dress uses a new head mold used only on one other doll ever, the Fashion Friends Swimsuit doll. **$15.00.**

K-Mart 1991 **Fashion Friends Pretty Teen** doll uses the Skipper doll body with a unique head mold not used since. Her box front states, "Wears all Skipper Fashions." **$15.00.**

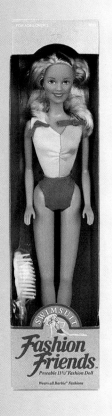

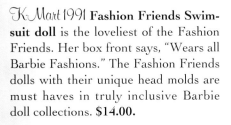

K-Mart 1991 **Fashion Friends Swimsuit doll** is the loveliest of the Fashion Friends. Her box front says, "Wears all Barbie Fashions." The Fashion Friends dolls with their unique head molds are must haves in truly inclusive Barbie doll collections. **$14.00.**

K-Mart 1992 **Pretty in Purple Barbie** (white or black) wears a purple lame party dress with white polka dot net overlay on the skirt and collar and a matching hairbow. **$12.00.**

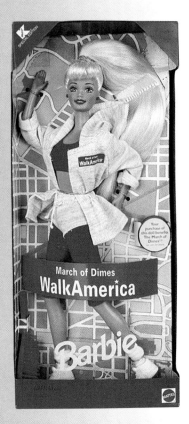

K-Mart 1998 **March of Dimes Walk America Barbie** (white or black) wears a gray hooded sweatshirt and shorts over a red top and leggings. Her box states, "Your purchase of this doll benefits the March of Dimes." K-Mart is the number one corporate sponsor of the March of Dimes. **$12.00.**

K-Mart 1999 **March of Dimes Walk America Barbie & Kelly Gift Set**, black, features Barbie doll with the Nichelle head mold with pink lips. African American Kelly uses the same head mold as Caucasian Kelly. **$20.00.**

K-Mart 1998 **K-Mart Barbie Fashions** include two inexpensive carded Barbie fashions shrink-wrapped together and sold for $3.00. **$8.00.**

K-Mart 1999 **March of Dimes Walk America Barbie & Kelly Gift Set** features Barbie and sister Kelly in matching red, white, and black jogging outfits. Barbie doll has the March of Dimes Walk America logo on her cap and jacket, and Kelly has the logo on her shirt. A red backpack allows Barbie doll to carry Kelly when the toddler gets tired. The box states that Mattel will donate $15,000 to the March of Dimes. **$18.00.**

K-Mart 2000 **Very Berry Barbie** (white or black) wears a white t-shirt under a striped jumper. A strawberry-scented locket and a strawberry ring are included for the child. She was originally scheduled to be called Tutti Fruity Barbie. **$14.00.**

K·Mart 2000 **Barbeque Bash Barbie** (white or black) wears a colorful striped t-shirt under black denim shorts overalls. A plastic barbeque grill, two hamburgers, a spatula, two cups, a cardboard bag of coal, potato chips, plates, and soda are included. **$15.00.**

K·Mart 2001 **It's My Birthday! Barbie,** white, features Barbie doll wearing a black floral-print sleeveless top with blue Capri pants and pink shoes. Party hats, gift boxes, and a cardboard gift bag are included. **$16.00;** black, **$35.00.**

K-Mart 2001 **It's My Birthday!** Playset includes a table, two chairs, a plastic cake with six pieces, cookies, plates, eating utensils, a drinking glass, bottled drinks, a candle, a platter, a cookie tray, flowers, a pair of earrings, a necklace, party hats, birthday cards, and gift boxes. **$15.00.**

K-Mart 2001 **Route 66 School Zone Barbie** (white or black) wears a colorful sheer blouse under a ROUTE 66 bra top, blue pants, and blue shoes, and she has a plastic blue ROUTE 66 lunchbox purse and cardboard school accessories. **$15.00.**

K-Mart 2001 **Route 66 Classroom** includes a chalk board with map print on back, a teacher's chair, a teacher's desk, three students' desks, three books, an apple, chalk, a computer, and two pens. **$15.00.**

K-Mart 2002 **Route 66 Adventure Barbie** (white or black) wears blue, khaki, and pea green floral-design camouflage style pants with a green belt, an olive green shirt featuring an American flag star symbol, and green boots. She carries a camera and a map and comes with mini postcards, a mini driver's license, an overnight case, and a cardboard suitcase. **$16.00.**

197

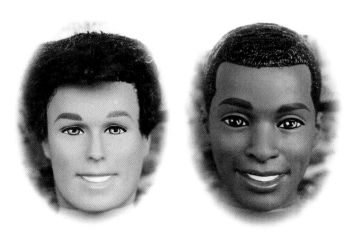

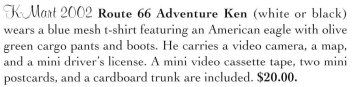

K-Mart 2002 **Route 66 Adventure Ken** (white or black) wears a blue mesh t-shirt featuring an American eagle with olive green cargo pants and boots. He carries a video camera, a map, and a mini driver's license. A mini video cassette tape, two mini postcards, and a cardboard trunk are included. **$20.00.**

K-Mart 2003 **SpongeBob SquarePants Barbie Gift Set** packages the blonde SpongeBob SquarePants Barbie sold at most stores with the large plush Beach Blastin' SpongeBob SquarePants talking toy. **$18.00.**

K-Mart 2003 **Barbie All Day Style Fashion Gift Pack** was available in several styles featuring five complete fashions including shoes and purses for "casual style and glitzy glamour." **$10.00 each.**

K-Mart 2003 **All Day Style Fashion Gift Pack.** Each version includes five fashions, three pairs of shoes, three hangers, two purses, and sunglasses. **$10.00 each.**

K-Mart 2003 **Cozy Home Playset** is a complete home for Barbie doll featuring a blue doorway with side wall, shelving, and a pink roof, a kitchen unit with a stove and a sink, a refrigerator, a kitchen table with two chairs, a serving cart, a couch and coffee table, a bed with a blue pillow and a comforter, a wardrobe with drawers, shelves, and hangers, a floor lamp, a hamper with lid, a cordless phone, and many food and beauty accessories. **$20.00.**

K-Mart 2003 **Barbie Fashion Avenue set** includes four complete fashions with footwear. **$15.00.**

K-Mart 2004 **Route 66 University Barbie**, white, wears a red blouse decorated with flowers, jeans with floral appliqués, and blue shoes. She has an easel with paintings, a cardboard portfolio, and a plastic case with tiny tubes of paint and a paint brush. Her box back states that she is studying fine arts. **$15.00**; black, **$25.00.**

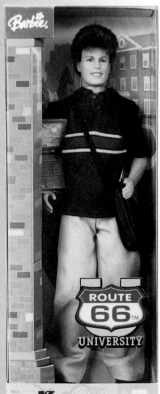

K-Mart 2004 **Route 66 University Ken** wears a blue polo with khaki pants and brown boots. He carries a laptop computer and a book bag. His box back states that he is studying computer graphics. **$18.00.**

Kool-Aid 1992 **Special Edition Barbie Fashion**, available for 40 Kool-Aid points, is a pink and purple miniskirt and top decorated with yellow dots (bottom left fashion). **$8.00.** A rare version of the same outfit has been found in a green, orange, and pink design (top left fashion). **$10.00.**

Kool-Aid 1993 **Special Edition Barbie Fashion**, a pink Kool-Aid logo top with leggings, was offered as a Kay-Bee store promotion (bottom right fashion). **$7.00.**

Kool-Aid 1993 **Collector's Edition Barbie Fashion** is a lime green and blue two-piece outfit bearing the Kool-Aid logo (top right fashion). It was available for 45 Kool-Aid points. **$5.00.**

Kool-Aid 1993 **Collector's Edition Barbie Doll from Wacky Warehouse** was available for 240 Kool-Aid points (about 20 canisters of Kool-Aid). She wears a casual beach outfit and comes with a bikini, a visor, and a Kool-Aid logo bag. **$20.00.**

Kool-Aid 1994 **Kool-Aid Wacky Warehouse Barbie** was advertised by Kool-Aid as a Special Edition 35th Anniversary Barbie doll. She was available for 300 Kool-Aid points (about 25 canisters of Kool-Aid). She wears a colorful blouse and wrap skirt over a yellow swimsuit and carries a Kool-Aid logo bag. She has been found in two distinct outfit versions. **$18.00.**

Kool-Aid 1996 **Kool-Aid Wacky Warehouse Barbie** wears a denim overalls fashion with the Kool-Aid logo on the bib and patches on the legs, and she comes with a matching backpack. **$15.00.**

Kraft 1994 **Special Edition Barbie Doll from Kraft Treasures** was available for 220 Kraft points (about 73 boxes of Kraft Macaroni and Cheese). She wears a blue Kraft logo hat, blue leggings under a Kraft Cheeseasaurus Rex logo dress and a vest, and she has a knapsack with the Kraft Treasures logo on it. **$20.00.**

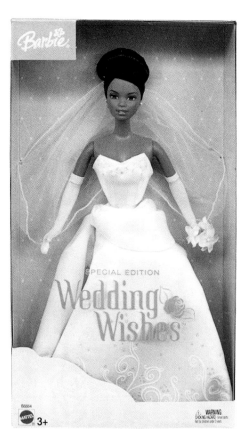

Kroger 2004 **Wedding Wishes Barbie** (white or black) wears a white wedding gown with ivory swirl designs on her bodice and dress, with tiny holographic glitter flowers. She has a net veil, white gloves, and a white floral bouquet. Her box back says, *"She imagines her wedding day, though it may be far away."* **$18.00.**

Kroger 2004 **Wedding Wishes Barbie Store Display** features the words *Wedding Wishes Barbie* surrounded by flowers, with six rows of Wedding Wishes Barbie dolls on the two levels of the display. **$20.00.**

Lady Lovelylocks 1989 **Starlight Blue Barbie** was offered as a mail-in premium for Mattel's Lady Lovelylock's line for Pixietail points and cash. Starlight Blue Barbie wears a blue party dress with shimmery overskirt. The doll came in a brown catalog box with blue pumps. The same doll in a pink box, called Fashion Play Barbie, was sold on the foreign market. **$20.00.**

Lara's 1995 **Barbie in Fur Coat** dolls were re-dressed Fun to Dress and Ruffle Fun Barbie dolls wearing real dyed mink coats. These were not authorized by Mattel. The dolls, sold for between $99.00 to $125.00, arrived in white Lara's Fur Accessories boxes. The more unusual colored minks such as yellow or green are more desirable to some collectors. The pink mink is even more limited, with only 200 produced. **$100.00.**

Lionel 1990 **Barbie 4-Fashion Gift Set** includes four fashions, shoes, and accessories. Note the yellow circle in the lower right corner stating that this set was exclusively at Lionel. **$20.00.**

Little Debbie Snacks

Little Debbie Snacks 1993 **Little Debbie Barbie** features a Barbie doll designed to look like the brunette Little Debbie mascot. She wears a blue and white checked dress with an apron and straw hat. **$25.00.**

Little Debbie Snacks 1996 **Little Debbie Barbie Series II** wears a long blue and white gingham dress and wide-brimmed hat, showing the Southern heritage of Little Debbie. The first version has bent arms. **$20.00.**

Little Debbie Snacks 1996 **Little Debbie Barbie Series II** was quickly changed to a straight-arms body. The color of the warning box on the doll's box fronts differs on this version of the doll. **$18.00.**

Little Debbie Snacks 1998 **Little Debbie Barbie Series III** evokes a sense of nostalgia in her tea party outfit, a blue and white gingham drop-waist sailor-style fashion with puffed sleeves, hat, and handbag. **$16.00.**

Little Debbie Snacks 1998 **Little Debbie Barbie Collector's Edition Figurine Set** includes three 4" Little Debbie Barbie figurines with rooted hair and fabric skirts depicting the 1993, 1996, and 1998 dolls. **$10.00.**

Little Debbie Snacks 2000 **Little Debbie Snacks 40th Anniversary Barbie** celebrates the 40th anniversary of the Little Debbie brand wearing a sparkly blue party dress with a silver rose on her bodice, a silver "Little Debbie" belt, and a silver purse. She has the Generation Girl head mold. The box reveals that in 1960 Ellsworth McKee developed a 49-cent family pack of twelve Oatmeal Creme Pies, placing a picture of his 3½-year-old granddaughter, Debra McKee, on the box, creating the Little Debbie brand. As of 2000, the McKee Foods Corporation operated six manufacturing plants, employing nearly 6,000 people, with product distribution to all 50 states and Canada. **$24.00.**

Little Debbie Snacks 2002 **Little Debbie Snacks Barbie** features brunette Barbie wearing a white shirt with blue and white checked Capri pants, a blue jacket, a white hat with a blue brim, and blue shoes, and she carries a cardboard bag containing packages of Oatmeal Creme Pies, Nutty Bars, and Fudge Brownies. **$20.00.**

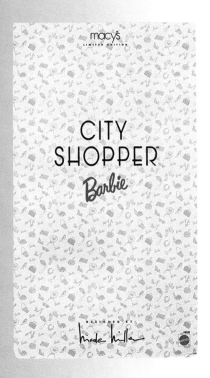

Macy's 1996 **City Shopper Barbie** is a redhead with green eyes wearing a one-piece Nicole Miller design dress with a matching jacket lined in Barbie accessory icons. She carries a matching purse and a Macy's shopping bag. **$38.00.**

Macy's 1997 **Anne Klein Barbie** doll's box quotes designer Anne Klein, "All women work, whether they stay home or go to an office. I design for these women." Anne Klein Barbie wears a black and white houndstooth jacket, a black skirt, black pantyhose, a red vest over a white dickey, a black belt with golden buckle featuring the signature Anne Klein lion's head design, and a golden chain-link necklace and earrings. She carries a black briefcase with a golden Anne Klein label. **$48.00.**

Mary Kay Cosmetics 2003 **Mary Kay Star Consultant Barbie** celebrates the 40th anniversary of Mary Kay Cosmetics dressed in a red jacket with a Ladder of Success pin, a white shirt, a black skirt, pantyhose, a pearl necklace, and black shoes. She carries a black purse. The box back states, "This special edition keepsake captures the spirit of women everywhere, embracing the vision of Mary Kay Ash and living the dream. Cherish this treasure as a symbol of 40 years of women helping women." **$125.00.**

Mattel 2002 **Bullet Train Barbie** is a Mattel reward doll honoring leadership among top Mattel employees in 2002. Barbie doll is dressed as a conductor carrying a pink suitcase with a "Catch the Bullet Train" sticker, and the box insert shows a train with the Mattel logo. The box back states, "THANKS FOR RIDING THE BULLET TRAIN TO SAVINGS. This specially packaged Bullet Train Barbie is proudly presented to you in appreciation and recognition for your dedicated leadership and service to the Bullet Train in 2002. This Barbie was specially created for this occasion and is one of only one hundred created. Your contributions to the Bullet Train have not only sped the train forward but also aided in the growth and success of Mattel. Many Thanks!" and it is signed by Kevin Farr and Joe Eckroth. This doll is basically the same as the playline Travel Train Fun Barbie but with unique packaging. **$100.00.**

Mattel Toy Store 2003 **Batik Princess Barbie**, the first Barbie doll created for Mattel Toy Clubs/Toy Stores, wears a ball gown made of pink chiffon Batik decorated with romantic pastel floral print, with a faux-pearl necklace and earrings. A cardboard photo frame is included. The box back states, "Traveling the continents in search of a unique Ball Gown, Barbie found herself on Java Island, Indonesia, and came across an exquisite fabric design locally called 'Batik.' She immediately fell in love with the style and with the help of her friends at Mattel Indonesia, created a beautiful gown fit for any grand event. When originally introduced, the Javanese reserved Batik solely for Javanese royalty." **$22.00.**

Mattel Toy Store 2004 **Barbie Mix 'Em Up Fashions** was created for the Mattel Toy Stores. She wears a satiny gold top with matching flared skirt, a faux fur wrap, and a "pearl" necklace. A gold handbag, gold strap pumps, gold pants, a white top with gold dots, black boots, a black coat with faux fur collar, a red vinyl purse, jeans, a shimmering black skirt, shimmering black turtleneck, a black "leather" tote, and black sunglasses are included for mix-and-match fun. **$20.00.**

Meijer 1992 **Something Extra Barbie** wears a blue party dress with sheer white polka dot overlay. She comes with a Meijer Barbie coupon book with $11.00 in coupons. **$14.00.**

Meijer 1993 **Collector's Edition Barbie Dollar** was available by mail to purchasers of Shopping Fun Barbie. For the receipt and the doll's UPC symbol, a dollar bill bearing Barbie doll's portrait sticker was sent. **$10.00.**

Meijer 1993 **Shopping Fun Barbie** wears a pink jacket with white polka dots over a white dress with a colorful circles-inside-squares-print dress, and she carries a Meijer shopping bag. Her coupon book, designed for the child as checks to be signed, contains $27.00 in coupons. **$12.00.**

Meijer 1999 **Horse Riding Barbie with Riding Club CD-ROM** couples the children's line Horse Riding Barbie in a European package with computer software for horse racing and adventure. **$18.00.**

Meijer 1999 **Tie Dye Barbie with Cool Looks Fashion Designer CD-ROM** packages the children's line Tie Dye Barbie with computer software to make fashions for Barbie using Fashion Fabric sheets and decorating supplies. **$18.00.**

Meijer 1999 **Twirlin' Make-Up Barbie and Magic Hair Styler CD-ROM** pairs the children's line Twirlin' Make-Up Barbie with Barbie doll hairstyling software. These CD-ROM sets, supposedly a $49.99 value, were also discounted and sold at Value City stores. **$18.00.**

Mercantile Stores 1996 **Special Occasion Barbie** is an exclusive shared by 13 finer department store chains (Bacons, Kastner Knott Co., de Lendrecies, Gayfers, Glass Block, Hennessys, J. B. White, Joslins, the Jones Store Co., Lion, Maison Blanche, McAlpin's, and Root's) associated with the Mercantile Stores Company, Inc. She wears a satiny blue gown with white faux fur trim, a fur hat, and blue pumps. **$28.00.**

Mercantile Stores 1997 **Special Occasion Barbie II** wears a velvety blue skirt, a silver lamé bodice with a large bow at the back, and shiny silver pumps. She carries a silver lamé purse. **$20.00.**

Mercantile Stores 1997 **Special Occasion Barbie II**, black, had very limited distribution and is very hard to find. **$28.00.**

Mervyn's 1984 **Ballerina Barbie** has the hairstyle of 1979's Ballerina Barbie, but her outfit has less detail, and this version uses the SuperStar Barbie head mold. She is the last doll to use the poseable Ballerina Barbie doll arm construction. She was also available on the foreign market. **$45.00.**

Mervyn's 1986 **Fabulous Fur Barbie** was available in Canada and Europe but was sold exclusively in the U.S. by Mervyn's. She wears a sparkly blue jumpsuit with iridescent belt and versatile white faux fur coat, comprised of a separate faux fur vest, sleeves, and fur extensions. **$50.00.**

Montgomery Ward 1972 **The Original Barbie** was created for the 100th anniversary of Montgomery Ward. She wears a black and white zebra-striped swimsuit like the 1959 Barbie, but her facial paint more closely resembles a 1961 Barbie. Unlike the original Barbie, she does not have earrings and her shoes are white instead of black. Dolls sold in the Montgomery Ward stores had painted fingernails and were available in rare pink window boxes. **$700.00.**

Montgomery Ward 1972 **The Original Barbie** is more commonly found in the Montgomery Ward brown catalog box. The dolls sold in the catalog boxes do not have fingernail polish. **$575.00.**

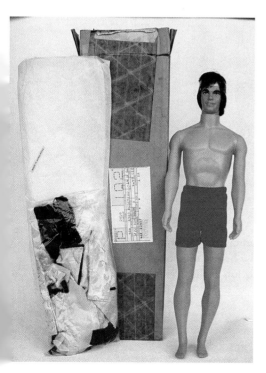

Montgomery Ward 1974 **Mod Hair Ken**, a children's line doll, was offered with a tuxedo as an exclusive in the 1974 Montgomery Ward catalog. Packaged in a brown catalog box with stock #7234 printed on the box, the doll wears red shorts and is wrapped in white tissue paper with a "MADE IN HONG KONG" label, with the tuxedo in a clear "Korea" bag beside him. The tuxedo has a blue brocade jacket with black lapels, a blue dickey with black bowtie, black pants, black socks, and black shoes. A sheet of brown hair stick-ons allows the doll to have a moustache, goatee, and sideburns. **$175.00.**

Osco 1992 **Picnic Pretty Barbie** wears a pink and white checked skirt with a yellow and white checked apron, a pink bodice, and a white hat with pink flowers on the brim. Her purse matches her skirt. **$14.00.**

Montgomery Ward 1978 **Malibu Barbie & Her Ten-Speeder Set** includes Malibu Barbie wearing a square-neck red one-piece swimsuit packaged in a brown catalog box with the Barbie Ten Speeder bicycle, both of which where available separately at most stores. She uses the Stacey head mold and has Francie doll's arms. Montgomery Ward first offered this set in 1974 and 1975. **$110.00.**

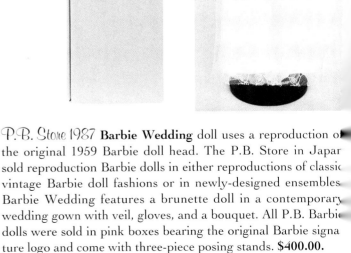

Otasco 1983 **Barbie & Ken Campin' Out Set** includes children's line Sunsational Malibu Barbie and Ken dolls re-dressed in red and white camping outfits. The tent, backpack, sleeping bag, and other camping accessories are basically the same as sold separately in the Barbie Campin' Out Play Pak #2318. **$50.00.**

P.B. Store 1987 **Barbie Wedding** doll uses a reproduction of the original 1959 Barbie doll head. The P.B. Store in Japan sold reproduction Barbie dolls in either reproductions of classic vintage Barbie doll fashions or in newly-designed ensembles. Barbie Wedding features a brunette doll in a contemporary wedding gown with veil, gloves, and a bouquet. All P.B. Barbie dolls were sold in pink boxes bearing the original Barbie signature logo and come with three-piece posing stands. **$400.00.**

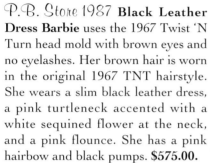

P.B. Store 1987 **Black Leather Dress Barbie** uses the 1967 Twist 'N Turn head mold with brown eyes and no eyelashes. Her brown hair is worn in the original 1967 TNT hairstyle. She wears a slim black leather dress, a pink turtleneck accented with a white sequined flower at the neck, and a pink flounce. She has a pink hairbow and black pumps. **$575.00.**

P.B. Store 1987 **Fur Coat Barbie** doll uses the 1967 Twist 'N Turn Barbie head mold with rooted eyelashes. This doll has straight hair and bangs in the style of the original Twist 'N Turn Barbie. She wears an original outfit, a leopard print coat with faux fur trim, a cream skirt, gloves, and a pillbox hat. **$450.00.**

P.B. Store 1987 **Gay Parisienne Barbie** wears a reproduction of the rarest Barbie doll fashion, 1959's Gay Parisienne. Purchasers of the P.B. Barbie dolls were allowed to choose the hair color they desired for their dolls as well as the head mold (1959 original or 1967 Twist 'N Turn), but all dolls have the modern straight-arms body. **$445.00.**

P.B. Store 1987 **Black Evening Barbie** is a brunette doll using the 1959 head mold wearing a re-creation of the vintage Solo in the Spotlight fashion with an added black faux fur wrap. **$375.00.**

P.B. Store 1987 **Red Kimono Barbie** uses the original 1959 Barbie head mold with the 1960's bubble cut hairstyle. The kimono is one of the more desirable P.B. fashions. This impressive kimono has a dark red obi with a gold floral design. **$425.00.**

P.B. Store 1987 **Black Kimono Barbie** uses the original 1959 Barbie head mold with a striking titian ponytail hairstyle with bangs. Her kimono is black with pink and red floral designs and a gold obi. **$500.00.**

P.B. Store 1987 **Uchikake Kimono Barbie** wears a bright red kimono with colorful floral designs, white stockings, and red slippers. She is unique because she comes with a molded black plastic geisha wig. **$550.00.**

P.B. Store 1987 **Summer Dress Barbie** uses the original 1959 Barbie head mold with a blonde bubble cut hairstyle. She wears a blue and white summer dress. **$400.00.**

P.B. Store 1987 **Green Gown Barbie** uses the Twist 'N Turn Barbie head mold with titian hair worn in a ponytail with bangs. She has brown eyes and rooted eyelashes. She wears a slim green gown with white floral designs and green and white bow accents, with a black flounce and black open-toe heels. **$475.00.**

P.B. Store 1987 **Pink Evening Barbie** uses the original 1959 Barbie head mold with medium brown hair. She wears a pink dress with silver glitter (fabric similar to the U.S. children's line Jewel Secrets Barbie) with silver bows, a long white satin coat, white pumps, a silver purse, and a pearl and rhinestone necklace. **$400.00.**

P.B. Store 1987 **Solo in the Spotlight Barbie** uses the 1967 Twist 'N Turn head mold with rooted eyelashes, but this doll has a variant hairstyle — bangs and a ponytail! Her outfit is a recreation of the vintage Solo in the Spotlight. **$415.00.**

P.B. Store 1987 **Red Gown Barbie** uses the 1967 Twist 'N Turn head mold in the original TNT hairstyle. She wears a slim red gown with sheer red floral-print overlay, accented with red bows and a black flounce, and black pumps. **$475.00.**

P.B. Store 1987 **White & Pink Dress Barbie** is a side-part bubblecut Barbie doll wearing a short pink dress with floral accents, a white faux fur wrap, and a hairbow. **$400.00.**

P.B. Store 1987 **Victorian Barbie** has the 1967 Twist 'N Turn head mold with brown eyes and rooted eyelashes. Her blonde hair is worn in a ponytail with bangs. She models a brown dress with white pantaloons. **$425.00.**

P.B. Store 1987 **Blue Dress Barbie** has the 1967 Twist 'N Turn head mold with brown eyes and no eyelashes. Her brown hair is worn in the original 1967 TNT hairstyle. She wears a blue dress with wide stripes and a white collar with floral trim and white pumps, and she carries a white purse. **$450.00.**

Pallendorf 1997 **Das Spielzeug Barbie** commemorates the 40th anniversary of Austria's Pallendorf store in a limited edition of only 100 dolls. These 100 dolls wears stylish two-piece suits with white satin lapels, matching hats, white tops, white gloves, and pumps. Five different colors of suits were available. Each doll comes with a Das Spielzeug shopping bag, a leather-look white purse, white earrings and a pearl necklace, a doll stand, and a wrist tag labeled "fashion dreams by E. Stelzer Vienna" on the front with the doll's individual number on the back. The dolls are redressed Puerto Rican Barbie dolls. $250.00.

Palmers 1996 **Palmers Barbie** is the first exclusive for the Palmers clothing store of Austria. Palmers Barbie wears a green employee uniform with a white *P*-logo blouse. She comes with panties, a bra, a Palmers shopping bag, shoes, and a green ten-shilling Pamers token. Only 1,500 dolls were made. **$75.00.**

Palmers 1996 **Palmers Barbie** second edition wears an employee apprentice uniform — a white shirt with a green pleated skirt and garter. She comes with a scarf decorated with the Palmers horse-drawn coach, a Palmers shopping bag, and a green ten-schilling Palmers token. Only 1,300 dolls were made. **$65.00.**

Palmers 1997 **Palmers Barbie** third edition features Splash 'n Color Teresa re-dressed in a bikini with a sheer black cover-up. A *P*-logo white towel, a Palmers shopping bag, black sunglasses, a green ten-schilling Palmers token, and a poster featuring a model wearing a life-size version of this fashion are included. Only 2,500 dolls were made. **$48.00.**

Palmers 1997 **Palmers Barbie** fourth edition is dressed as an angel with golden wings, a long white satin robe, and a sheer white nightgown with panties. She comes with a white pillow, a Palmers shopping bag, a poster of a model wearing this fashion, a green Palmers ten-shilling token, and a golden Palmers token dated 1997. **$45.00.**

Palmers 1998 **Palmers Barbie** fifth edition wears a green carriage driver's uniform with a green top hat, stockings, and black boots. She comes with a Palmers Christmas card, a Palmers shopping bag, a green Palmers ten-shilling token, and a golden 5 Euro token. **$40.00.**

Palmers 1999 **Palmers Millennium Barbie** sixth edition wears a holographic silver skirt with a "jeweled" bra top, a gray jacket with "jeweled" trim, holographic silver boots, and a holographic hair band. A silver "2000" memory book and a green Palmers five–Deutsche mark token are included. **$75.00.**

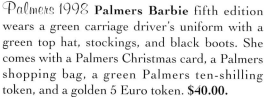

Radio Shack 1993 **Earring Magic Barbie** Software Pak contains a children's line Earring Magic Barbie doll plus two computer games, Barbie and Barbie Design Studio. Although originally sold for $49.99, a surplus of reduced-price dolls hit the market, causing the value to fall. **$15.00.**

Planet Hollywood 1997 **Planet Hollywood Barbie** was designed for the Planet Hollywood chain of restaurants but was never released.

Radio Shack 1996 **Sparkle Beach Barbie Wire-Controlled Sun Rider** includes a helmet for Barbie doll. **$15.00.**

Radio Shack 1998 **Remote Control City Nights Cycle** is nearly identical to the 1995 Toys "R" Us Remote Control City Nights Cycle, but this set says, "Custom Manufactured in China for Radio Shack," and includes a pink helmet for Barbie doll, which the Toys "R" Us cycle lacks. **$12.00.**

Retail Stores 1995 **Barbie Bunny** by Mattel was an Easter promotion for select retail stores' toy departments. One winner per store received this 36" tall pink plush bunny wearing a Barbie-logo bow. **$40.00.**

Russell Stover Candies 1996 **Russell Stover Candies Special Edition Barbie** is packaged in an Easter basket with six bags of real candy. Collectors are divided on whether to keep the doll intact inside the basket with the unopened candy or to remove the boxed doll and discard the candy. Two versions are available — Barbie doll wearing pink and white checked shorts, a matching jacket, and a white bunny t-shirt, or Barbie doll dressed in a floral-print dress and straw hat. Each doll carries a plastic basket. **$15.00.**

Russell Stover Candies 1997 **Russell Stover Candies Special Edition Barbie Sample** doll is packaged in a plain white box. This sample doll wears a darker floral-print dress than the doll that was mass produced, and she also has a black collar, black pantyhose, and a black hairbow. She is shown in the photo on the right, next to one of the 1997 mass-produced dolls. **$65.00.**

Russell Stover Candies 1997 **Russell Stover Candies Special Edition Barbie** is available in either a pink dress with a floral-design collar and a purple bow at the bodice or in a pastel floral-print dress with pink collar and white bow at the bodice. **$15.00.**

Russell Stover Candies 1997 **Russell Stover Candies Special Edition Barbie**, black, is only available wearing the pastel floral-print gown with a pink collar and white bow at the bodice. She uses the Christie head mold. **$15.00.**

Sara Lee 1993 **Sara Lee Barbie** is exclusive to the Philippines' Sara Lee clothing company. Sara Lee Barbie wears a pink "I (heart) Sara Lee" shirt, pink and white striped shorts, a headband, wristbands, and pink gymshoes. **$65.00.**

Sears 1970 **New 'n Wonderful Walking Jamie** introduces Barbie doll's best friend Jamie, who uses the Twist 'N Turn Barbie head mold with brown eyes and rooted eyelashes. She has a side-part flip hairstyle worn, with a pink scarf, in blonde, brunette, or redhead hair colors. She wears a yellow minidress with pink and orange checks, an elastic orange belt with a silver buckle, and orange boots. When the button in her back is pressed, her arms swing, her head turns, and her legs move back and forth. **$495.00.**

Sears 1970 **Walking Jamie Furry Friends Set** is a Sears exclusive gift set that includes Walking Jamie in her original yellow knit dress with an orange belt, a pink scarf, and orange boots, with an orange and pink furry coat with matching hat, shoes, a gray male poodle with a collar and leash, doggie treats, a bowl, and a bone. **$1,000.00.**

Sears 1971 **Jamie Party Penthouse Case** is a six-sided carry case and penthouse home for Jamie featuring a dramatic window view of the city, two storage compartments, an illustrated fireplace, and furniture. **$195.00.**

Sears 1971 **Jamie Studio Apartment and Carry Case** is a single doll case with one storage compartment and illustrated graphics depicting Jamie's bedroom. **$45.00.**

Sears 1972 **Walking Jamie Strollin' in Style** is a Sears exclusive gift set that includes Jamie wearing a unique red version of her original yellow knit mini-dress with a blue belt, a blue scarf, and red boots, along with a blue pantsuit with yellow trim, blue pilgrim shoes, a white poodle with a blue collar, and a blue and yellow ball. **$1,250.00.**

224

Sears 1972 **Barbie Mountain Ski Cabin** was sold by Sears in 1972 and 1974. The vinyl playcase opens to reveal a cabin with bunk beds, a closet, cupboards, and a fireplace with mantle. An Aspen poster is on the wall. **$40.00.**

Sears 1973 **Barbie Goin' Boatin' Set** features a two-seat 15" long yellow boat with "motor," two oars, a trailer hitch, a fishing rod, a tackle box, and a fish. **$60.00.**

Sears 1974 **Barbie Baby Sits** uses the baby Sweets from Mattel's The Sunshine Family line, wearing a dress with a bonnet and diaper, along with the following babysitting accessories: a pink and white checked apron for Barbie, a bathtub, a blanket, two bottles, a dish, a teddy bear, a duck, a bar of soap, a bib, a towel, a pillow, a tray, and a list of emergency phone numbers. Even though packaged for Barbie doll, the baby in this set wears The Sunshine Family wrist tag! **$72.00.**

Sears 1974 **Barbie's Miss America Beauty Center** is the first time Barbie doll is identified as Miss America. From 1972 through 1979, an 11½" Miss America doll distinct from Barbie was sold by Mattel. In this set, the large 1972 Barbie Beauty Center head, modeled from 1967's Twist 'N Turn Barbie doll's head mold, is used for Miss America. The head is 6" tall and stands 11½" tall when attached to the neck base. The box says, "Make Barbie pretty for the Miss America Pageant." She has Growin' Pretty hair; a ponytail section can be pulled out long and then shortened with a pull ring at the back of her head. Beauty accessories include a compact with blue and green eyeshadow, cheek blusher, lipstick, an eyebrow pencil, sponge applicators, and false eyelashes. Three barrettes, three ribbons, a brush, a comb, 12 bobby pins, and four rollers are included. Barbie doll wins the competition, as a silvery crown and Miss America medallion come with the set. **$75.00.**

Sears 1974 **Barbie's Sweet 16 Mix 'N Match** set includes 11 pieces of red, white, and blue clothing. **$150.00.**

Sears 1974 **Wardrobe Builders** for Barbie and Ken dolls include several outfits for each. **$125.00 each.**

Sears 1975 **Gold Medal Barbie and Her U.S. Olympic Wardrobe** repackages the children's line Gold Medal Barbie with her original red, white, and blue swimsuit and gold medal with an exclusive red, white, and blue towel and two extra fashions. The extra skating fashion consists of a red, white, and blue skating dress, red tights, white ice skates, and an additional gold medal. The parade fashion features a pleated white dress with a red and blue top, a blue belt, a white hat with red band, white shoes, a red purse, and a third gold medal. **$150.00.**

Sears 1975 **Gold Medal Barbie Winter Sports** is a Sears catalog exclusive sold only in the pink, illustrated catalog box. A children's line Gold Medal Barbie Skier, wearing her red and blue ski jumpsuit, her #9 racing number, a blue belt, a red hat, red goggles, white boots, and a gold medal, is packaged with yellow skis and blue ski poles along with an exclusive After Ski fashion: an ivory blouse, a red, white, and blue print skirt, and blue pilgrim shoes. **$95.00.**

Sears 1975 **Olympic Gymnast Set** pairs the children's line Gold Medal P.J. Gymnast with the Olympic Gymnast Set #7420 (which is basically just a high bar with side supports and a base) in one box. The front left corner of the box states that this set, "also includes P.J. doll with her own balance beam, warm-up jacket and gold medal!" This set is rare. **$185.00.**

Sears 1975 **Barbie and Ken Set #9046** includes a camisole-style top and floral skirt for Barbie, and slacks, a shirt with floral-print sleeves, and boots for Ken. **$95.00.**

Sears 1975 **Barbie and Ken Set #9047** includes matching plaid fashions for the dolls, with a cape and beret for Barbie. **$95.00.**

Sears 1975 **Barbie and Ken Set #9048. $95.00.**

Sears 1975 **Barbie Gown #9049** includes a lovely coral gown with sheer overskirt and matching jacket, a hand mirror, a gold clutch purse, a necklace, and shoes. **$175.00.**

Sears 1975 **Quick Curl Barbie's Miss America Beauty Center** contains the same basic styling head as the 1974 set, but instead of Growin' Pretty Hair, this head has Quick Curl hair, in which tiny wires are rooted with the hair to give great styleability. A Quick Curl curler is included. Only two barrettes come with this set, and the bobby pins and rollers are deleted; the other accessories are otherwise the same as the 1974 set. **$45.00.**

Sears 1976 **Quick Curl Barbie Miss America Beauty Center** has a modified box photo that shows the styling head without eyelashes. The 1976 box has a new warning statement in the lower left corner. **$36.00.**

Sears 1975 **Barbie's Bathe 'n Beauty Place** is a bathroom setting with a real working shower, a floral shower curtain, a ruffled vanity cover with a matching vanity stool, a bath mat, a towel, a mirror, a brush, a comb, a bath brush, and play soap. **$40.00.**

Sears 1975 **Barbie's Pool Party** includes a 28" x 28" plastic patio mat, an item not included with the Barbie's Pool Party sets sold in most stores. **$45.00.**

Sears 1975 **Barbie's Room-fulls** combines the Country Kitchen and Firelight Living Room, which were sold separately at most stores, in this illustrated catalog box. **$115.00.**

Sears 1975 **World of Barbie Sleep 'n Keep Case** features Barbie doll in a white dress with blue floral print design next to a Barbie doll in orange slacks and a blue gingham blouse with vest. The case opens up to reveal a fold-out bedroom with two beds. **$25.00.**

#9001

#9002

#9003

#9004

Sears 1975 **Barbie Best Buy Fashions** and **Ken Best Buy Fashions** are very hard to find. **$95.00 each.** (Nineteen of the Sears fashions on this page and the next are courtesy of Carmen Varricchio.)

#9006

#9007

#9008

#9009

#9010

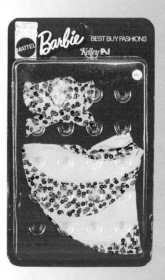

#9011

#9682

#9683

#9684

Sears 1976 **Barbie Best Buy Fashions** and **Ken Best Buy Fashions** now use the updated *Barbie* and *Ken* name logos on the packages. **$85.00 each.**

#9685

#9686

#9687

#9658

#9696

#9697

#9698

#9699

232

Sears 1976 **Barbie Baby-sits** was sold in 1976 in a pink store box with changes to the baby's outfit and accessories. This version contains the baby wearing a robe over a diaper and includes these accessories: Barbie doll's pink apron, a phone list, a bonnet and baby dress, a bathtub, a cradle, a highchair, a blanket, a washcloth, a bar of soap, a ducky, a teddy bear, a baby dish, two bottles, and a bib. The note in this set gives Barbie doll instructions on when to bathe and feed the baby and is signed by Mrs. Jones, eliminating any reference to the Sunshine Family. This set was offered through 1982, and the baby has been found with four robe variations. **$36.00.**

Sears 1976 **Barbie Fashions #9650** is a ballerina set with a real record featuring music from *The Nutcracker Suite*. The record included with this set was clear-colored when first released, but was changed to red since the clear record was not clearly visible inside the package. **$55.00.**

Sears 1976 **Barbie Fashions #9663 and #9664. $75.00.**

Sears 1976 **World of Barbie Fashion Doll Case** uses the updated *Barbie* name logo, and features an illustration of Barbie doll wearing a pink blouse with white polka-dots and blue pants. **$18.00.**

Sears 1976 **Ballerina Barbie Stage** is two feet long and features a backstage dressing room with a practice bar and mirror, a vanity table, a vanity seat, a comb, a brush, a hand mirror, and the colorful stage-front setting. **$55.00.**

Sears 1976 **World of Barbie Sleep 'n Keep Case** uses the updated *Barbie* name logo, and the fashions shown are color variations of those on the 1975 Sleep 'n Keep case. **$20.00.**

Sears 1977 **Growing Up Skipper & Her 2-in-1 Bedroom** packages the children's line Skipper 2-in-1 Bedroom with Growing Up Skipper doll in an illustrated white catalog box. The playset changes from a little girl's room with bunk beds and a ladder, a desk, a desk lamp, a growth chart, and a reversible picture, to a teenager's room with a canopy bed, a vanity, and a hanging lamp. Growing Up Skipper is the controversial doll who grows "slim and tall and curvy" when her left arm is turned all the way around counter clockwise, adding ¾" to her height and some cleavage. For a young girl look, Skipper wears a red and white checked miniskirt, a red bodyshirt with a blue collar, red socks, and red shoes. As a teenager, Skipper removes her blue collar and adds a blue scarf and trades her miniskirt for a long red and white checked skirt, and she changes her flat red shoes for white platform sandals. **$150.00.**

234

Sears 1977 **Growing Up Skipper Fashions #9659** combines several of the children's line mix-and-match Growing Up Skipper Fashions in one package. **$65.00.**

Sears 1977 **Barbie Best Buy Fashions** and **Ken Best Buy Fashions. $85.00 each.**

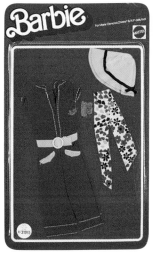

#2051

#2052

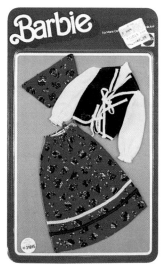

#2053

#2054

#2055

#2056

#2057

#2058

#2059

#2060

Sears 1977 **Barbie Fashions** have a star by the *Barbie* name on each package. In 1978, Barbie Fashions featuring mix-and-match styles and Ken Fashions were available. **$95.00 each.**

#2050

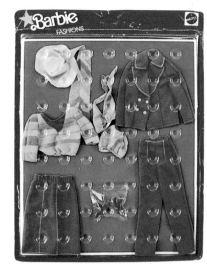

#2061

#2062

#2063

1978 #2579

1978 #2580

1978 #1036

1978 #2582

Sears 1977 **Barbie Dune Buggy and Tow Bar** is Barbie doll's 13" long yellow Dune Buggy with pink underbody, black bucket seats, an antenna with "Barbie" pennant, a "Barbie" license plate, and pink and orange racing stripes. A tow bar is included for hitching the vehicle to the Star Traveler Motorhome, sold in most stores. **$55.00.**

Sears 1977 **Barbie Racing Bike and Bike Rack** contains a special hot pink version of the 1974 Barbie's Ten Speeder bicycle with white handlebars, a night light, and a basket. An exclusive bike rack is included for attaching to the Star Traveler Motorhome. **$45.00.**

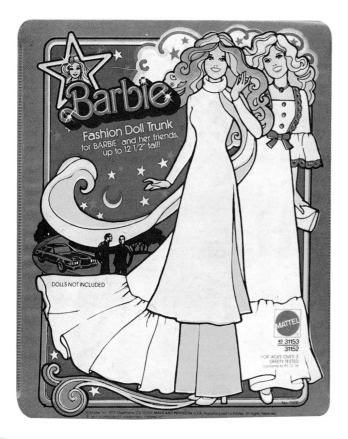

Sears 1977 **Barbie Fashion Doll Trunk** features an illustration of a doll in a long yellow top with yellow bell-bottom pants, and a second doll in a long white gown with pink trim. **$18.00.**

Sears 1977 **Barbie Sleep 'n Keep Case** features Barbie doll in a long white nightgown and robe and a second Barbie doll wearing a pink nightgown. **$18.00.**

Sears 1977 **SuperStar Barbie Photo Studio** contains a back-drop with a garden setting, a SuperStar background, and an island scene. Also included are a photographer's camera, a studio light, a dressing room, a chair, a brush, a comb, and a mirror. The set was packaged in a pink illustrated catalog box in the U.S. and in a photo box in Canada. $48.00.

Sears 1979 **Ken Fashion Favorites #1804** includes two Ken Fashion Collectibles in one package. $55.00.

Sears 1978 **SuperSize Barbie On the Go** wardrobe includes a blue jacket, a skirt, a cape with faux fur collar, a scarf, a suitcase, a makeup case, and hair and makeup accessories for use with the 18" SuperSize dolls. $40.00.

Sears 1982 **Quick Curl Christie Beauty Center** features a Christie styling head in an illustrated catalog box. $36.00.

Sears 1986 **Celebration Barbie** is the second Barbie doll designed to commemorate a retailer's 100th anniversary; Montgomery Ward issued an "Original Barbie" in 1972 for its centennial. Celebration Barbie doll is dressed in a silver lamé jumpsuit under a silver lamé skirt with sheer pink overskirt, a pink stole, and a large "diamond" necklace. She has a fabric jewelry holder and a silver wrist tag that reads, "Celebration Barbie Doll Sears 100th Anniversary." The Sears catalog boasted that she is dressed in her "most glamorous gown ever." She cost $14.99 from the Sears catalog. $28.00.

Sears 1987 **Star Dream Barbie** wears a white bodysuit, a sheer white gown, a glittery belt, and a glittery tiara with a "jewel." She carries a bouquet of roses. $20.00.

1988 **Skating Star Barbie** from Canada was sold to commemorate the 1988 Calgary Winter Olympics. She is the same as Star Dream Barbie except instead of a long skirt, she has a pair of ice skates. **$32.00.**

Sears 1988 **Lilac & Lovely Barbie** wears a lilac bodysuit, a lacy change-around skirt and stole, and fingerless gloves. **$22.00.**

Sears 1989 **Evening Enchantment Barbie** wears a shimmering white top with a long blue skirt that reverses to a form-fitting sparkly white skirt, and she has a blue rosette with "pearl" in her curly hair. **$18.00.**

Sears 1990 **Lavender Surprise Barbie** wears a ruffled lavender minidress with overskirt that can be worn short as packaged or pulled lower for an ankle-length gown. **$15.00.**

240

Sears 1990 **Lavender Surprise Barbie**, black, was not pictured in the Sears Christmas catalog. She is the first Sears exclusive black Barbie doll. She uses the Christie head mold. **$18.00.**

Sears 1991 **Southern Belle Barbie**, called Glamour Barbie in the 1991 Sears catalog, offers three ways to wear her sheer peach gown: as a minidress, a short ruffled party dress, or a full-length Southern belle fashion with a lavender cummerbund, a parasol, and a white hat. **$16.00.**

Sears 1991 **Barbie Evening Fashions** contains three full-length dresses — a purple lace ruffled fashion, a hot pink and iridescent white layered party dress, and a magenta and gold lamé gown. These outfits were packaged in a white catalog box. They are hard to find. **$25.00.**

Sears 1991 **Barbie Commemorative Medallion** was available in the 1991 Sears Christmas catalog. The silver-plated medallion bears the inscription, "30th Anniversary Barbie Authorized Commemorative Medallion" and comes with a velvety Barbie-logo pouch. The medallion was redeemable by mail to purchasers of the 1991 Happy Holidays Barbie doll, or it was sold separately in the catalog for $10.00. **$15.00.**

Sears 1992 **Blossom Beautiful Barbie**, called Flower Princess Barbie in the 1992 Sears catalog, is dressed in a mint green gown, and she has brilliant green eyes. Gold-speckled white tulle overlays her gown, and a white rosettes petal design at her waist adds to her floral theme. She is the first and only doll in the Sears Flower Princess Barbie Collection. Sold only briefly, the series ended with the closing of Sears's catalog division. Originally sold for $49.99, she is the most expensive Sears exclusive Barbie doll to date. **$65.00.**

Sears 1992 **Dream Princess Barbie** wears a blue ball gown that can be converted to a short dress with cape. She wears an iridescent white crown. She was reduced to half price when Sears decided to close its catalog division in the spring of 1993 and sold all toys at clearance, offering collectors some once-in-a-lifetime bargains such as Bob Mackie's Platinum Barbie and Starlight Splendor Barbie dolls for $42.00, Swan Lake Barbie for $30.00, and the 1992 Happy Holidays Barbie for $4.99! **$15.00.**

Sears 1992 **Sun Sensation Barbie Backyard Party Set** includes the children's line Sun Sensation Barbie repackaged in a slim white box, along with a 12" x 18" vinyl pool, basketball hoop, and a picnic table with accessories. **$25.00.**

Sears 1992 **Sachi Dog & Honey Cat** repackages the plush Sachi dog with a collar, tail ruffle, ear ruffle, bandana, baseball cap, sunglasses, and flying disc and accompanied by the plush Honey cat with a collar, headband, tail ruffle, sun hat, shoulder purse, carrier basket, pillow, and brush inside a white Sears catalog box. Sachi and Honey were sold separately at most stores. **$65.00.**

Sears 1992 **Shani Beach Dazzle Plus 2 Fashions** features Barbie doll's friend Beach Dazzle Shani doll packaged in a white mailer box with two additional outfits from the Shani Sizzling Style series, #5968, a black gown with gold lamé coat, and #5969, an orange, gold, and black jacket, a matching skirt, and orange pants. This is a hard-to-find item. **$55.00.**

Sears 1993 **Enchanted Princess Barbie** was sold exclusively in Canada in a French and English box. She is dressed in silver lamé with a lavender skirt with a sparkly star in her hair, and she carries a ribboned scepter. **$20.00.**

Sears 1994 **Silver Sweetheart Barbie** was available in the United States through a Sears Shop at Home Barbie Collectibles catalog. She wears a blue full-length tulle gown accented with a silver lamé collar and hairbow. **$17.00.**

Sears 1995 **Ribbons & Roses Barbie** wears a white satin and taffeta dress with a sheer floral print overskirt, and she has an oversized golden bow at her waist and golden glitter on her bodice. **$15.00.**

Sears 1996 **Evening Flame Barbie** is Sears' first brunette exclusive Barbie doll. She wears a gown flocked with crimson and gold flowers and icy white satin bodice edged in gold trim and detailed with a red bow and fingerless white gloves. **$15.00.**

Sears 1996 **Evening Flame Barbie Prototype** differs from the mass-produced doll in several ways. The prototype wears a red gown with red flocking, while the regular doll has a white gown with red flocking. The prototype has a thin gold band around her waist, while the regular doll has a chain-style gold belt around her waist. The prototype has a solid red bow on her bodice, while the mass-produced doll has a red bow with golden edging. The prototype has lovely links of golden rings in her hair band, while the regular doll has a threaded golden strip in her hair. **$75.00.**

Sears 1997 **Blue Starlight Barbie** wears a metallic blue ballgown with raised collar. She has upswept brown hair accented with a jewel. **$14.00.**

Sears 1998 **Pink Reflections Barbie** is the first Sears exclusive doll to use the Mackie head mold; she has brown hair and brown eyes. She wears a patterned satiny light pink ballgown with silver accents and a large silver bow at her waist. **$18.00.**

Sears 2000 **Barbie Evening Recital with Kelly, Stacie, and Tommy Gift Set** features Barbie with a baton conducting Kelly with her cello, Stacie with her flute, and Tommy with his trumpet. This set was shared with F.A.O. Schwarz and JCPenney. Excess stock sold at Ames for $14.99 in 2001. **$32.00.**

Sears 2003 **Sears 50 Barbie** celebrates the 50th anniversary of Sears Canada. Barbie doll wears a satiny lavender floral-print dress and carries a lavender purse. The box front has a golden "Sears 50" with the words *Quality, Value, Service, Trust*. The doll is very similar to the Big Lots 2003 Summer Garden Barbie. **$15.00.**

See's Candies 2000 **See's Candies Barbie** features Barbie doll in her very first job, a See's Candies salesperson! She wears a white dress with black trim and pantyhose, and she has a hairnet in her hair; her uniform is practically identical to those worn by See's employees in the 1920s and 1930s. The box reveals, "Founder Mary See began selling her wonderful confections in Los Angeles in 1921 with the motto, 'Quality Without Compromise.' 'Quality Without Compromise' has always been true for the people behind See's candy counters, so when Barbie doll went to apply for her first job, she picked See's Candies. Barbie had always found that a present of See's made anyone happy on a birthday, the holidays, or for a hostess gift when she was invited to dinner. Barbie also knew that helping customers select their favorites would be fun, and it was! Of course, See's knew that Barbie, with her friendly personality, beautiful smile, and sunny disposition, would make a perfect addition to the See's family. One of Barbie doll's favorites is Milk Bordeaux, a Valentine's gift from Ken." A cash register is included. **$45.00.**

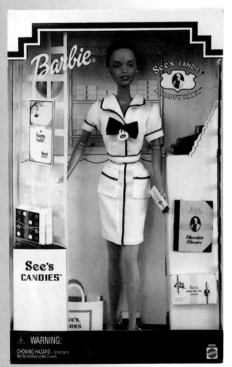

See's Candies 2000 **See's Candies Barbie**, black. **$50.00.**

See's Candies 2001 **I Left My Heart in San Francisco Barbie** (white or black) features Barbie doll wearing a chic satiny jacket cinched at the waist, a full, long black skirt, a faux fur hat with netting covering her hair, which is atop her head in a stylish chignon, short black gloves, and pantyhose. The box states, "Barbie doll's ensemble takes you back in time to an era of elegance when details were everything." The story on the box relates how Barbie doll visited the City by the Bay, rode a cable car, crossed the Golden Gate Bridge, dined at a fabulous restaurant, and shopped at Union Square, with her favorite stop the original See's Candies shop on Polk Street. The box states that Charles A. See, a pharmacist-turned-chocolate-salesman, founded See's Candies in 1921. Three San Francisco postcards are included. **$36.00.**

Service Merchandise 1991 **Blue Rhapsody Barbie** wears a gold-speckled sheer layered blue gown with a gold lamé bodice. Her matching hair fashion also serves as a boa. Incredibly, each of the Service Merchandise exclusive Barbie dolls prior to 1998 originally sold for under $20.00 each! **$35.00.**

Service Merchandise 1992 **Satin Nights Barbie** wears a black and white satin gown. One version has all-white earrings and studs and a plain white one-piece necklace. The second version has silver stud earrings and a shiny strung pearl necklace. **$25.00.**

Service Merchandise 1993 **Sparkling Splendor Barbie** wears a slim red silhouette wrap-around gown with red mesh on the bodice, a red flared sparkly overskirt, and a hat with bow. **$20.00.**

Service Merchandise 1994 **City Sophisticate Barbie** wears an elegant belted gold coat with black satin lapels over a black skirt and a black hat with a golden adornment. In the excitement over Barbie doll's 35th anniversary in 1994, many store exclusives like this disappeared quickly and forced secondary prices higher. **$27.00.**

Service Merchandise 1995 **Ruby Romance Barbie** wears a dramatic red gown with a black bow and a black and red hair decoration. She was so popular that she never made it into Service Merchandise's Christmas catalog. **$22.00.**

Service Merchandise 1996 **Sea Princess Barbie** has an elaborate upswept hairstyle and wears a blue and sea green gown with a lavender bodice. The box states that she reigns over the underwater kingdom of Atlantis. **$18.00.**

Service Merchandise 1997 **Dream Bride Barbie** (white or black) wears a lovely white wedding gown with a double-strand pearl necklace and upswept hair. A cut-out wedding archway is on the box back. The Caucasian Dream Bride Barbie reappeared in some Service Merchandise stores for the Christmas 1998 season. **$20.00.**

Service Merchandise 1998 **Evening Symphony Barbie** is the first Service Merchandise Barbie doll to use the Mackie head mold. She wears a golden top with sheer sleeves and a long turquoise skirt as she goes to the symphony. **$15.00.**

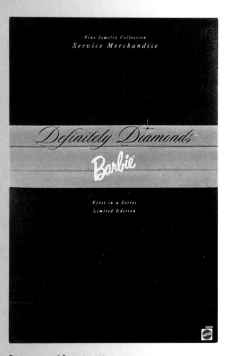

Service Merchandise 1998 **Definitely Diamonds Barbie** is the first and only doll in the Fine Jewelry Collection, which was designed to showcase the beauty and elegance of authentic jewels. On the evening of the opera, Definitely Diamonds Barbie wears a classic black velvet gown lined in pink, a ruffled stole of black organza, a pink charmeuse cummerbund, and a necklace and earrings set that contains three diamonds, with a total weight of one point, set in 10 karat gold. Her earring posts are sterling silver. **$65.00.**

Shopko/Venture 1991 **Blossom Beauty Barbie** wears a rose, green, and purple print skirt with a rose bodice, a purple jacket, and a matching hat. **$18.00.**

Shopko/Venture 1992 **Party Perfect Barbie** wears a shimmering floral-print slim gown with a pink train and a hairbow. **$16.00.**

Singapore Airlines 1992 **Singapore Girl** was only sold aboard Singapore Airlines planes. The first edition has dull makeup and light pink lips and was sold in a brown box labeled "Genuine Barbie." This is hard to find. **$75.00.**

Singapore Airlines 1994 **Singapore Girl** second edition was widely available. She has red lips and vivid makeup and was sold in a pink box. Mattel Canada labeled the POG milk cap bearing this Singapore Girl's picture "Barbie," so she should be considered a Barbie doll. **$30.00.**

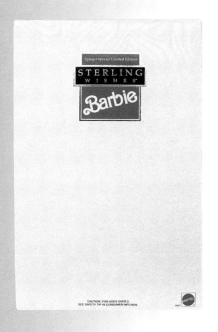

Spiegel 1991 **Sterling Wishes Barbie** wears a silver lamé gown with flocked black velvet design, fingerless gloves, and a hairbow. She originally sold for $49.99. **$45.00.**

Spiegel 1992 **Regal Reflections Barbie** wears an exquisite midnight blue, black, and gold evening gown with an elegant hair ornament. She was an incredible value at only $49.99 originally. **$65.00.**

252

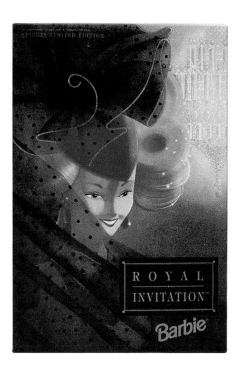

Spiegel 1993 **Royal Invitation Barbie** wears a fuchsia satin gown with golden accents, a black and pink diamond-design overskirt covering a black petticoat, and a matching hat. She originally sold for $49.99. **$28.00.**

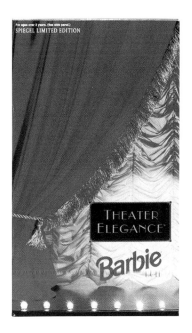

Spiegel 1994 **Theater Elegance Barbie** wears a long velvety black gown with a beaded pink floral appliqué, a pink shawl with "crystal" drops, and black lace gloves. She quickly sold out at $49.90 in 1994 during the Barbie-doll-collecting frenzy that came with Barbie doll's 35th anniversary. **$55.00.**

Spiegel

Spiegel 1996 **Shopping Chic Barbie**, black, uses the Asha head mold. Most dolls wear the metallic knit dress, but some Caucasian and African American dolls have been found with a smooth gold lamé dress like the one used on the 1994 Happy Holidays Barbie. The doll shown uses the gold lamé version. The Shopping Chic dolls originally sold for $59.99 each, but Spiegel clearanced remaining black dolls for $14.99 in early 1999. **$28.00.**

Spiegel 1995 **Shopping Chic Barbie** wears a gold metallic knit sleeveless dress under a black coat with faux leopard collar and cuffs and matching hat and purse. Her poodle is the same as the one in the Classique Fifth Avenue Style fashion. **$30.00.**

Spiegel 1996 **Summer Sophisticate Barbie** wears a 1950s-style slim pastel silk-look dress, a pink bolero jacket with a porcelain rose on her lapel, and a pink hat with floral trim. She comes with a purse, glasses, and a Barbie-logo travel bag. Her issue price was $59.99, but Spiegel reduced excess inventory of this doll for $14.99. **$30.00.**

Spiegel 1997 **Winner's Circle Barbie** is a lovely redhead in equestrian attire — a scarlet velveteen riding jacket, a golden brocade vest, a golden striped ascot with a golden key charm, a black skirt, leggings, boots, and a black hat. Issued at $59.00, her price was reduced to $14.99 by Spiegel. **$25.00.**

Spiegel 1997 **Winner's Circle Barbie,** black, was planned but never released. A prototype using the Asha head mold is shown in this Mattel photo.

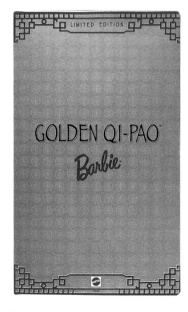

Spiegel 1998 **Golden Qi-Pao Barbie** was designed to celebrate the first anniversary of the British return of Hong Kong to China. *Qi-Pao* means "long dress" and has survived political change and revolution to become the traditional dress worn by Chinese women on special occasions. The golden color symbolizes good luck, wealth, and prosperity. This Qi-Pao features a layer of golden lace covering a solid golden background, with tiny crystals and golden rosettes. The faux jade butterfly brooch signifies beauty. Barbie doll uses the Diva head mold and wears her hair in an updated version of the chignon. **$58.00.**

Spielzeug-Ring 1993 **Secret Hearts Barbie Deluxe Gift Set** commemorates the 25th anniversary of the Spielzeug-Ring store of Germany. A "25 Jahre SPIELZEUG RING" sticker is on the box window, and a "Mattel GmbH of West Germany" sticker is on the box bottom. This set is otherwise identical to the Sam's Club set. **$75.00.**

Target 1989 **Gold & Lace Barbie** wears a gold lamé bodysuit, a matching skirt with lacy white overskirt, and a glittery white jacket. Each of the Target exclusive Barbie dolls sold through 1993 originally retailed for approximately $10.00. **$16.00.**

Target 1989 **30th Anniversary *Barbie Magazine* Plus A Special Fashion** pairs the *Barbie Magazine* with an exclusive pink dress for Barbie doll. The magazine is a fun retrospective on Barbie doll's first 30 years. This was a great value for $2.99. **$10.00.**

Target 1990 **Barbie Dress 'N Play** combines the Travel Time, Winter Ski Set, and Exercise Center playsets, which were sold separately at most stores, into one package for Target. **$20.00.**

Target 1990 **Party Pretty Barbie** wears a black dress with lacy white overskirt and a lacy white jacket. She carries a tiny black purse. One version has plain white lace on the dress and jacket, while a second version has a sparkly, textured lace-trimmed overskirt and jacket. **$14.00.**

Target 1991 **Cute 'N Cool Barbie** wears a retro 1960s-look geometric print top, leggings, and a headband, and she has an extra matching scarf, a purple skirt, and a purple tank top to mix and match for 12 different looks. $15.00.

Target 1991 **Golden Evening Barbie** is the hardest to find Target exclusive Barbie doll. She wears a velvety black dress with a gold floral design on the bodice and a short lacy overskirt with a gold lamé jacket. $20.00.

Target 1992 **Bathtime Fun Skipper** was made to accompany the popular Bathtime Fun Barbie doll available at most stores; their swimsuits even match. She is packaged with pink foam soap to be used to create foam fashions on the doll. $15.00.

Target 1992 **Dazzlin' Date Barbie** is the most popular of Target's four 1992 exclusive dolls since she is glamorously dressed in a satiny aqua dress with lacy black trim and matching jacket. $15.00.

Target 1992 **Pretty In Plaid Barbie** doll's box boasts that she has "the latest look." She wears a floral skirt, a checked jacket, a scarf, stockings, and a hat with flowers on the brim. $14.00.

258

Target 1992 **Wild Style Barbie** wears a black leather-look jacket, a yellow shirt, print leggings, a belted blue denim miniskirt with fringe, and a satiny pink baseball cap. **$14.00.**

Target 1993 **Baseball Barbie** has a *B*-logo baseball cap and a *B*-logo bag to go with her red, white, and blue baseball uniform with yellow midriff. **$15.00.**

Target 1993 **Golf Date Barbie** is all set for golfing, with a golf club, golf cup, and three golf balls. She wears a diamond-print blue vest and blue shorts. A coupon for a free game of miniature golf is included with the doll. **$18.00.**

Target 1994 **Barbie Living Room Collection** features a black piano, a sofa, a coffee table, a fireplace and mantle, a bookshelf, and a grandfather clock in Target's blue gift collection box. This is very hard to find. **$26.00.**

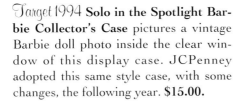

Target 1994 **Solo in the Spotlight Barbie Collector's Case** pictures a vintage Barbie doll photo inside the clear window of this display case. JCPenney adopted this same style case, with some changes, the following year. **$15.00.**

Target 1995 **Steppin' Out Barbie** wears a satiny pink dress with black collar, black cuffs, a black belt with jeweled belt, and a black pillbox hat. **$15.00.** The prototype doll wears a red and white version of the same dress. **$75.00.**

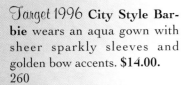

Target 1996 **City Style Barbie** wears an aqua gown with sheer sparkly sleeves and golden bow accents. **$14.00.**

Target 1996 **City Style Barbie Prototype** has a satiny white heart-print dress and purse that use the material from Target's 1996 Valentine Barbie doll's skirt and collar. The silver-dotted sheer purple sleeves and overskirt are borrowed from the Toys "R" Us 1995 Purple Passion Barbie. The aqua collar, cuffs, and earrings are the same as used on the mass-produced 1996 City Style Barbie. Mattel sample makers may occasionally sew fashions using various leftover materials to determine if the outfit style or fit is correct, disregarding whether the resulting combination matches. **$65.00.**

Target 1996 **Pet Doctor Barbie**, brunette, is exclusive to Target, while the blonde and African American versions are regular children's line dolls. Barbie doll wears paw-print pants and a white doctor's coat. Her cat meows and her dog barks when buttons on their pet bed are pushed. **$20.00.**

Target 1996 **Valentine Barbie** wears a satiny white heart-print skirt and collar with a red bodice and hairbow. She comes with two cardboard cards for the child. **$14.00.**

Target 1997 **City Style Barbie** wears a satiny purple and black dress with velvety black bodice and black fishnet stockings. She carries a matching purple and black purse. **$15.00.**

Target 1997 **Valentine Romance Barbie** wears a red dress with white hearts and lacy white sleeves. **$12.00.**

Target 1997 **Happy Halloween Barbie & Kelly Gift Set** features Barbie doll wearing a cat-in-a-pumpkin sweatshirt, black leggings, an orange headband, and orange shoes as she escorts sister Kelly, wearing a pumpkin costume, trick-or-treating. A flashlight and treat bag are included. According to Target, this is by far their best-selling exclusive in recent years. **$25.00.**

Target 1997 **Target 35th Anniversary Barbie** celebrates the 35th anniversary of Target in a metallic scarlet gown with gold-dotted cream tulle and a satiny underskirt. A "Target 35th Anniversary Exclusive Edition" hangtag is on the doll's right wrist. The box back features a history of Target since the first store opened in Roseville, Minnesota, in 1962 and reveals that as of 1997, Target had 804 stores in 39 states. **$16.00.**

Target 1998 **Valentine Date Barbie** wears a satiny red dress with a white collar and cuffs and golden heart accents, white pantyhose, and red pumps. She carries a red heart-shaped purse and comes with a cut-out picture frame. **$12.00.**

Target 1997 **Target 35th Anniversary Barbie**, black, is Target's first African American Barbie doll exclusive. She uses the Christie head mold. **$16.00.**

Target 1998 **City Style Barbie** has brown hair and wears a two-piece velvety purple suit with iridescent white trim, white pantyhose, and purple pumps. She carries an iridescent white purse. Some versions of this doll have stiff, upturned hair, while other dolls have soft, straight, and silky hair covered in a clear plastic hair shield. **$14.00.**

Target 1998 **Club Wedd Barbie**, black, is the first store exclusive African American doll to use the Mackie head mold. **$18.00.**

Target 1998 **Club Wedd Barbie**, blonde or brunette, promotes the Target Club Wedd bridal registry. Club Wedd Barbie wears a satiny white gown adorned with golden rosettes and with golden floral-design panels, sheer gold-specked over-skirt, a veil with golden headband, white pumps, and pearl jewelry. **$16.00.**

Target 1998 **Barbie Bride Case** features a photo of the blonde Club Wedd Barbie. The plastic case has a compartment for a doll, a closet with a clothes bar, and five accessory bins. **$10.00.**

Target 1998 **Easter Egg Hunt Barbie & Kelly Gift** includes Barbie doll wearing a yellow jumper with a white t-shirt, a pink and white checked hat, socks, and white gymshoes, along with Kelly wearing pink and white checked overalls, a white t-shirt, yellow shoes, and bunny ears. Both dolls carry white baskets, and Barbie doll carries an Easter bunny identical to the one carried by the 1996 grocery Easter Basket Barbie. **$20.00.**

Target 1998 **Halloween Party Barbie & Ken Gift Set** features Barbie and Ken dolls in matching pirate costumes. Ken doll has chest-length rooted brown hair. This is the second Ken ever with an earring (the first was the controversial Earring Magic Ken of 1993). **$27.00.**

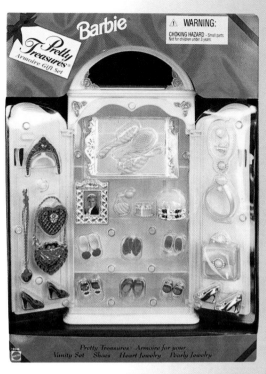

Target 1998 **Power Wheels Tommy & Kelly** features Tommy driving a motorized blue Power Wheels Jeep vehicle while Kelly and her puppy ride in the trailer; the Power Wheels Kelly & Tommy set sold at most retail stores in 1998 featured a pink Jeep and trailer and featured Kelly as the driver. **$36.00.**

Target 1998 **Pretty Treasures Armoire Gift Set** includes a white armoire, a vanity set with a mirrored tray and a framed photo of Ken, magenta heart jewelry and purse, pearl jewelry and purse, and eight pairs of shoes. **$15.00.**

Target 1999 **Valentine Style Barbie** wears a satiny skirt depicting hearts growing on vines, a satiny red jacket, white pantyhose, and a heart choker. She carries a heart-shaped purse. **$12.00.**

Target 1999 **Valentine Style Barbie**, black, uses the Asha head mold with light skin. **$14.00.**

Target 1999 **Club Wedd Barbie** (blonde, brunette, or black) wears a satiny white wedding gown with net overskirt, a lacy bodice with two pink ribbons at the waist, short white gloves, and a veil with hairbow. She carries a bouquet of three flowers. $15.00.

Target 1999 **Easter Bunny Fun Barbie & Kelly Gift Set** includes Barbie and Kelly dolls dressed in matching spring bunny-print dresses with lilac hats, sheer white pantyhose, and lilac shoes. The plush bunny has a tag that says, "To: Kelly From: Barbie." Kelly carries a white basket. $24.00.

Target 1999 **Easter Bunny Fun Barbie & Kelly Gift Set**, black, features Barbie doll with the Nichelle head mold. Both black dolls in this set have blue eyes. $25.00.

Bed with cat

Dining table and chairs

Table accessory set

Sofa

Adult and child chairs with cat

Target 1999 **Barbie Décor Collection** includes seven sets of high-quality furniture made for the European market and sold exclusively in the U.S. by Target. Bed and dining table sets, **$20.00 each**; all others, **$15.00 each.**

Checked chair and ottoman with dog

Floral chair and ottoman with dog

Target 1999 **Fashion Avenue Barbie Easter Fashion** features a pink top with a yellow egg-print dress, pink shoes, and a pink purse. **$10.00.**

Target 1999 **Kelly & Tommy Soccer Set** includes the dolls in blue and yellow soccer uniforms with a soccer ball and goalie net. **$32.00.**

Target 1999 **Halloween Fun Barbie & Kelly Gift Set** (white or black) features Barbie and Kelly in orange and black cat costumes with tails and cat ears headbands. **$24.00.**

Target 1999 **Halloween Fun Li'l Friends of Kelly Gift Set** features Deidre as a butterfly, Jenny as a witch, Kayla as a princess, and Tommy as a skeleton. **$28.00.**

Target 1999 **Xhilaration Barbie** (white or black) wears a gray vest over a white T-shirt and a plaid skirt, plus she comes with a hooded sweatshirt and a keepsake box. Barbie has a butterfly barrette in her hair, and a child-size butterfly barrette is included. The white doll uses the Generation Girl Barbie head mold, while the black doll has the Christie head mold. **$18.00.**

Target 2000 **With Love...Barbie** wears a pink Valentine's Day dress with shiny pink hearts and swirls. She carries a cardboard candy box. **$14.00.**

Target 2000 **With Love...Barbie**, black, uses the Nichelle head mold with blue eyes and pink lips. **$16.00.**

Target 2000 **Easter Egg Party Barbie & Kelly Gift Set** (white or black) includes brown-eyed Barbie doll in a mint green spring dress with flowers and bunny designs, sheer pantyhose, and a straw hat with pink ribbon, and includes Kelly in a pink bunny suit. An Easter scene with reusable vinyl stickers is included. **$18.00.**

Target 2000 **Halloween Party Kelly** is dressed as a purple-haired alien with a silver lamé spacesuit and glittery silver antennae, **Halloween Party Deidre** is a pumpkin, **Halloween Party Jenny** is a pumpkin, **Halloween Party Kayla** is a ghost, and **Halloween Party Tommy** is a cowboy. **$10.00 each.**

2000 **Halloween Shelly** is the Canadian equivalent of the U.S. Kelly, except the Halloween Party Shelly as an alien has *white* hair! **$40.00.**

Target 2000 **Holiday Collection Fashion Avenue** was available in either a blue gown with silver snowflake designs and white faux fur trim or a red gown with golden snowflake designs and white faux fur trim. **$15.00 each.**

Target 2000 **Pajama Fun Barbie** was exclusive to Target, while Pajama Fun Skipper, Courtney, and Skipper were sold at most stores. Barbie wears blue pajamas with a pink robe and yellow slippers. She comes with a Magic Date Ball, glow-in-the-dark hair decorations, an inflatable pillow, and a tote bag that transforms into a sleeping bag. **$14.00.**

Target 2000 **Pajama Fun Furniture Bed Set** includes a bed, a fabric pillow, an inflatable heart pillow, pretend magazines, a laptop computer, a basket, and beauty accessories. **$15.00.**

Target 2000 **Pajama Fun Bear** is a plush beanbag bear with a silver *B* on its chest and a pink ribbon around its neck. The cardboard tag attached to its ear is pre-priced $2.99. **$6.00.**

Target 2000 **Pajama Fun Furniture Couch Set** includes a couch, fabric pillows, an inflatable daisy pillow, a coffee table, two end tables, a popcorn bowl, two glasses, a cola bottle, two pretend magazines, an aquarium, and a table lamp. **$15.00.**

Target 2000 **Pajama Fun Trunk Playset** is a roll-along trunk that opens into a house containing a bed that transforms into a bathtub, a TV that folds down to a vanity, a secret pop-up jewelry box, a cassette player, two compact discs, two CD cases, a Lava lamp, a mobile phone, three pairs of shoes, six hangers, a purse, a necklace, a hair dryer, two perfume bottles, lipstick, a makeup jar, two cups, a cola bottle, a popcorn bowl, and a sticker album with stickers. **$45.00.**

272

Target 2000 Pet Lovin' Puppy Twins and Kelly Giftset includes Kelly dressed in a blue floral sundress, two plush puppies with plastic heads, a pet carrier, two bottles, two dishes, two bones, and two leashes. **$25.00.**

Target 2001 Valentine Friends Kelly & Marisa (white or black) wear coordinating satiny pale pink and dark pink with floral design fashions. Three markers, five sheets of colored papers, a sticker sheet, a stencil, two doll-sized cards, and two child-sized cards are included. **$22.00.**

Target 2001 Easter Garden Hunt Barbie & Kelly Gift Set (white or black) features Barbie doll wearing a pastel floral-print glittery Easter dress and a hat with pink ribbon, and Kelly wearing a matching dress with pink hair band and pink panty-hose. Both dolls hold white baskets. The Easter Garden Hunt game with five stand-up character cards and 20 matching character eggs is included. **$22.00.**

273

Target 2001 **Halloween Party Kelly** is a witch, **Chelsie** is a pumpkin, **Deidre** is a pumpkin, **Jenny** is a kitty, and **Tommy** is a vampire. This 2001 series is the rarest of all the Halloween Party Kelly dolls. **$15.00 each.**

Target 2001 **Halloween Princess Barbie** wears a purple dress and sheer cape with orange and gold spider web designs. Barbie doll has a spider hair ornament, and a spider ring is included for the child. **$20.00.**

Target 2001 **Home For the Holidays Barbie**, white or black, wears a golden top with a satiny red skirt and pantyhose. Two stockings, a toy bear, a toy trumpet, and a gold present ornament are included. **$18.00.**

Target 2002 **My Li'l Valentine Kelly** is dressed as a regal Queen of Hearts, with a cardboard crown. **$10.00. My Li'l Valentine Nikki** is dressed as Cupid, with a cardboard bow and arrow. **$17.00.**

Target 2002 **Easter Eggie! Kelly** (white or black) is dressed as a li'l bunny, in a pink and white bunny suit with plastic bunny ears; **Easter Eggie! Liana** is dressed as a li'l egg, with a broken-eggshell hat, and **Easter Eggie! Melody** is dressed as a li'l lamb, in a plush white suit with hood and black trim. **$8.00 each.**

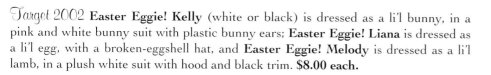

Target 2002 **Kelly Pretty Kitty Giftset** includes Kelly wearing a satiny pink dress with white overskirt, her cat Lily, a vanity, a chair, a hair dryer, a mirror, a brush, a comb, two shampoo bottles, and a perfume atomizer. $16.00.

Target 2002 **Perrr-fectly Halloween Barbie** is dressed as a cat, with a pink dress with black faux fur collar and cuffs, boots, and a cat ears headband. A black cat with pink leash is included. $15.00.

Target 2002 **Halloween Party Kelly** is dressed in a vinyl pumpkin costume, **Deidre** is a pumpkin, **Jenny** is a genie, **Lorena** is a witch, and **Tommy** is a scarecrow. $8.00 each.

Target 2002 **Barbie Holiday Stocking** packages the Sunshine Day Barbie sold in most stores with child-size sunglasses, a bubble pendant, a puzzle watch, a lip gloss compact, a diary with pencils, a coin purse, hair clips, a compact mirror and a comb, and a flower ring. $15.00.

Target 2003 **Li'l Heart Kelly and friends** are dressed in costumes inspired by the little candy hearts with messages of endearment. Li'l Heart Kelly wears a "BE MINE" placard, Li'l Heart Belinda wears a "KISS ME" placard, and Li'l Heart Jenny wears a "SWEET" placard. **$8.00 each.**

Target 2003 **Easter Garden Kelly** is a li'l bunny in her plush pink and white rabbit suit with plush ears, **Easter Garden Melody** is a li'l flower in her pink top with green petal dress and flower petal hat, **Easter Garden Melody** is a li'l lamb in her plush lamb costume with black ears, gloves, and socks, and **Easter Garden Nikki** (top of next page) is a li'l chick in her yellow chick costume with orange leggings; **$8.00 each. Easter Garden Tamika** (top of next page) is a li'l chick in her yellow chick costume with orange leggings; **$18.00.**

Target 2003 **Halloween Fortune Barbie** is a green-eyed fortune teller wearing a purple top, gold hoop earrings and a medallion necklace, a striped skirt, and a bandana. She comes with a crystal ball and six good luck cards. **$15.00.**

Target 2003 **Halloween Party Kelly** is dressed as a black and red spider, **Halloween Party Belinda** is a cat, **Deidre** is a witch, **Jenny** is a witch, **Nikki** is a pumpkin in a plush, satiny orange costume, and **Tommy** is a dragon. **$8.00 each.**

Target 2003 **Barbie Holiday Stocking Gift Set** includes a green-eyed Barbie doll with the Generation Girl Barbie head mold wearing a short version of the grocery 1999 Holiday Surprise Barbie doll's dress, along with a diary, a coin purse, a play watch, hair clips, a compact mirror with comb, sunglasses, and a flower ring. **$14.00.**

Target 2003 **Christmas Morning 2003 Barbie** wears red pajamas featuring snowman and snowflake designs. She carries a plush teddy bear, and her cardboard gift box contains a silver snowflake ornament on a silver cord for the child. **$12.00.**

Target 2003 **My Scene Chelsea** is one of three surplus My Scene dolls that Mattel offered to Target in very limited quantities packaged with working My Scene FM radios with earphones. Barbie doll was not offered in this series. Chelsea has streaked brown hair and brown eyes and comes with a yellow FM radio. **$17.00.**

Target 2003 **My Scene Delancey** has teal green eyes and platinum blonde hair with brown streaks. She is packaged with a brown My Scene FM radio. **$17.00.**

Target 2003 **My Scene Madison** has blue eyes and curly, dark brown hair with blonde highlights. She is packaged with a purple My Scene FM radio. **$17.00.**

Target 2004 **Valentine Darlings Kelly and Belinda** debut a new, over-sized Kelly head dated 2003. Valentine Darlings Kelly is dressed as a fairy wearing a satiny red heart-print dress with tulle underskirt, heart antennae, and iridescent wings, and Valentine Darlings Belinda is dressed as Cupid in a sheer pale pink pierced-heart design dress with iridescent wings and strap-on sandals. **$6.00 each.**

Target 2004 **Hoppy Spring Kelly** (white or black) wears a pink and white plush bunny suit with a bunny ears headband accented with a pink bow. **Hoppy Spring Marisa** wears a purple and white plush bunny suit with a bunny ears headband accented with a purple bow. These dolls use the enlarged, new Kelly head mold. A spring base is included with each doll. **$6.00 each.**

Target 2004 **Halloween Party Kelly** (white or black) is a witch, **Kerstie** is a pumpkin, **Melody** is a tiger, **Nikki** is a ghost, and **Tommy** is a vampire. **$10.00 each.**

Target 2004 **Boo-tiful Halloween Barbie**, the "ghostess with the mostess," has a large head with white hair. She wears a white dress with a sheer white shawl and shoes. A ghost Halloween ring is included for the child. **$15.00.**

Target 2004 **My Scene Shopping Spree Delancey** wears jeans, a sweater, and glasses, and she comes with a "d" purse, a cell phone, a striped shirt, an "Xhiliration" skirt, a boxed boom box, a coin purse, four CD cases, a magazine, a red Target shopping basket, three perfume/lotion bottles, and a cardboard Target bag. **$18.00.**

Toys "R" Us 1984 **Crystal Ken**, black, is the first Toys "R" Us exclusive Barbie family doll. The 1984 children's line had white versions of Crystal Barbie and Crystal Ken and a black Crystal Barbie, but there was no date for black Crystal Barbie, so Toys "R" Us offered this black Crystal Ken with painted afro and a white suit. **$24.00.**

Toys "R" Us 1984 **Ken Dream 'Vette** is Ken doll's powder blue Corvette with dark blue interior. The California license plate reads, "KEN." The car's features include a TV/telephone/radio console, luggage rack, bucket seats with headrests, super tread tires with custom wheel covers, and bumper guards. Nearly all vehicles are made for Barbie doll, so this Dream 'Vette is especially desirable and hard to find. **$55.00.**

Toys "R" Us 1986 **Dance Sensation Barbie** is the first Toys "R" Us Barbie doll exclusive, although her outfits were sold separately at most stores. Her dance outfit combines to form ten different looks. **$28.00.**

1984 **Dance Sensation Spectacular Fashions** contains most of the outfit pieces used with Dance Sensation Barbie. $15.00.

Toys "R" Us 1986 **Vacation Sensation Barbie** wears a blue jumpsuit and has a shorts outfit and a swimsuit and skirt. All three fashions are from the "B" Active Fashions series, with the addition of luggage and travel accessories. $25.00.

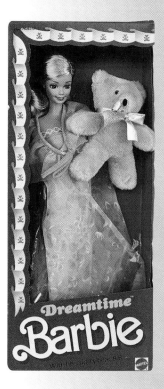

Toys "R" Us 1988 **Vacation Sensation Barbie** is a reissue of the 1986 set featuring the same fashions in different colors. Barbie doll now wears a pink and white jumpsuit and has violet eyes, while her 1986 predecessor has aqua eyes. Both boxes use the same pictures of the 1986 doll and fashions. $28.00.

1985 **Dreamtime Barbie** has a shade of purple nightgown and peignoir. The box states that Barbie doll's bear is named B.B., for *Barbie's Bear*. This doll was sold by most retailers and is shown here for comparison to the Toys "R" Us edition. $20.00.

Toys "R" Us 1988 **Dreamtime Barbie** is a reissue of the original playline 1985 Dreamtime Barbie. The Toys "R" Us doll's box is dated 1988 and her outfit is more pink than purple in this set. Nowhere on the box is the plush pink teddy bear's name mentioned. **$20.00.**

Toys "R" Us 1988 **Show 'N Ride Barbie** is dressed for horseback riding with a red jacket, riding pants, and a top with a "B" collar. She has an extra blue skirt for awards shows and has a horse blanket and four horseshoes for her horse. The doll's pants have been found in both cream or brown colors. **$25.00.**

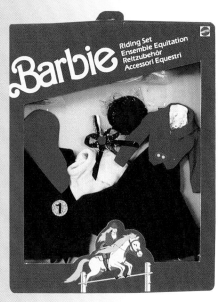

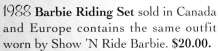

1988 **Barbie Riding Set** sold in Canada and Europe contains the same outfit worn by Show 'N Ride Barbie. **$20.00.**

Toys "R" Us 1988 **Tennis Stars Barbie & Ken** features the dolls in coordinating pink and blue tennis outfits. The tennis net is unique to this set. **$27.00.**

Toys "R" Us 1989 **Denim Fun Barbie Cool City Blues!** dolls wear denim fashions that were sold separately at most stores. **$26.00.**

Toys "R" Us 1989 **Party Treats Barbie** is the first all-original Barbie doll and fashion for Toys "R" Us. She wears a pink party dress, with balloons appliqué on her bodice, a shimmery lace overskirt, and sleeves. Toys "R" Us advertising proclaimed, "It's Barbie's 30th birthday, and she's looking sweet as can be in her candy-striped outfit." **$15.00.**

Toys "R" Us 1989 **Pepsi Spirit Barbie** was also called Pepsi Generation Barbie and Pepsi Picnic Barbie in Toys "R" Us advertising. The Pepsi name appears on five pieces of this doll's red, white, and blue ensemble: on her shirt, belt, denim jacket, blanket, and beach bag. These dolls have been found with red earrings, with earring holes where red earrings were originally intended, or with no earrings and no earring holes. Interestingly, Mattel's relationship with Pepsi-Cola dates back to 1974, when Barbie, Ken, Skipper, and Francie dolls wore Pepsi-Cola-print Best Buy fashions and had miniature cola bottles. **$45.00.**

Toys "R" Us 1989 **Pepsi Spirit Skipper** matches her big sister with her red, white, and blue Pepsi ensemble. She comes with a white beach blanket/bag, although the box photos picture it as red. **$42.00.**

Toys "R" Us 1989 **Sweet Roses Barbie** doll's pink gown changes for every room; she has a short dress for the living room, an apron for the kitchen, a bodysuit for the bedroom, and a long gown for parties. Toys "R" Us called Sweet Roses Barbie a Special 30th Anniversary Collector's Item in its advertising, which also included the Pink Jubilee Barbie logo. **$16.00.**

1990 **Home Pretty Barbie**, a regular children's line doll, is identical to Sweet Roses Barbie minus the miniskirt. **$10.00.**

Toys "R" Us 1990 **Cool Looks Barbie** wears an orange and pink top with matching tiered skirt and leggings and a black print vest. This fashion was initially intended for Barbie doll's teen cousin Jazzie. **$12.00.**

Toys "R" Us 1990 **Dream Date Skipper** is a European doll in an English-language box sold exclusively in the U.S. by Toys "R" Us. She wears a blue gown with a bow-design net overskirt. She has beautiful reddish hair with blonde bangs and a long blonde hairpiece. The Dream Date name was used in 1983 with Barbie, Ken, and P.J. dolls. **$17.00.**

Toys "R" Us 1990 **Doctor Barbie** is a reissue of the regular children's line Doctor Barbie of 1988. The Toys "R" Us doll wears silver-painted earrings, while the original wears clear plastic earrings with "diamonds." **$20.00.**

Toys "R" Us 1990 **Western Fun Barbie Gift Set** includes Western Fun Barbie dressed in a blue bodysuit, a pink fringed jacket, and a Southwestern-style skirt, and also comes with her horse Sun Runner. This set was also sold by Children's Palace and several other toy stores. The doll in this set was made in Mexico and has experienced facial discoloration and yellowing; the oils in her face have caused her lips to lose their color. Only a few different dolls were made in Mexico for sale in the U.S. during this time, but most of them have suffered similar discoloration. **$25.00.**

Toys "R" Us 1990 **Winter Fun Barbie** wears a white ski fashion, a white jacket with white faux fur trim, a matching hat, and boots. She comes with skis, ski poles, and sunglasses. **$18.00.**

Toys "R" Us 1991 **Barbie & Friends Gift Set** finds Barbie, Ken, and Skipper dolls wearing Disney fashions and Mickey Mouse–ears hats. A red Mickey Mouse balloon is included. The Barbie and Ken dolls in this set were repackaged in a 1993 Euro Disney gift set, but the Ken doll used in that set has a newer head mold. This set should not be confused with the 1983 Barbie & Friends set. **$32.00.**

Toys "R" Us 1991 **Beauty Pageant Skipper** doll's box says, "Talent and charm win the beauty contest." She wears a swimsuit under her ruffled dress with boa and has a "Skipper" sash. She was sold as a children's line doll in Europe called Beauty Teen Skipper. **$15.00.**

Toys "R" Us 1991 **My First Barbie Deluxe Fashion Gift Set** was shared by Toys "R" Us, Sears, and others. My First Barbie, dressed in pink as a ballerina, has nine different articles of clothing to combine into five different outfits. My First Barbie dolls have unbending, smooth plastic legs for easy dressing. **$16.00.**

Toys "R" Us 1992 **School Fun Barbie**, black, was introduced later than the white doll and therefore has the new, slimmer *Barbie* name logo on her box and a different box design. **$15.00.**

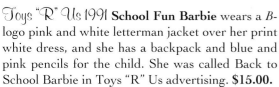

Toys "R" Us 1991 **School Fun Barbie** wears a *B*-logo pink and white letterman jacket over her print white dress, and she has a backpack and blue and pink pencils for the child. She was called Back to School Barbie in Toys "R" Us advertising. **$15.00.**

Toys "R" Us 1991 **Ski Fun Midge** is a European doll packaged in an English box and sold exclusively in the U.S. by Toys "R" Us. Baby boomers will remember freckle-faced Midge, Barbie doll's best friend from the 1960s. Mattel reintroduced Midge to a new generation of children in 1988. Ski Fun Midge has freckles and red hair, as does her 1963 predecessor. **$20.00.**

Toys "R" Us 1991 **Sweet Romance Barbie** wears a blue lamé top with gloves and a long blue skirt. She has a child-size locket that contains solid fragrance. **$18.00.**

Toys "R" Us 1991 **Wedding Day Kelly & Todd Gift Set** was sold through both Toys "R" Us and JCPenney. The dolls are part of the children's line Midge Wedding Party. *Barbie Magazine* called this flower girl Kelly the sister of Barbie doll, while ring bearer Todd was called Ken doll's brother, but Mattel does not recognize that relationship, and this Kelly is nothing like Barbie doll's baby sister Kelly. In the 1960s, Barbie doll's twin siblings were named Tutti and Todd, but by 1991 the name *Tutti* was no longer in vogue, so this Kelly was paired with Todd. The Kelly and Todd dolls in this set share the same head mold, but the prototype Todd doll has molded, painted hair (see photo on far right), not flocked as used in the set. **$20.00.**

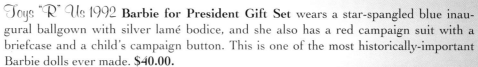

Toys "R" Us 1992 **Barbie for President Gift Set** wears a star-spangled blue inaugural ballgown with silver lamé bodice, and she also has a red campaign suit with a briefcase and a child's campaign button. This is one of the most historically-important Barbie dolls ever made. **$40.00.**

Toys "R" Us 1992 **Barbie for President Gift Set**, black, is shown in the second style box with stars on the top banner. The first style box has the official Presidential seals on the box fronts where the stars are, as seen on the white doll's box. **$34.00.**

Toys "R" Us 1992 **Cool 'N Sassy Barbie** (white or black) wears a blue print jacket, yellow leggings, a yellow top, and a sheer pink skirt. **$13.00.**

Toys "R" Us 1992 **Fashion Brights Barbie** (white or black) wears a pink teddy and comes with 14 fashion pieces that combine for eight different looks. **$15.00.**

Toys "R" Us 1992 **Radiant in Red Barbie** is a vision in red from the red bow in her red hair to the hem of her gown. This doll was an instant favorite with collectors. **$22.00.**

Toys "R" Us 1992 **Radiant in Red Barbie**, black, is the first black exclusive Barbie doll to use a lighter skin tone. Some dealers have called this doll ethnic or even Hispanic because of the lighter skin, but she does use the black Christie head mold and Toys "R" Us advertising refers to the doll as black. **$20.00.**

Toys "R" Us 1992 **Spring Parade Barbie** is dressed in her Easter best — a lavender skirt with a shimmering white bodice and a white hat, and she carries a basket of flowers. Dolls sold prior to Easter 1992 have a "Perfect for Easter" sticker on the box's window. **$16.00.**

Toys "R" Us 1992 **Spring Parade Barbie**, black, was sold in the white doll's box with stickers of her new stock number placed over the white doll's numbers. Even the photo on the box back shows the white doll. Dolls remaining in stores after Easter 1992 had a yellow "Toys 'R' Us Limited Edition" sticker placed over the "Perfect for Easter" sticker so that leftover dolls would not appear outdated. **$16.00.**

Toys "R" Us 1992 **Totally Hair Courtney** is Skipper doll's best friend, which means they are the same size and can share the same wardrobe. Courtney wears a blue Pucci-style dress with a green hair decoration, and she comes with a tube of Dep styling gel for her ankle-length hair. **$17.00.**

Toys "R" Us 1992 **Totally Hair Skipper** was created to complement her sister Totally Hair Barbie doll, the best-selling Barbie doll of all time. She wears a pink Pucci-style minidress with matching leggings and has a pink hair decoration. **$15.00.**

Toys "R" Us 1993 **Dream Wedding Barbie** wears a white wedding gown with tulle overskirt and veil. She is packaged with flower girl Stacie, wearing a pink dress and white hat, and ring bearer Todd, in a white tuxedo. This is a "dream" wedding because Mattel prefers to let children decide whether or not Barbie and Ken dolls will marry. **$35.00.**

Toys "R" Us 1993 **Dream Wedding Barbie**, black, comes with the first black Todd doll made; black Todd dolls were available in 1993 and 1994 only in this Toys "R" Us set. **$40.00.**

Toys "R" Us 1993 **Love-to-Read Barbie Deluxe Gift Set** features Barbie doll, wearing a floral-print white dress with purple and white striped sleeves and border, along with two of Mattel's Heart Family baby dolls, each wearing fashions using the same material as Barbie doll's dress. *My Little Book of Mother Goose Rhymes* is included. Mattel donated one dollar of the sale from each set to Reading Is Fundamental, Inc. **$20.00.**

Toys "R" Us 1993 **Malt Shoppe Barbie** is dressed in a 1950s-style blue poodle skirt with a pink sweater and a scarf. A free ice cream cone coupon for use at Dairy Queen is included. **$16.00.**

294

Toys "R" Us 1993 **Moonlight Magic Barbie**, black, uses a light skin tone. **$22.00.**

Toys "R" Us 1993 **Moonlight Magic Barbie** dazzled collectors with her coveted black hair, pale skin, and beautiful black gown with golden glitter, overskirt, and golden hairbow. **$25.00.**

Toys "R" Us 1993 **Police Officer Barbie** (white or black) is part of the Toys "R" Us Career Collection. Barbie doll wears a blue uniform with a hat and comes with a gold and white dress for the Police Awards Ball, a child-size Barbie Police Department badge (with badge number 77, the same as the Mattel designer's husband's badge), and a cardboard German Shepherd police dog. **$40.00.**

Toys "R" Us 1993 **School Spirit Barbie** is essentially a reissued School Fun Barbie doll wearing the same basic outfit as the 1991 edition made with different fabrics. Barbie doll's dress uses material from the K-Mart Fashion Friends Casual Wear Fashions #7484 and #7485. The box back shows Barbie doll standing in front of a high school building. **$12.00.**

Toys "R" Us 1993 **School Spirit Barbie**, black, has a light skin tone, in sharp contrast to her 1991 counterpart with dark skin. **$14.00.**

Toys "R" Us 1993 **Sea Holiday Barbie** is a foreign market Barbie doll sold exclusively in the U.S. by Toys "R" Us, F.A.O. Schwarz, and independent doll shops. The doll's play camera was initially supposed to contain lip gloss for the child, but the cameras were altered before they actually reached stores. Shown here is the first-style box featuring a photo of a child applying lip gloss. **$16.00.**

Toys "R" Us 1993 **Sea Holiday Barbie** doll's box was changed to eliminate any reference to lip gloss. Boxes now read, "See Barbie and friends through pretend camera," and the photo on the box front only shows the camera. **$14.00.**

Toys "R" Us 1993 **Spots 'n Dots Teresa** is the first retail store exclusive Teresa doll. She wears the same outfit as Barbie doll, but usually Barbie doll's friends wear outfits in different colors even if the style is identical. **$19.00.**

Toys "R" Us 1993 **Spots 'n Dots Barbie** wears a Dalmatian-print top with a tiered red skirt and a hairbow. She has a Dalmatian dog first used with the 1992 Pet Pals Kevin doll. **$17.00.**

Toys "R" Us 1993 **Western Stampin' Barbie with Western Star Horse** pairs the playline Western Stampin' Barbie, wearing a silver lamé dress with a blue fringed jacket, blue boots with spurs, and a blue cowboy hat, with her horse with combable mane. **$22.00.**

Toys "R" Us 1994 **African American Collection Asha** is the first in this unique series which presents dolls dressed in authentic clothing reflecting the African American heritage. The name *Asha* means "life" in Swahili and was first used in the discontinued Shani doll line (officially listed by Mattel as Barbie Doll's Friends), which consisted of Shani, Asha, Nichelle, and Jamal. Each of the girl dolls used a different head mold and had various shades of darker skin. Barbie doll has now used Shani, Asha, and Nichelle dolls' head molds. In this series, Asha uses Shani's head mold, even though the original 1991 Asha had her own head mold. **$22.00.**

Toys "R" Us 1995 **African-American Collection Asha**, second edition, also wears a dress utilizing West Africa's Kente cloth (a cotton fabric woven on narrow looms in 4" strips and edge-sewn together), known as the fabric of royalty in earlier times and used here on the head wrap and borders of Asha's flared purple-dotted orange skirt with golden-sheen wrap. **$20.00.**

Toys "R" Us 1996 **African-American Collection Asha**, third edition, wears a shimmering one-piece gown and matching headband, with a large waist bow. **$20.00.**

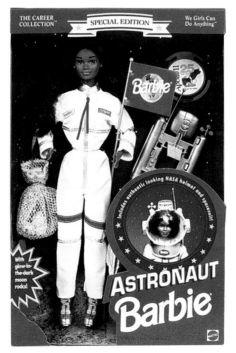

Toys "R" Us 1994 **Astronaut Barbie** (white or black) is from the Career Collection. An earlier Astronaut Barbie sold at most stores in 1986 wore a magenta lamé and silver spacesuit. The 1994 Astronaut Barbie commemorates the 25th anniversary of the Apollo 11 moonwalk wearing a white spacesuit with gray boots. The box back advertises NASA's Space Week "'94, July 16 – 24." The doll comes with a child's badge inscribed, "Apollo 11 25 1969 – 1994 The Eagle Has Landed." Glow-in-the-dark moon rocks and a Barbie flag are included. This doll is on permanent display at the Smithsonian Institute. **$28.00.**

Toys "R" Us 1994 **Emerald Elegance Barbie** (white or black) has a satiny blue bodice, an emerald-green skirt with shimmering net overskirt, a matching jacket, and a hair decoration. **$20.00.**

Toys "R" Us 1994 **Party Time Barbie** wears a blue party dress with lacy white trim, with a coral bow at her waist and in her hair. She is packaged with a child's real wristwatch. **$12.00.**

Toys "R" Us 1994 **Party Time Teresa** wears a mint green party dress with lacy white trim, with a pink bow at her waist and in her hair. She is packaged with a real child's wrist watch. **$12.00.**

Toys "R" Us 1995 **Party Time Barbie**, black, wears the same dress as the white doll and has a similar style watch, but she wasn't available until 1995. **$12.00.**

Toys "R" Us 1994 **Quinceanera Teresa** wears a tiered sheer pink party dress with a crown, pearl necklace, and bouquet as she celebrates her fifteenth birthday. The box is in both English and Spanish, since the Quinceanera celebration is popular in Mexico and Latin America. **$18.00.**

Toys "R" Us 1994 **Home For the Holidays** is a Christmas playset including a Christmas tree, a baby grand piano and bench, a mantel, a couch, a scooter, a teddy bear, a candleabra, a coffee pot, cups and saucers, a tray, and a picture frame. This is very hard to find. **$35.00.**

Toys "R" Us 1995 **Bicyclin' Barbie** is a reissue of the playline 1994 Bicyclin' Barbie in a different box that is 1" smaller than the original. The Toys "R" Us Bicyclin' Barbie doll's box is dated 1994, has the new choking hazard warning symbol in the lower left front of the box, and misspells the word *pedals* as *peddles* on the box front in the phrase, "She peddles by herself!" The 1994 doll has the word *pedals* spelled correctly on her box front, plus the 1994 doll's box back features an ad for Epcot's Magical World of Barbie live show, which the Toys "R" Us doll's box omitted. **$14.00.**

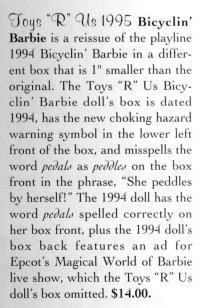

Toys "R" Us 1994 **Bicyclin' Barbie**, black, is a reissue of the 1994 black Bicyclin' Barbie in a 1995 box that misspells the word *pedals* as *peddles* on her box front. Bicyclin' Barbie dolls used new, poseable bodies with flat feet that were first used on the 1994 Gymnast Barbie dolls. **$14.00.**

Toys "R" Us 1995 **Dr. Barbie** (white or black) is a reissue of the playline 1994 Dr. Barbie wearing a blue dress and white doctor's coat, but this Toys "R" Us edition has three baby patients while the 1994 doll comes with just one. A battery-operated stethoscope detects her patients' heartbeats. Three of four different babies were randomly inserted in the package, but the black-haired Hispanic baby in the purple towel is the least common. **$20.00.**

Toys "R" Us 1994 **International Pen Friend Barbie** wears a satiny blue jacket with white collar and cuffs, a world flag-print dress, and a red cap. Included with the doll are forms to assist a child in locating pen pals. **$13.00.**

Toys "R" Us 1995 **Fire Fighter Barbie** (white or black) is from the Career Collection. She has fire fighter pants, a shirt and turnout coat with "Barbie Fire Rescue 1," a yellow helmet, an emergency bag, a beeper, a child-size "Barbie Fire Rescue" badge, and a Dalmatian. **$45.00.**

Toys "R" Us 1995 **My Size Bride Barbie**, brunette, is the first three-foot-tall Barbie doll exclusive. She wears a white wedding gown and veil and is simply a brunette version of the playline blonde doll. The My Size Bride Barbie dolls use the 1977 SuperStar Barbie Fashion Face head mold. **$95.00.**

Toys "R" Us 1995 **POG Fun Barbie** wears multicolored striped shorts and a matching shirt with a blue skirt with white polka dots and a matching headband. She is packaged with five POG milk caps, a Barbie-logo slammer, and a hand-bag. Two of her milk caps picture the POG Fun Barbie doll. **$10.00.**

Toys "R" Us 1994 **POG Barbie** is the name used on the Canadian version of POG Fun Barbie. Both versions showed up at Toys "R" Us. **$10.00.**

Toys "R" Us 1995 **Purple Passion Barbie** wears a sparkly purple skirt with satiny purple bodice and a purple hair decoration. She has lovely silky red hair. **$20.00.**

Toys "R" Us 1995 **Purple Passion Barbie**, black, has a light skin tone. She comes in one of two box styles; one has the Barbie name printed directly on the window that extends to the bottom of the box, while the other has a shorter window with the Barbie name printed directly on the cardboard box. **$20.00.**

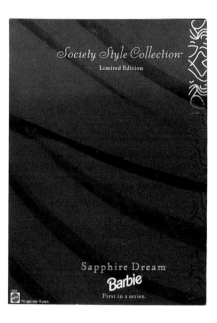

Toys "R" Us 1995 **Sapphire Dream Barbie** is first in the Society Style Collection. She has rooted eyelashes and wears a sapphire blue velvet gown with a sheer gold-accented cape with rhinestone jewelry and a blue hair decoration. Each doll in the Society Style Collection cost $49.99. **$32.00.**

Toys "R" Us 1995 **Sunflower Barbie** wears a pink sunflower-print dress with a black and white checked bodice accented by a large daisy, along with a matching hat. A heart-shaped purse containing fragrance is included for the child. **$11.00.** Mattel's pre-production doll has a pink and white checked top with a hat and skirt made using fabric from Hill's Polly Pocket Barbie. **$55.00.**

Toys "R" Us 1994 **Sunflower Teresa** wears a purple sunflower-print dress with a pink and white checked bodice accented by a large daisy, along with a matching hat. A heart-shaped purse containing fragrance is included for the child. **$11.00.**

Toys "R" Us 1995 **Super Talk! Barbie** (white or black) is a reissued version of the popular playline 1994 Super Talk! Barbie in a 1995-dated box that is 1" smaller than the 1994 box. The new warning symbol is in the upper left corner of the reissued dolls' boxes, and the Toys "R" Us edition has a new stock number. This Doll says over 100,000 things, using a computer chip that randomly combines phrases into coherent sentences. For instance, Barbie doll might say, "Let's go/to the mall/with Skipper/on the weekend" when one presses the button in her back. A second press of the button might produce a newly-combined sentence like, "Let's go/to the beach/with Ken/on Saturday." **$15.00.**

Toys "R" Us 1995 **Travelin' Sisters Playset** contains Barbie, Skipper, Stacie, and Kelly dolls in matching fashions featuring red Scottish Terrier–print fabric, blue denim-look material, and white with black polka dots. Plastic luggage is included. **$38.00.**

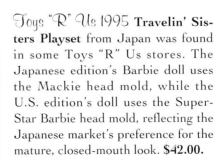

Toys "R" Us 1995 **Travelin' Sisters Playset** from Japan was found in some Toys "R" Us stores. The Japanese edition's Barbie doll uses the Mackie head mold, while the U.S. edition's doll uses the Super-Star Barbie head mold, reflecting the Japanese market's preference for the mature, closed-mouth look. **$42.00.**

Toys "R" Us 1995 **Wedding Party Barbie Deluxe Set** (white or black) depicts Barbie doll's dream of a garden wedding, as she wears a white wedding gown with lacy white bodice and sleeves, accompanied by flower girl Stacie in a yellow dress and ring bearer Todd in a white tuxedo. **$38.00.**

Toys "R" Us 1995 **Western Stampin' Barbie With Western Star Horse**, black, contains a black Barbie doll with a light skin tone dressed in a red and gold western outfit similar to that worn by the 1993 playline Western Stampin' Tara Lynn; the Toys "R" Us doll has different fringe and also comes with red riding pants; included is her Western Star Horse. **$25.00.**

1993 **Western Stampin' Tara Lynn** is shown here so collectors can see the differences between the fringe and gold border on her vest and that on the doll above. Tara Lynn has a gold belt buckle, which the Barbie doll lacks. She uses the Steffie head mold. **$24.00.**

Toys "R" Us 1995 **Winter Sports Barbie and Ken** are foreign-market dolls sold in the U.S. by F.A.O. Schwarz, JCPenney, and Toys "R" Us. The dolls, bodysuits, knee pads, and ice skates are taken from the 1995 U.S. Hot Skatin' playline dolls, while the jackets, snowboards, skis and ski poles, sunglasses, and boots are original to this set. **$16.00.**

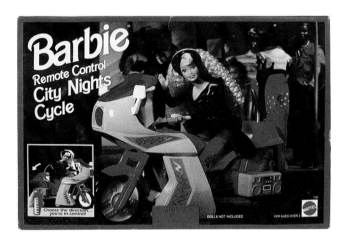

Toys "R" Us 1995 **Winter Sports Midge** is a foreign-market doll sold in the U.S. exclusively by Toys "R" Us. The doll, bodysuit, knee pads, ice skates, and skirt are taken from the U.S. 1995 Hot Skatin' Midge, while the jacket, snowboard, skis and ski poles, sunglasses, and boots are original to this set. **$18.00.**

Toys "R" Us 1995 **Remote Control City Nights Cycle** is a purple, pink, and aqua vehicle that operates by remote control. **$15.00.**

Toys "R" Us 1996 **Native American Barbie** is the only Dolls of the World Collection doll exclusive to one retailer. She wears an authentically styled blue "buckskin" dress with turquoise fringe and moccasins. She uses the Diva head mold. **$30.00.**

Toys "R" Us 1996 **Birthday Fun Kelly Gift-set** contains Barbie doll and Kelly doll, and Kelly doll's friend Chelsie doll wearing party outfits. A plastic birthday cake and three plastic balloons are included. **$24.00.**

Toys "R" Us 1996 **Dr. Barbie**, black, is noticeably different from her 1995 counterpart, as this 1996 edition uses a lighter skin tone. **$22.00.**

Toys "R" Us 1996 **Dr. Barbie** is basically the same doll as the 1995 edition with a larger box, which now includes a child's badge depicting a heart inside a cross and a card with rules for caring for the baby. **$20.00.**

Toys "R" Us 1996 **Crystal Splendor Barbie** has platinum blonde hair and wears a satiny white bodice and long sparkly white skirt. She originally cost $24.99. **$20.00.**

Toys "R" Us 1996 **Crystal Splendor Barbie**, black, has a light skin tone. The photo on the back of the box (at left) shows this doll with the Asha head mold instead of the Christie head mold that was actually used. **$20.00.**

Toys "R" Us 1996 **Got Milk? Barbie** (white or black) is based on the popular Got Milk? national advertising campaign. Barbie doll wears cow-print short overalls with a pink t-shirt. A tray of cookies, a plastic milk carton, and a cup are included for the doll, while the child gets a plastic "B" straw. **$11.00.**

Toys "R" Us 1996 **My Size Bride Barbie**, red-head, arrived at Toys "R" Us while its brunette My Size exclusive was being clearanced for $86.90. The redheads were given the same clearance price and disappeared quickly. **$100.00.**

Toys "R" Us 1996 **Olympic Gymnast Barbie**, redhead, was sold only at Toys "R" Us, while blonde and black dolls were available at most stores. She wears a red, white, and blue competition uniform with a 1996-dated gym bag. Two versions of the box exist; the version with "SPECIAL EDITON" at the top is harder to find. **$18.00.**

Toys "R" Us 1996 **Pink Ice Barbie** is the first in a new series. She has rooted eyelashes and the Mackie head mold. She wears a pink silk shantung gown adorned with beads and sequins and pink marabou feathers. Toys "R" Us advertising proclaimed, "Barbie has taken fashion to a glamorous new height." She is the most expensive Toys "R" Us exclusive to date, with an original retail of $149.99, but she was clearanced in 2000 for $30.00. **$56.00.**

Toys "R" Us 1996 **Radiant Rose Barbie** (white or black) is second in the Society Style Collection. Barbie has rooted eyelashes and long dark red hair adorned with a red satin flower, and she wears a red velvet sleeveless ball gown with a row of roses draped over her right shoulder and extending to her waist and a red foil print satin overskirt. **$35.00.**

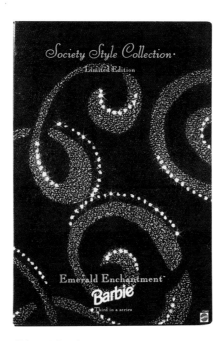

Toys "R" Us 1997 **Emerald Enchantment Barbie** is third in the Society Style Collection. She wears an emerald green taffeta dress, a velvet skirt with golden glitter swirl pattern, an emerald green chiffon-like shawl, and a tiara with rhinestones. She has blonde hair with green eyes and rooted eyelashes. **$36.00.**

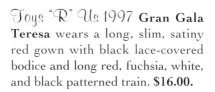

Toys "R" Us 1997 **Gardening Fun Barbie & Kelly Gift Set** includes Barbie, wearing white garden-print capri pants, a blue denim shirt, and a blue and white striped hat with flower on the brim, and Kelly, wearing blue and white striped overalls over a green t-shirt. A basket with flowers, a pail, a shovel, a spade, a watering can, a trowel, and a cardboard shelf are included. **$20.00.**

Toys "R" Us 1997 **Gran Gala Teresa** wears a long, slim, satiny red gown with black lace-covered bodice and long red, fuchsia, white, and black patterned train. **$16.00.**

Toys "R" Us 1997 **101 Dalmatians Barbie** (white or black) wears a Dalmatian-print vest, a white skirt with black spots, and a matching headband. She carries a red bone-shaped purse and sunglasses while holding the leash of a Dalmatian with golden dog tag. This dog was first used with the 1992 Pet Pals Kevin doll. **$17.00.**

Toys "R" Us 1997 **101 Dalmatians Teresa.** The doll's box back features a maze with a double-decker London bus, three-story townhouses, Big Ben, and a bridge — the locales in Disney's 1961 animated classic. **$17.00.**

Toys "R" Us 1997 **Oreo Fun Barbie** celebrates the 95th anniversary of the Oreo cookie, the best-selling cookie in America. She wears an Oreo cookie–print baseball jacket, a white t-shirt with the Oreo logo, a blue skirt, a headband, and black gymshoes. She comes with an Oreo purse, cups, plates, and a cardboard box of Oreo cookies. **$16.00.**

Toys "R" Us 1997 **Paleontologist Barbie** (white or black) is from the Career Collection. She wears belted khaki shorts, a dinosaur-print shirt, a pink scarf, a hat, socks, and boots. She carries a backpack and canteen and comes with two toy dinosaurs (which vary from set to set), a map, a dinosaur badge for the child, and cardboard fossils. **$25.00.**

Toys "R" Us 1997 **Sapphire Sophisticate Barbie** (white or black) is last in the Toys "R" Us glamour doll series. She wears a sapphire blue ballgown accented with blue and silver jeweled buttons. **$20.00.**

Toys "R" Us 1997 **Share a Smile Barbie** wears a pink denim miniskirt with a matching vest, a pink headband, a white t-shirt, and pink tennis shoes. Barbie doll's friendship necklace doubles as a child's bracelet, and a separate child-sized friendship necklace is included for the child. **$10.00.**

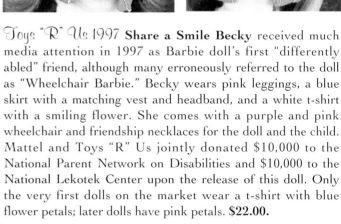

Toys "R" Us 1997 **Share a Smile Becky** received much media attention in 1997 as Barbie doll's first "differently abled" friend, although many erroneously referred to the doll as "Wheelchair Barbie." Becky wears pink leggings, a blue skirt with a matching vest and headband, and a white t-shirt with a smiling flower. She comes with a purple and pink wheelchair and friendship necklaces for the doll and the child. Mattel and Toys "R" Us jointly donated $10,000 to the National Parent Network on Disabilities and $10,000 to the National Lekotek Center upon the release of this doll. Only the very first dolls on the market wear a t-shirt with blue flower petals; later dolls have pink petals. **$22.00.**

Toys "R" Us 1997 **Share a Smile Christie** wears a purple denim miniskirt with a matching vest and headband and a white t-shirt with a smiling flower. **$12.00.**

Toys "R" Us 1997 **Show Parade Barbie with Her Star Stampin' Horse** includes Barbie with the bend and move Gymnast body wearing an original parade fashion, a horseshoe-print bodysuit with silver lame fringe on the bodice and cuffs, a silver lame scarf, a pink hat, and short pink boots. Her horse's hooves stamp stars or hoofprints. Earrings for the child are included, along with a saddle, bridle, reins, and five stars for the horse's mane or tail. **$22.00.**

Toys "R" Us 1997 **Show Parade Barbie with Her Star Stampin' Horse**, black, uses the Christie head mold with dark skin. The black doll's horse has a dark brown mane and tail, while the Caucasian doll's horse has a blonde mane and tail. **$22.00.**

Toys "R" Us 1997 **Wedding Fantasy Barbie & Ken Gift Set** features Barbie doll's "wonderful dream" of marrying Ken doll. Barbie doll wears a lovely ivory wedding gown with lacy white overskirt and sleeves, a veil with hair bow, pumps, and she holds a single white flower. Ken doll wears an ivory tuxedo. A wedding cake (with a real photo of Barbie and Ken on top), table service, and a gift box are included. **$36.00.**

Toys "R" Us 1997 **Fashion Avenue Spectacular Seasons Gift Set** contains one fashion for each season; the winter fashion has an adorable Santa's helper cap with white faux fur trim. The back of the box features a calendar cut out showing a doll modeling each fashion. **$20.00.**

Toys "R" Us 1998 **Charity Ball Barbie** is "proud to be the beautiful guest of honor as the first Toys "R" Us Children's Charity Collection Barbie doll," according to the box. She wears a black and silver gown. Toys "R" Us donated $100,000 to Children's Organ Transplant Association, Inc. (COTA) when it sold this doll. **$22.00.**

Toys "R" Us 1997 **Barbie Kool-Aid Stand Playset** features a working drink dispenser, three packets of Kool-Aid drink mix, two child-size glasses, four doll-size glasses, four sun visors, four pairs of doll sunglasses, stickers, and two mixing spoons. **$15.00.**

Toys "R" Us 1998 **Charity Ball Barbie**, black, uses the Asha head mold with a light skin tone. Except for the three dolls in Toys "R" Us Asha series, *all* of the African American Barbie dolls exclusive to Toys "R" Us prior to 1998 use the Christie head mold. **$22.00.**

Toys "R" Us 1998 **Golden Anniversary Barbie** commemorates Toys "R" Us' 50th anniversary. The box front features a red AIDS-awareness ribbon, and each box lists the serial number of the doll inside. Only 25,000 dolls were produced. To celebrate the 50th anniversary of Toys "R" Us, Mattel and Toys "R" Us jointly donated $50,000 to the Children Affected by AIDS Foundation (CAAF). Barbie doll wears a gown of golden brocade with heart-shaped neckline and fitted bodice which drops into a full pleated skirt, trimmed with golden and white lace and with matching capped sleeves. She has golden hair worn in a simple, elegant bob, and she has a red AIDS awareness ribbon on her bodice. She cost $99.99. **$65.00.**

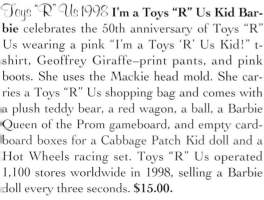

Toys "R" Us 1998 **I'm a Toys "R" Us Kid Barbie** celebrates the 50th anniversary of Toys "R" Us wearing a pink "I'm a Toys 'R' Us Kid!" t-shirt, Geoffrey Giraffe–print pants, and pink boots. She uses the Mackie head mold. She carries a Toys "R" Us shopping bag and comes with a plush teddy bear, a red wagon, a ball, a Barbie Queen of the Prom gameboard, and empty cardboard boxes for a Cabbage Patch Kid doll and a Hot Wheels racing set. Toys "R" Us operated 1,100 stores worldwide in 1998, selling a Barbie doll every three seconds. **$15.00.**

Toys "R" Us 1998 **I'm a Toys "R" Us Kid Barbie**, black, uses the Nichelle head mold with light skin tone. Both the Caucasian and African-American dolls come in two styles of boxes; the earlier box style is shown with the white doll, whose shopping bag and upper right box corner have a white background printed with "Toys 'R' Us 50th Anniversary." The black doll is shown in the later box; the shopping bag and upper right corner each have a new purple background printed with "Toys 'R' Us 50 Years Forever Fun." **$15.00.**

317

Toys "R" Us 1998 **Kelly & Ginger Gift Set** features Kelly in a denim jumper over a red and white t-shirt, riding in her red wagon. Also included are a flying disk, a brush, a dog food bowl, a bone, and Ginger, the plush dog that really walks, barks, and pulls Kelly doll's wagon! **$35.00.**

Toys "R" Us 1998 **Winter Ride Barbie Gift Set** is an exclusive shared with F.A.O. Schwarz and several other retailers. Barbie doll wears a white brocade patterned gown with faux-fur accents and a matching hat, and rides sidesaddle upon her mare. **$35.00.**

Toys "R" Us 1998 **35th Anniversary Midge** reproduces Barbie doll's first best friend, with titian hair and wearing a reproduction of her original yellow and orange swimsuit with white open-toe heels. Also included are reproductions of the original Midge box and the 1963 Senior Prom fashion #951, which is an ice blue and sea green gown with a green satin bodice and a blue and green tulle overskirt, with green open-toe shoes. A golden purse is also included, although the vintage Senior Prom fashion did not come with a purse. $45.00.

Toys "R" Us 1998 **Pilot Barbie**, white or black, from the Career Collection, has short hair and wears a blue pilot's jacket with pink trim, matching pants, a scarf, a blue pilot's cap, and pink shoes. She comes with a suitcase with adjustable handle, a passport, a luggage tag, and tickets, along with a "B" wings badge for the child. The box states that only two percent of the world's commercial pilots are women. $25.00.

Toys "R" Us 1998 **Wild Style Barbie** wears a silver lamé minidress, sheer white pantyhose, a tiger-print coat with black faux fur collar and cuffs, and black boots. Black sunglasses complete her cool look. $12.00.

Toys "R" Us 1998 **Wild Style Teresa** wears a gold lamé minidress, sheer white pantyhose, a leopard-print coat with black faux fur collar and cuffs, and black boots. She carries black sunglasses. $12.00.

Toys "R" Us 1999 **Fashion Fun Barbie Gift Set** includes a blue and silver lamé mix-and-match wardrobe. She uses the Generation Girl Barbie head mold. **$20.00.**

Toys "R" Us 1998 **Barbie Doll Display** is a clear plastic case with the Barbie logo on the front, back, and lid. The Barbie Doll Display is 16" tall, 10" wide, and 4" deep. The black case features Midnight Princess Barbie in the large box photo, and the pink case features Barbie as Cinderella in the large box photo. **$15.00 each.**

Toys "R" Us 1999 **Generation Girl Barbie Gift Set** pairs Generation Girl Barbie doll with Generation Girl Lara or Generation Girl Nichelle playline dolls available separately, and comes with a chapter book for the child. Barbie debuts a new head mold that is now used on most playline Barbie dolls. These sets were shared with Sam's Club. **$32.00.**

Toys "R" Us 1999 **101 Dalmatians Barbie** (strawberry blonde, brunette, or black) wears a red 101 Dalmatians t-shirt, a Dalmatian-print vest, a black leather-look skirt, Dalmatian-print socks, Dalmatian-rim sunglasses, and black shoes. She comes with two Dalmatian puppies and a tiny Dalmatian-print backpack. The black doll uses the Nichelle head mold. **$16.00.**

Toys "R" Us 1999 **Toy Story 2 Tour Guide Barbie** features Barbie doll as she appeared in the Disney movie, along with Woody, Buzz Lightyear, and Hamm finger puppets. **$15.00.**

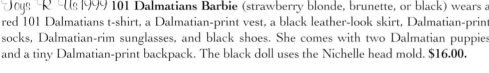

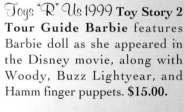

Toys "R" Us 1999 **Pink Inspiration Barbie** (blonde or brunette) wears a satiny pink gown with silver-dotted pink tulle train and long pink gloves. The doll might more aptly be called Pink Invitation Barbie since her box back shows Barbie doll's pink invitation to an annual celebration and goes into detail about the proper etiquette in replying to an invitation and the meaning of RSVP. The Toys "R" Us register receipt for the dolls refers to her as "Barbie at the Ball." **$18.00.**

Toys "R" Us 1999 **Pink Inspiration Barbie**, black, uses the Nichelle head mold with light skin. **$18.00.**

321

Toys "R" Us 1999 **Barbie Fashion Avenue Coat Collection** features five quality coat ensembles. **$12.00 each.**

Yellow #22158

Leopard #22157

Red #22160

Blue #22159

White #22156

Toys "R" Us 1999 **Space Camp Barbie** has strawberry blonde hair. She is packaged in a clever spaceship-style box with accessories like packets of freeze-dried space food, a U.S. Space Camp Wings diploma, space travelers' checks, a red and silver duffel bag, and a red cap "floating" near her. She wears a blue astronaut flight suit with black boots. A child-size U.S. Space Camp badge is included. **$18.00.**

Toys "R" Us 1999 **Space Camp Barbie**, black, uses the Nichelle head mold. **$18.00.**

Toys "R" Us 1999 **Toys "R" Us Toy Store** is the same as the Barbie Toy Store sold at most stores, except this set is customized for Toys "R" Us with a Toys "R" Us sign, Toys "R" Us shopping bags and gift boxes, and even Barbie-doll sized Geoffrey money included. **$15.00.**

Toys "R" Us 2000 **Generation Girl Dance Party Chelsie** is an aspiring folk music singer/songwriter from London. Chelsie Peterson wears a pink dress with a matching shrug, a necklace, a silver bracelet, pink shoes, and glasses. She carries a striped purse and comes with a bandeau top, a wrap skirt, a drum, drum sticks, a flute, a tambourine, maracas, and a world music guide. **$20.00.**

323

Toys "R" Us 2000 **Let's Drive Student Driver Barbie and Skipper Dolls Gift Set** features Barbie doll as the passenger and Skipper behind the wheel of a white car. Also included are a first aid kit, a cell phone, a 2000 Driver Handbook, Skipper doll's driver's license, and a driver's license for the child. **$40.00.**

Toys "R" Us 2000 **President Barbie 2000**, Hispanic, is historically important since she is the first Hispanic Barbie doll to run for the nation's highest office. She uses the Teresa head mold and is harder to find than her Caucasian and African-American counterparts. **$35.00.**

Toys "R" Us 2000 **President Barbie 2000** (white or black) is the second Barbie doll to be sold as a presidential candidate, following her 1992 election bid. Barbie doll wears a blue satin campaign suit with blue pantyhose, and she comes with a red inaugural gown, "Barbie for President" cardboard signs, bumper stickers, and a "Barbie for President" badge for the child. The bottom fronts of the boxes are either red or blue. **$30.00.**

Toys "R" Us 2000 **Royal Romance Barbie Gift Set** includes Barbie wearing a velvety purple dress with glittery silver swirls and a velvety purple-hooded, silver-lined cape. She sits sidesaddle on her white stallion. **$45.00.**

Toys "R" Us 2000 **Sign Language Barbie** (white or black) has a specially-molded hand for signing "I love you." She wears a blue top with a blue sweater, a checked skirt, white socks, and shoes, and she comes with a cling-on board/chalkboard, chalk, and vinyl sticker pictures for use in teaching American Sign Language. **$28.00.**

Toys "R" Us 2000 **Barbie Coat Collection Styles** include five high-fashion winter ensembles.

Eskimo Pink Fashion. $12.00.

Off The Slopes Fashion. $12.00.

Mezzanine Mink Fashion. $18.00.

Standing Ovation Fashion. $12.00.

Velvet & Vivaldi Fashion. $16.00.

Toys "R" Us 2000 **Barbie Lingerie Collection Styles** include four bedtime styles.

Breakfast Nook Fashion. $10.00.   Dreamscape Fashion. $8.00.   Lottery Lounge Fashion. $8.00.   Satin Slumber Fashion. $10.00.

Toys "R" Us 2001 **Bedtime Stories Gift Set With Barbie and Kelly** (white or black) features Barbie wearing Three Little Bears–print pajamas, a teal tank top, and pink slippers, and reading to Kelly, who has ringlet curls and is wearing a teal nightshirt, a diaper, and slippers. A stuffed bear and *The Three Little Bears* book are included. $18.00.

Toys "R" Us 2001 **Bedtime Stories Bed** is a pink canopy bed with teal bedding. A teddy bear is included. **$15.00.**

Toys "R" Us 2001 **Cowgirl Kelly & Pony Giftset** (white or black) includes Kelly, dressed in a cowgirl fashion with a blue hat and blue boots, along with her pony, whose head moves up and down. A saddle, blanket, reins, a bucket, a feed bag, carrots, a brush, and a car are included. **$20.00.**

Toys "R" Us 2001 **Grand Hotel Barbie** (white or black) wears a blue top and blue skirt with a jacket, pink scarf, and sunglasses. She has a sparkly pink top and long pink skirt for nighttime. Two purses, a hatbox, a suitcase, and two pairs of shoes are included. **$16.00.**

Toys "R" Us 2001 **Let's Camp! Barbie, Stacie, and Kelly Gift Set** includes the three green-eyed sisters wearing camping outfits. A tent, three sleeping bags, a leaf booklet, binoculars, and a lantern are included. Caucasian set, **$40.00**; African American set, **$65.00.**

Toys "R" Us 2001 **Renaissance Rose Barbie Giftset** includes golden-haired Barbie, dressed in a pink and blue gown, riding sidesaddle on her horse to the Renaissance Faire. **$40.00.**

Toys "R" Us 2001 **Spanish Teacher Barbie** (white or Hispanic) will speak up to 60 words and phrases in both English and Spanish when the button in her back is pressed. Flash cards, a quiz, an easel, and a notebook key chain for the child are included. **$22.00.**

Toys "R" Us 2001 **The Tale of the Forest Princess Barbie**, white or black, wears a green dress with golden trim and a yellow overskirt. She carries a basket and a bell and comes with two blue birds, an owl, a squirrel, a raccoon, three rabbits, and a 24-page Golden Book. **$35.00.**

Blue coat #50481. $10.00.

Toys "R" Us 2001 **Barbie Coat Collection** styles feature four fabulous looks for covering up in style.

Russian coat #50482. $12.00.

Red poncho #50484. $10.00.

Yellow raincoat #50483. $14.00.

Toys "R" Us 2001 **Barbie Lingerie Collection Styles** includes four bedtime or breakfast looks for Barbie.

Blue robe #50435. $8.00.   Cherry pajamas #50438. $10.00.   Clouds nightgown #50437. $8.00.   Pink pajamas #50436. $8.00.

Toys "R" Us 2001 **Skipper Prom Styles** feature four choices to allow Skipper to dress simply elegant or terrifically trendy on the biggest night of the year. A tiny flower corsage comes with each fashion.

Blue #50148. $9.00.   Orange #50146. $9.00.   Pink #50149. $9.00.   Purple #50147. $9.00.

Toys "R" Us 2002 **Baby Doctor Barbie**, white or black, wears a pink floral top, pink pants, and a white doctor's coat. Two baby patients in robes, an exam table, diapers, an ear checker, a reflex hammer, a stethoscope, three tongue depressors, a medicine bottle, a clipboard, two baby bottles, and a doctor's bag are included. **$20.00.**

Toys "R" Us 2002 **Dress Up Friends Kelly & Liana** includes Kelly dressed as a fairy princess with a star wand and Liana dressed as a movie star with sunglasses. A wedding gown, ballerina costume, mirror/vanity, cardboard trunk, hat box, and purse are included. **$18.00.**

Toys "R" Us 2002 **Dress Up Friends Kelly & Nia** (black) includes Kelly dressed as a princess and Nia dressed as a movie star. **$18.00.**

Toys "R" Us 2002 **Friends of the World** set features three Kelly dolls dressed in costumes of foreign lands, including brunette Kelly from Spain wearing a satiny pink dress with black dots and lace trim, blonde Kelly from Holland wearing a tulip-grower's costume with "wooden" shoes, and black Kelly from Kenya wearing a plaid rubeka dress with a collar necklace; she is accompanied by a young lion. **$18.00.**

Toys "R" Us 2002 **Let's Grocery Shop! Barbie & Kelly** (white or black) features Barbie doll pushing Kelly in a shopping cart inside the grocery store. A shelf unit with a bag dispenser and scale, a check-out stand with cash register, 13 mini food packages, and 9 mini food pieces are included. **$25.00.**

Toys "R" Us 2002 **Mother Goose Storytime Barbie and Kelly Doll-and-Book Gift Set** (white or black) depicts Barbie doll reading to her little sister Kelly. Barbie doll's blue pants feature the cat and the fiddle, a cow jumping over the moon, and a dish running with a spoon! A 28-page *My Little Golden Mother Goose Storybook*, a plastic pig, and a plastic goose in a bonnet are included. $20.00.

Toys "R" Us 2002 **Toys "R" Us Times Square New York Barbie** (white or black) wears a pink Barbie-logo shirt, a colorful skirt, a blue jacket with faux fur collar and cuffs, pantyhose, and blue boots. She carries a Toys "R" Us Times Square shopping bag and comes with miniature Magic 8 Ball, UNO, See 'n Say, and Rock-a-Stack toys. She was only sold at the Toys "R" Us Times Square New York store. A cardboard New York souvenir picture frame is included. $25.00.

Toys "R" Us 2002 **Toys "R" Us Times Square New York Barbie**, black, was originally designed with the World Trade Center Twin Towers featured prominently on the doll's box front, on the box liner, on the doll's shopping bag, on the box back, and on the cardboard picture frame. The doll was scheduled to go into production shortly before Sept. 11, 2001, but the tragic events of that day caused Mattel to scrap plans for packaging with the WTC images, and only a few pre-production samples are in existence. **$300.00.**

Toys "R" Us 2002 **Kelly Seashore 4" X 4" Playset** features a Jeep Wrangler and includes a "Kelly" beach chair, a "Tommy" beach chair, towels, an umbrella, a starfish, a lobster, sunglasses, a lotion bottle, and a pail. **$10.00.**

Toys "R" Us 2003 **Kelly Tea For Three** (white or black) includes Kelly in a blue dress with pink floral accents, two chairs, a table, tea service for three, plush Piggie, plush Bear, a necklace, a boa, a tutu, wings, a purse, a hat box, and a dessert tray. **$16.00.**

Toys "R" Us 2003 **My Scene Nolee Styling Head** has purple eyes, long rooted eyelashes, and black hair with brown streaks. Four hair extensions, two hair clips, four hair twists, six rubber bands, a choker/headband, and a brush are included. **$20.00.**

Toys "R" Us 2003 **Barbie Dresses That Dazzle** includes two assortments of fashions. **$10.00 each.**

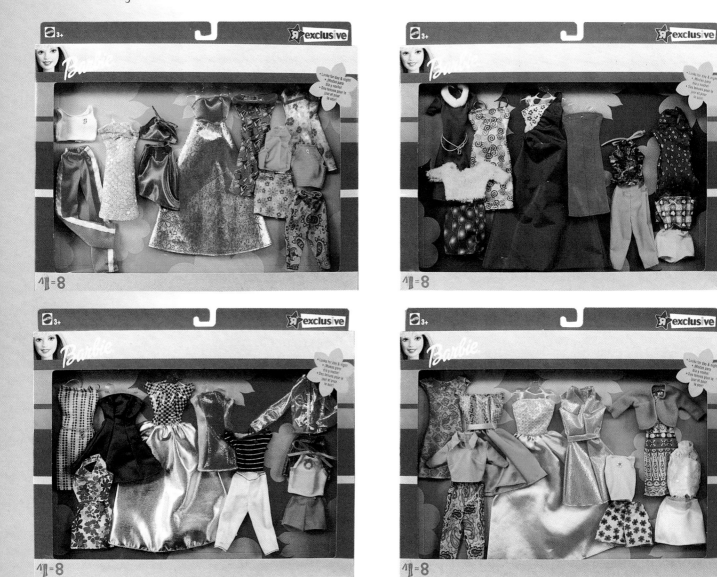

Toys "R" Us 2003 **Barbie Looks for Day & Night** includes four different assortments of fashions. **$10.00 each.**

Toys "R" Us 2003 **Barbie Mix 'n Match!**, available in two assortments, includes four complete fashions, three pairs of shoes, two purses, and one pair of sunglasses. **$10.00 each.**

Toys "R" Us 2003 **Barbie Trendy & Bright, Day or Night!** is available in two assortments. **$10.00 each.**

Toys "R" Us 2003 **Ken Trendy & Bright, Day or Night!** is available in two assortments. Each offers four two-piece fashions and two pairs of shoes for Ken. **$10.00 each.**

Toys "R" Us 2003 **Barbie Keychain Fashions** are inexpensive casual fashions for Barbie packaged inside a vinyl Barbie-size carr case with an attached key chain clasp. Four fashions with shoes were available in blue, pink, purple, or red cases. **$4.00 each.**

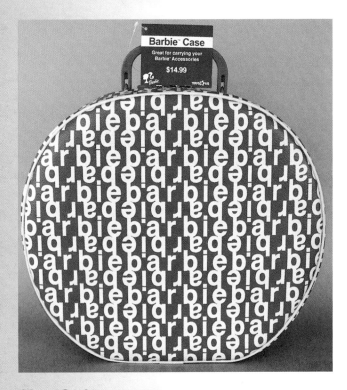

Toys "R" Us 2003 **Barbie Case**, a child-size hatbox-style carrying case with zipper and an interior mirror, was a free gift with any Barbie purchase totaling $35.00 or more in October 2003. **$15.00.**

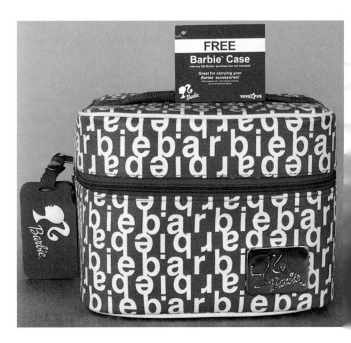

Toys "R" Us 2003 **Barbie Case**, a child-size cosmetics case with a mirror in the lid and a luggage tag, was a free gift with any Barbie purchase totaling $20.00 or more. **$10.00.**

Toys "R" Us 2003 **Barbie Biking Fun.** $10.00.

Toys "R" Us 2003 **Radio Control Corvette** is Barbie doll's hot pink car. **$24.00.**

Toys "R" Us 2003 **Sweet Shoppin' Fun** includes a plastic sweet shop unit with doorway, counter, and display case, a table with two chairs, a cash register, a gumball machine, a drink machine, four cake boxes, shopping bags, gift boxes, cooking utensils, trays, table service, and sweets. $15.00.

Toys "R" Us 2004 **Barbie as Batgirl** packages the playline Barbie as Batgirl, sold at most stores, with Batgirl's motorcycle, only available in this set. $30.00.

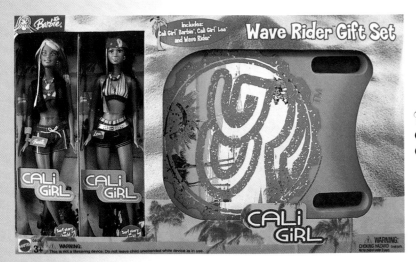

Toys "R" Us 2004 **Cali Girl Barbie Wave Rider Gift Set** packages the playline Cali Girl Barbie and Cali Girl Lea with a child-size wave rider. $15.00.

Toys "R" Us 2004 **Barbie Dream House Playset** features a working elevator, a doorbell that dings, a kitchen with a sink and a stove, a living room with a sofa, a bedroom and nursery with a canopy bed and a crib, a bathroom with a bathtub, and a balcony. $100.00.

Toys "R" Us Native Spirit Collection 2001 **Spirit of the Earth Barbie** wears a floor-length brown coat trimmed in white faux fur. Her brown and tan "buckskin" dress features an eagle design and has long fringe accents. She wears cloth boots, a head-band, and a bead necklace with medallion. She uses the Goddess of Africa head mold. $200.00.

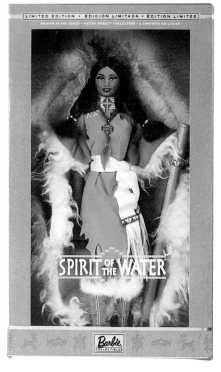

Toys "R" Us Native Spirit Collection 2002 **Spirit of the Water Barbie** is dressed for a rain dance in a turquoise "suede" dress with white fringed belt, a long turquoise coat with white trim, fringed turquoise boots with white faux fur trim, a beaded necklace, and a feather hair ornament. She uses the Lara head mold. **$65.00.**

Toys "R" Us Native Spirit Collection 2003 **Spirit of the Sky Barbie** wears a white "leather" skirt with "suede" fringe, a matching shirt with belt, a black and white necklace, silver hair clips on her thigh-length braids, and cloth boots. She carries a blanket and a dream catcher. She uses the Goddess of Africa head mold. **$95.00.**

Toys "R" Us 2003 **Legends of Ireland The Bard Barbie** is a redheaded traveling poet in ancient Ireland. She plays a golden Irish harp as she recited her lyrical tales. **$50.00.**

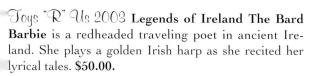

Toys "R" US 2004 **Barbie for President 2004** (white, black, Hispanic, or Asian) wears a red pantsuit with a white top, black shoes, and a red, white, and blue scarf. She carries a black handbag and black sunglasses and has a "Barbie for President" sign and a "Barbie for President" badge for the child. Her box states, "I am running for President of the United States because I love this country. I also care about education, the environment, and the arts. I want to inspire and lead. Together we can change the world!" **$25.00 each.**

Toys "R" Us 2004 **Happy Family Hometown Fair** (black or white) includes Midge, Alan, and their children, Ryan and Nikki. The fair features a carousel, a ring toss game, popcorn, soda, a bear prize, and a balloon. **$32.00.**

Toys "R" Us 2004 **Legends of Ireland Faerie Queen Barbie** is Queen Medb (Maeve), the ruler of the enchanted land of Tir Nan Og, dressed in a rich green gossamer gown with a golden crown and a scepter. A tiny trickster, she is said to be no bigger than an agate stone. She comes to mortals as they sleep, bringing dreams of love. **$30.00.**

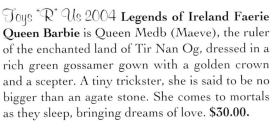

True Value 1978 **SuperStar Barbie Fashion Change-abouts** contains a re-dressed SuperStar Barbie doll wearing a print gown with coat along with an apron, a long skirt, pink pants, and a strapless pink top. **$100.00.**

Vedes 1993 **Vedes Star Barbie** from Germany commemorates the 90th anniversary of the Vedes store. She wears a pink and silver gown first worn by Wal-Mart's Anniversary Star Barbie of 1992. She comes with children's perfume, lip gloss, and nail polish and wears a "Vedes Star Barbie" banner and "Vedes 90" hangtag. **$45.00.**

Wal-Mart 1987 **Pink Jubilee Barbie** commemorates Wal-Mart's 25th anniversary. With a pink faux fur stole, a long pink skirt and bodice, a silver belt, tights, and a long pink cape, the doll boasts ten glamorous looks. **$24.00.**

Wal-Mart 1989 **Pink Jubilee Barbie Store Display** features Pink Jubilee Barbie posed on a black base inside her mirrored-back display case that has the Wal-Mart Twenty-Fifth Anniversary logo on the left front side and the Barbie and Mattel logos on the right front sides. **$100.00.**

1987 **Party Pink Barbie** from Canada, Europe, and Mexico is the same as Pink Jubilee Barbie, but with all references to Wal-Mart deleted. **$18.00.**

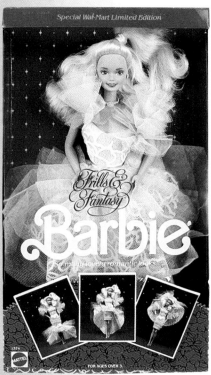

Wal-Mart 1988 **Frills & Fantasy Barbie** wears a shimmering blue minidress with a change-around overskirt. **$18.00.**

1989 **Garden Party Barbie** is a children's line doll wearing a lavender version of Frills & Fantasy Barbie doll's gown. **$14.00.**

Wal-Mart 1989 **Lavender Looks Barbie** wears a short lavender minidress under a dotted net overskirt that doubles as a coat. **$17.00.**

Wal-Mart 1990 **Dream Fantasy Barbie** wears a silver lame bodysuit with a long sheer skirt and a matching boa, which can also be worn as a short party dress. **$20.00.**

Wal-Mart 1991 **Bathtime Fun Barbie** is a regular children's line doll, but Wal-Mart commissioned an exclusive version packaged with a 10-pack of Barbie trading cards. A yellow sticker on the box window identifies the doll as having a "Free 10-Pack of Barbie Trading Cards Inside." The doll has a yellow, pink, and blue swimsuit and wears foam soap fashions. **$18.00.**

Wal-Mart 1991 **Ballroom Beauty Barbie**, wearing a slim iridescent dress with tiered tulle overskirt, a boa, and a hair ornament, has six different dance looks. **$18.00.**

Wal-Mart 1992 **Anniversary Star Barbie** celebrates Wal-Mart's 30th anniversary. She wears a pink party dress with a sheer overskirt with silvery accents, and she has a "30th Anniversary" sash and a "Wal-Mart 30th Anniversary" hangtag. **$20.00.**

Wal-Mart 1993 **SuperStar Barbie** wears a star-studded pink gown with iridescent bodice, and she has a star-shaped "Barbie Special Edition" hangtag. She is packaged with a white statuette award for her movie performance and a movie poster. The same statuette in silver was issued with the 1989 children's line SuperStar Ken doll. **$18.00.**

Wal-Mart 1993 **SuperStar Barbie**, black, has a very light skin tone and lavender eyes, and despite some collectors who call her ethnic or Hispanic, both her Christie head mold and Wal-Mart advertising indicate she is an African American edition. **$24.00.**

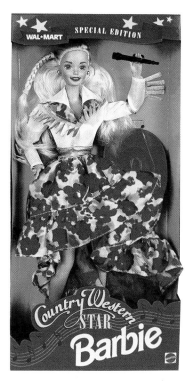

Wal-Mart 1994 **Country Western Star Barbie** carries a microphone and is dressed in a white blouse with golden fringe and a floral print skirt. Her dress material is the same as used for the Classique Flower Shower jacket. She has a pink cowboy hat and pink boots. **$16.00.**

Wal-Mart 1994 **Country Western Star Barbie**, Hispanic. All Wal-Mart exclusive Hispanic Barbie and Teresa dolls use the 1992 Teresa head mold. **$16.00.**

Wal-Mart 1994 **Country Western Star Barbie**, black, is the most difficult of this series to locate. She has the Christie head mold. **$18.00.**

Wal-Mart 1994 **Country Star Western Horse** is Wal-Mart's exclusive horse for the Country Western Star dolls. The horse wears a saddle blanket and leg wraps made of the same fabric used in the dolls' skirts. **$20.00.**

Wal-Mart 1994 **Toothfairy Barbie** is dressed in a pink and purple fairy costume. She has cardboard wings and an iridescent pouch in which to place the child's tooth. The doll has white legs with molded-on slippers. **$15.00.**

Wal-Mart 1995 **Toothfairy Barbie** was reissued in a blue and pink outfit and in a newly-designed box. The 1994 version has violet eyes, while this edition has blue eyes. **$14.00.**

Wal-Mart 1995 **Country Bride Barbie** (white, black, or Hispanic) wears a white-dotted Swiss gown trimmed in pink gingham piping and a veil with a pink gingham headband, and she carries a daisy bouquet. **$15.00.**

1995 **Braut Barbie** from Europe was intended to be a second Vedes exclusive but became a children's line doll there instead. The banner across the top front of the box was left blank where the store name was to have been. **$18.00.**

Wal-Mart 1996 **Skating Star Barbie** is dressed in a blue skating costume with a pink iridescent bodice, white faux fur trim, silver snowflake accents, and ice skates. **$12.00.**

Wal-Mart 1996 **Skating Star Barbie**, Hispanic, has lavender eyes. **$12.00.**

Wal-Mart 1996 **Skating Star Barbie**, black, is packaged in a box that inexplicably features a photo of the Caucasian doll on the back, yet the box's stock number is correct for the black doll. **$12.00.**

351

Wal-Mart 1996 **Sweet Magnolia Barbie** (black, white, or Hispanic) wears a satiny pastel floral-print gown with lavender bodice and a white straw hat. She carries a parasol. **$13.00.**

Wal-Mart 1996 **Sweet Magnolia Barbie Horse & Carriage Set** includes a blonde horse with combable mane and tail and a covered carriage with rolling wheels and room for two passengers. **$25.00.**

Wal-Mart 1997 **Pretty Choices Barbie**, blonde, wears a lavender dress accented with silver bows at the neckline, with a silver polka dot overskirt, a silver crown, and stockings. She comes with two hair bows, a headband, and a comb for styling her ankle-length hair. Wal-Mart donated $1.00 from each doll to the Children's Miracle Network. Some blonde dolls were packaged with their right arms up, while most were sold with both arms at their sides. **$14.00.**

Wal-Mart 1997 **Pretty Choices Barbie,** brunette, uses the SuperStar Barbie head mold with ankle-length brown hair and brown eyes. Even though the stock number on the box was changed for the brunette, only the blonde doll is shown in back-of-box photos. **$16.00.**

Wal-Mart 1997 **Shopping Time Barbie** (white or black) wears a belted blue jumper over a red and white striped shirt. She carries a Wal-Mart shopping bag. **$10.00.**

Wal-Mart 1997 **Pretty Choices Barbie**, black. **$16.00.**

Wal-Mart 1997 **Skating Dream Barbie** wears a white skating costume with golden accents and a faux fur collar and ice skates. The box back has a cut-out award medal proclaiming, "FIRST PLACE 1997 ICE SKATING CHAMPION." $14.00.

Wal-Mart 1997 **Shopping Time Teresa.** $10.00.

Wal-Mart 1997 **Wal-Mart 35th Anniversary Barbie** (white or black) wears a lovely satiny pink ballgown with sheer pink overlay speckled in silver, with a large silver lamé bow at her waist. She wears a "Wal-Mart 35 Anniversary" hangtag on her wrist. $17.00.

Wal-Mart 1997 **Wal-Mart 35th Anniversary Teresa** is the most popular of the Wal-Mart 35th anniversary dolls. **$19.00.**

Wal-Mart 1997 **Wal-Mart 35th Anniversary Barbie Decoupage Ornament** features a photo of the blonde doll next to a Christmas tree. **$10.00.**

Wal-Mart 1998 **Portrait in Blue Barbie** wears an indigo blue gown with swirls of golden paisley. The box back states, "Everyone was so excited about the newest painting in the museum: a portrait of Barbie! The artist captured not only her beauty, but the gleam of kindness in her eyes as well." **$16.00.**

Wal-Mart 1998 **Portrait in Blue Barbie**, black, uses the Asha head mold with light brown skin tone. **$16.00.**

Wal-Mart 1998 **Puzzle Craze Barbie** (white or black) and Puzzle Craze Teresa wear yellow puzzle-print pants, pink t-shirts with yellow collars, and pink boots. They carry clear yellow purses containing puzzle pieces that when put together show the doll walking in the park. **$9.00 each.**

Wal-Mart 1998 **Holiday Decorating Kit** includes a cardboard fireplace, a Christmas tree, gift boxes, a Wal-Mart gift bag, and holiday decorations for Barbie doll's home. **$10.00.**

Wal-Mart 1998 **Toothfairy Barbie** wears a pink costume with iridescent skirt and cardboard wings. She comes with an iridescent pouch with a blue ribbon. She has flesh-tone legs with molded-on pink slippers. **$12.00.**

Wal-Mart 1999 **Blazin' Trails Barbie** has the Super-Star head mold and wears an authentic Western fashion as she rides her horse, which has a rooted brown mane and tail streaked like Barbie doll's hair. **$36.00.**

Wal-Mart 1999 **Jewel Skating Barbie** (white or black) wears a pink ice skating costume with white faux fur collar and cuffs and ice skates. Both the white and black dolls use the Mackie head mold. **$12.00.**

Wal-Mart 2000 **Barbie Tea Time Gift Set with Her Friends Li'l Bear & Cozy Bunny** (white or black) includes Barbie doll in a teapot/teacup/floral-print pink dress and a blue hat adorned with flowers, having tea with her plush bear and plush bunny. A table with two chairs and tea service is included. Ames sold excess sets in 2001 for $12.99 with a pink sticker covering the "Wal-Mart Special Edition" printed in the upper left corner. **$22.00.**

Wal-Mart 2001 **Party Party Party Barbie, Christie, and Teresa** are day-after-Thanksgiving specials for Wal-Mart. They wear striped swimsuits and sunglasses and come with four additional fashions perfect for a picnic, a beach party, a tea party, and a dance. **$15.00 each.**

Wal-Mart 2001 **Tooth Fairy Christie** wears a pink fairy costume with silvery glitter, iridescent wings, and molded on slippers. This is the first time Christie has represented the Tooth Fairy. **$15.00.**

Wal-Mart 2001 **Star Skater Barbie and Teresa** wear ice skating costumes with white faux fur collars and cuffs and ice skates. **$14.00 each.**

Wal-Mart 2001 **Tooth Fairy Barbie** wears a purple fairy costume with silvery glitter, iridescent wings, and molded-on slippers. She carries a cardboard wand and comes with a cloth pouch for the child's tooth. **$15.00.**

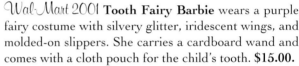

Wal-Mart 2002 **Purses Galore Barbie, Christie, and Teresa** were day-after-Thanksgiving sale dolls. Each doll wears a floral top, a vinyl skirt, and matching boots. A drum purse, a box bag, and an evening bag are included, along with a reusable sticker sheet for decorating her skirt, purses, and boots with "PURSE-onality galore." Barbie was available in pink or purple, Christie was available in orange, and Teresa was available in blue or green. **$12.00 each.**

Wal-Mart 2002 **Sleepover Girls Barbie & Kelly Gift Set** (white or black) includes Barbie doll wearing yellow pajamas and Kelly wearing a pink nightgown and robe, along with sleeping bags, a CD player, a toy CD, a soda bottle, soda glasses, a bowl of popcorn, a storybook, a cardboard teddy bear, and a cardboard pizza. **$18.00.**

Wal-Mart 2002 **Spot Scene Barbie, Christie, and Teresa** wear trendy dresses with Dalmatian-spotted skirts, matching headbands, and boots. An unspotted Dalmatian with bandana can be decorated with spots, and a key chain/picture frame is included for the child. The 2001 Spot Scene dolls were sold at most stores with slightly different fashions, including a beret and knee-high socks with shoes and minus the key chain/picture frame. **$9.00 each.**

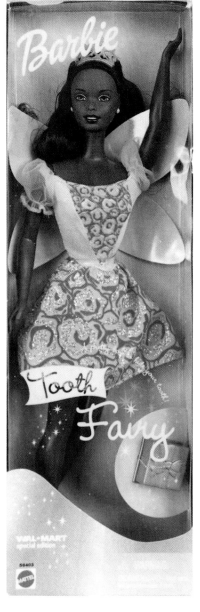

Wal-Mart 2002 **Tooth Fairy Barbie** (white or black) wears a fairy costume with floral designs on the bodice and sparkly glitter on the skirt, iridescent wings, a tiara, and molded-on slippers. A plastic box for the child's tooth is included. **$12.00.**

Wal-Mart 2003 **Happy Family Midge & Baby** features Barbie doll's best friend Midge as a new mother with her newborn daughter. The doll sold at most stores simulates pregnancy with a removable tummy panel that can hold the baby inside. Wal-Mart objected, so Mattel altered the dolls, omitting the pregnant feature from dolls sold at Wal-Mart and deleting the box text referring to Midge being pregnant and removing photos of her large belly. **$20.00.**

Wal-Mart 2003 **Happy Family Midge & Baby**, black, also lacks the simulated pregnancy feature if purchased at Wal-Mart. She uses the Teen Skipper head mold, while the white Happy Family Midge has the Diva head mold. **$22.00.**

Wal-Mart 2003 **Hawaiian Vacation Barbie & Kelly Gift Set** (white or black) features Barbie and Kelly in pink floral-print swimsuits with sarongs, sunglasses, and sandals. Two beach chairs and beach toys are included. K-B sold excess sets with blue stickers covering the "Wal-Mart Special Edition" text on the box front. **$16.00.**

361

Wal-Mart 2003 **Barbie & Skipper Pajama Fun Tote** (white or black) includes Barbie wearing starry pajama bottoms and a pink sleeveless top, her teenage sister Skipper with freckles and pigtails wearing satiny short pajama shorts with a matching top, and a child-size pink vinyl tote for carrying the dolls and their sleepover accessories along. K-Mart sold excess sets in 2004. **$18.00.**

Wal-Mart 2003 **My Scene A Ride in the Park Barbie, Madison, and Nolee** are day-after-Thanksgiving specials for Wal-Mart. The dolls are nearly identical to the My Scene Hanging Out Barbie, Madison, and Nolee dolls sold at most stores except that each Wal-Mart doll has jointed elbows and comes with a bicycle, a riding helmet, a dog, and accessories. **$15.00 each.**

362

Wal-Mart 2003 **Birthstone Collection** features Barbie dolls wearing birthstone jewelry and gowns in corresponding colors. Each doll in the series wears the same style of gown, which is decorated with glitter and worn with a sheer floor-length wrap. The (simulated) birthstone is in the necklace. Since ancient times, birthstones have been considered lucky for the people born in that month. As shown on the shelf display shown here, the Caucasian Birthstone Barbie dolls were released four at a time during the course of the year, in the spring, summer, and fall. African American versions of each 2003 edition were released in the winter of 2003. Each doll in this collection retailed for $24.99.

363

Wal-Mart 2003 **January Garnet Barbie**, white or black, wears a garnet, a deep red stone that has long symbolized fire, faith, and loyalty. In recent times, this stone has also come to represent a light heart and enduring affections. Dreaming of this jewel was said to foretell enormous wealth or the possibility of solving a mystery. Wearing a garnet was believed to encourage productivity and success in business. **$32.00.**

Wal-Mart 2003 **February Amethyst Barbie**, white or black, represents the amethyst, a rich purple jewel long symbolizing royalty and power. It was believed to assist in attaining fame in the arts. During the Middle Ages, the amethyst was used as medication, thought to sharpen intellect and protect against sorcery. According to Arabian legend, this gem protected against nightmares. **$32.00.**

Wal-Mart 2003 **March Aquamarine Barbie**, white or black, represents the aquamarine, a sparkling blue-green jewel believed to have washed ashore from the jewel caskets of the sirens, the sea nymphs of Greek mythology. It was thought that an aura of authority surrounded the wearer of an aquamarine. If you dreamed of this jewel, it was said you would soon experience new happiness and make new friends. **$32.00.**

Wal-Mart 2003 **April Diamond Barbie**, white or black, represents the diamond, called the King of Gems, the hardest mineral on earth. The diamond has come to symbolize eternal love. Its cold, sparkling fire is breathtaking and said to endow the wearer with matchless strength, bravery, and courage. The jewel was also said to attract friends, guarantee success, and assure good fortune. **$32.00.**

Wal-Mart 2003 **May Emerald Barbie**, white or black, features Barbie doll wearing a faux emerald, a brilliant green gem thought to bring its owner eternal love and protection from accidents. Some even believed that wearing an emerald enabled one to predict the future. In ancient Egypt, Cleopatra owned the earliest emerald mines and prized these jewels above all others. **$32.00.**

Wal-Mart 2003 **June Pearl Barbie**, white or black, represents a natural pearl, which is extremely rare. Pearls symbolize gentleness, purity, and a happy marriage. In China they represent wealth, power, and longevity. An Indian myth tells that pearls are dewdrops that fell from heaven. Ancient Greeks believed them to be drops of water flung from the goddess Aphrodite's body as she emerged from the sea. **$32.00.**

Wal-Mart 2003 **July Ruby Barbie**, white or black, represents the ruby, a fiery red gem believed to bring its owner health, wealth, and wisdom. The ruby symbolizes passion, beauty, and royalty. Napoleon gave Empress Josephine a magnificent suite of ruby jewelry. Other legends tell that Catherine of Aragon, first wife of King Henry VIII, was forewarned of her downfall by seeing her ruby darken. **$32.00.**

Wal-Mart 2003 **August Peridot Barbie**, white or black, represents the peridot, believed to bring the wearer a happy marriage, eloquence, and self-esteem. The jewel is thought also to hold the power to deepen friendships. Egyptian pharaohs owned and wore the finest peridots. Peridots were also prized in the Ottoman Empire; Turkish sultans collected what may be the world's largest collection. **$32.00.**

Wal-Mart 2003 **September Sapphire Barbie**, white or black, represents the sapphire, a brilliant blue gem symbolizing purity of the soul. The jewel was thought to provide comfort, courage, and strength, and to bestow spiritual enlightenment on the wearer. Others believed the sapphire would assure peace, hope, truth, and prosperity. **$32.00.**

Wal-Mart 2003 **October Opal Barbie**, white or black, represents the opal, a stone which comes in a rainbow of colors which shift and shimmer as the light plays across its surface. The opal has long been a symbol of hope, fidelity, and purity. Opals are said to enhance the wearer's psychic powers and give access to past lives. Some believed that wearing an opal brought good luck and prosperity. **$32.00.**

Wal-Mart 2003 **November Topaz Barbie**, white or black, represents the yellow topaz (also known as champagne or golden topaz), which was believed to strengthen the mind, increase wisdom, and draw love near. Wearing a topaz was thought to protect against injury, sudden death, and evil spells. **$32.00.**

Wal-Mart 2003 **December Turquoise Barbie** was only available as an African American in 2003. The first edition uses the Mackie Neptune Fantasy head mold (the same head mold used on all of the Caucasian dolls in this series), while the second edition uses the Goddess of Africa head mold. She represents the turquoise, a blue-green, opaque mineral which is a symbol of good fortune and success, believed to bring the wearer prosperity. An Oriental adage told that the gift of turquoise bestowed happiness and good fortune. The symbol of Persian monarchy was the famed Peacock Throne, which was covered in jewels including turquoise. **$32.00.**

369

Wal-Mart 2003 **Color Kelly** is dressed as a pink crayon with pink tights, pink shoes, and a pink crayon-shaped hat, **Color Deidre** is dressed as an orange crayon, **Color Jenny** is dressed as a blue crayon, and **Color Lorena** is dressed as a purple crayon. Each doll comes with one crayon, and the box back flap opens for a two-panel coloring scene. $10.00 each.

Wal-Mart 2003 **Red, White & Cute Kelly, Belinda, Deidre, and Liana** were released to coincide with the Fourth of July holiday. The dolls wear red, white, and blue fashions, and each comes with an animal toy. $10.00 each.

370

Wal-Mart 2004 **January Garnet Barbie** begins a second series of Birthstone Barbie dolls. For 2004 the dolls' dresses and jewelry remained the same, but each doll was sold using a different hair color and hairstyle from the 2003 releases. The 2003 versions have two strands of hair sewn to their gowns' bodices, while the 2004 editions have their hair completely pulled back. The boxes are very similar for both years, but the 2004 editions have the new "3+" age recommendation on the lower box front, and the stock numbers are different. $30.00.

Wal-Mart 2004 **February Amethyst Barbie $30.00.**

Wal-Mart 2004 **March Aquamarine Barbie $30.00.**

Wal-Mart 2004 **April Diamond Barbie $30.00.**

Wal-Mart 2004 **May** Emerald Barbie $30.00.

Wal-Mart 2004 **June** Pearl Barbie $30.00.

Wal-Mart 2004 **July** Ruby Barbie $30.00.

Wal-Mart 2004 **August** Peridot Barbie $30.00.

Wal-Mart 2004 **September Sapphire Barbie $30.00.**

Wal-Mart 2004 **October Opal Barbie** is an African American doll using the Mackie Neptune Fantasy head mold. **$30.00.**

Wal-Mart 2004 **November Topaz Barbie $30.00.**

Wal-Mart 2004 **December Turquoise Barbie** is Caucasian with blonde hair, unlike the 2003 edition which was only available in an African-American version. **$30.00.**

Walgreen's 2000 **Movie Star Barbie** is a foreign-market doll sold exclusively in the U.S. by Walgreen's. She has violet eyes and wears a transforming slim purple gown with silver starburst designs and comes with a silver lamé jacket, a silver lamé purse, purple sunglasses, and body glitter. **$25.00.**

Walgreen's 2000 **Movie Star Teresa** was only available in the U.S. at Walgreen's. She has a transforming day-to-night pink fashion with silver starbursts, a silver lamé jacket, pink sunglasses, and a purse, and she comes with body glitter for the child. **$25.00.**

Warner Bros. Studio Store 1999 **Barbie Loves Tweety** includes Barbie doll wearing khaki pants, a blue shirt illustrated with Warner Bros. characters, a WB-logo hat, and white tennis shoes, along with a plush Tweety Bird carrying a shopping bag. The box back states, "Friends tell friends if their feathers are ruffled when leaving the dressing room" and "Friends tell friends if a puddy tat is hiding behind the clothes rack." **$25.00.**

Warner Bros. Studio Store 2000 **Sleepover Party Barbie** wears her yellow Tweety Bird pajamas with yellow slippers and rests on her yellow Tweety Bird sleeping bag. The cardboard television in the package has a dial that changes the cartoon scene on the TV screen. **$25.00.**

Warner Bros. Studio Store 2001 **Barbie Doll in Scooby-Doo, Where Are You! The Great Amusement Park Caper** features Barbie doll as a detective wearing a pink floral-print top bodysuit with a satiny pink belted jacket and pink-framed sunglasses. She carries a flashlight and a decoder magnifying glass to help her find the crooks hidden in the scene on the box back, and she comes with a pencil, notepad, and camera. **$30.00.**

Warner Bros. Studio Store 2001 **The Powerpuff Girls Barbie** wears a pink Powerpuff Girls top and shimmery pink pants with pink clogs. She comes with an inflatable pink chair, which can be decorated with Powerpuff Girls stickers. The box back features punch-out trading cards of the Powerpuff Girls, Blossom, Bubbles, and Buttercup. **$32.00.**

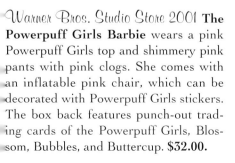

Wessco 1995 **International Travel Barbie** wears a satiny fuchsia dress, a satiny white travel coat decorated with the names and icons of international cities, and a white hat with blue band. She comes with a suit bag and two pieces of luggage. Some dolls have a blue bow on the dress bodice, while others have a pink bow. Dolls purchased in duty-free stores have Wessco's gold sticker on the box window. $20.00.

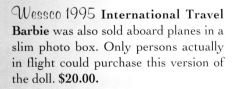

Wessco 1995 **International Travel Barbie** was also sold aboard planes in a slim photo box. Only persons actually in flight could purchase this version of the doll. **$20.00.**

Wessco 1996 **International Travel Barbie** second edition wears a black and white checked suit with a pink belt, sheer white stockings, and a black hat. She has an upturned short hairstyle and comes with a *B*-logo garment bag, a *B*-logo hat case, a hanger, sunglasses, a *B*-logo jewelry bag, and a golden charm bracelet for the child. **$22.00.**

Wessco 1997 **Carnival Cruise Barbie** is dressed for her first "Fun Ship" vacation in a red and white top, a blue jacket, white "Carnival" shorts with a red belt, a white captain's hat, and red shoes. She carries red sunglasses and a "Carnival" tote bag. Wessco sold her for $50.00. **$22.00.**

Wessco 1996 **International Travel Barbie**, second edition, was sold in a slim box for in-flight purchase like the first International Travel Barbie. **$24.00.**

White Swan Hotel 2002 **Going Home Barbie** is a special souvenir doll created by Mattel Hong Kong as a gift to adopting parents staying at the White Swan Hotel in Guangzhou, China. Barbie wears a pink dress with a blue floral-print bodice. Her Chinese baby has black hair and brown eyes and wears a pink romper with a white bib featuring two bears. The box front states, "For ages 14 and over" and "This is not a toy," and the box back states, "This souvenir is presented by Mattel (HK) Ltd, to adopting parents of Chinese orphan children staying at the White Swan Hotel, Guangzhou, China." Since the doll was not offered for sale in stores and was only given to adopting parents staying at the White Swan Hotel, the doll is very rare, especially since most new parents wish to keep the doll as a souvenir of the adoption. **$400.00.**

White Swan Hotel 2003 **Going Home Barbie** second edition wears the lavender sweater and blue scarf from the 2001 "Concert on the Green" Fashion Avenue, along with light blue floral-print Capri pants. Her Chinese baby wears a pink romper with white dots and a brown bear-face bib. **$295.00.**

White Swan Hotel 2004 **Going Home Barbie** third edition wears an off-the-shoulders blue blouse with pink floral print, a tan "suede" skirt, and a tan "suede" hat. Her Chinese baby wears a playsuit with a yellow and white gingham top and white shorts with blue and green flower designs. **$275.00.**

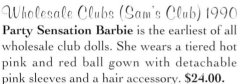

Wholesale Clubs 1991 **All American Barbie with Star Stepper Horse** packages the playline All American Barbie, with a denim skirt featuring an American flag design at the waist, a matching vest, a pink shirt, and two pairs of Reebok gymshoes, with her Star Stepper horse. **$22.00.**

Wholesale Clubs (Sam's Club) 1990 **Party Sensation Barbie** is the earliest of all wholesale club dolls. She wears a tiered hot pink and red ball gown with detachable pink sleeves and a hair accessory. **$24.00.**

Wholesale Clubs (Sam's Club) 1991 **Jewel Jubilee Barbie** wears a white and golden ball gown with a gold lamé shawl, a large gold waist bow, and a gold hairbow. A "ruby" accents her gown. She is the second glamour Barbie doll for Sam's Club. **$28.00.**

Wholesale Clubs (Pace Club) 1992 **Barbie Deluxe 100 Piece Gift Set** features several different inexpensive dolls repackaged with a vanity and mirror, a chair, and four extra fashions. The set shown here includes a 1992 Fashion Play Barbie redressed in a pink skirt with a black bodice with white polka dots. **$36.00.**

Wholesale Clubs (Pace Club) 1992 **Barbie Deluxe 100 Piece Gift Set** was also sold with the 1992 Sun Sensation Barbie doll packaged with four different fashions, including the one worn by the doll in the other Deluxe 100 Piece Gift Set. **$36.00.**

Wholesale Clubs 1992 **Dream Wardrobe Barbie** includes a repackaged 1991 Fashion Play Barbie in her original purple and white teddy along with eight additional fashions. **$20.00.**

Wholesale Clubs (Sam's Club) 1992 **Peach Blossom Barbie**, third in Sam's Club's series of glamour Barbie dolls, wears a sheer peach gown with sparkly overlay. Some leftover dolls were sold in Wal-Mart, Sam's Club's parent store. **$20.00.**

Wholesale Clubs (Pace Club) 1992
Rollerblade Barbie Snack and Surf Set
includes the playline Rollerblade Barbie with
Flicker 'n Flash Rollerblade skates, a hot dog
stand, and a surfboard with sail. The sparking
action of the skates caused safety concerns, so
Mattel offered to replace these skates with non-
sparking skates. **$28.00.**

Wholesale Clubs (Pace Club) 1992 **Royal
Romance Barbie** wears a beautiful blue lamé gown
with silver overlay, blue fingerless gloves, and a
matching blue and silver hair accessory. She is one
of the hardest wholesale club dolls to find. **$36.00.**

Wholesale Clubs (Sam's Club)
1992 **Sparkle Eyes Barbie
Dressing Room And Fashion
Set** includes the children's line
Sparkle Eyes Barbie with inset
blue rhinestone eyes, wearing a
silver minidress with sparkly
tiered pink tulle skirt and boa.
Also included are three extra
party dresses and a dressing
room play set. **$32.00.**

Wholesale Clubs (Pace Club) 1992 Sun Sensation Barbie Spray & Play Fun includes the children's line Sun Sensation Barbie with a 12" x 18" Spray and Play vinyl pool, a mountain bike, and extra fashions. This set is hard to find. **$30.00.**

Wholesale Clubs (Pace Club) 1992 Very Violet Barbie is Pace Club's first glamour Barbie doll. She wears a tiered violet ball gown with matching hair rosette. Although a Pace exclusive in the U.S., Very Violet Barbie was a Mattel France premium mail-away doll; the doll could be obtained for 120 package points until Jan. 31, 1994. **$26.00.**

Wholesale Clubs 1992 Fantastica Barbie wears an authentic white Mexican dance dress in the style of the Tapatia dancers of Mexico. She is the first Barbie doll to use the 1992 Teresa head mold. **$40.00.**

Wholesale Clubs 1993 **Barbie 10-Fashion Gift Set**. Four styles were available. **$20.00 each.**

Wholesale Clubs (Sam's Club) 1993 **Festiva Barbie** wears an authentic Mexican folk dance costume reflecting the countryside of Michoacan, Mexico. The box says that Barbie doll is dancing the Las Sonajas, the Rattle Dance. She uses the Teresa head mold. **$42.00.**

Wholesale Clubs (Sam's Club) 1993 **Dressing Fun Barbie Lots of Fashions Gift Set** contains a playline 1991 Hawaiian Fun Barbie in her yellow, pink, and green bikini repackaged with nine additional fashions. The first version of the box says, "Barbie and Lots of Fashions To Play With" and includes Hawaiian Fun Barbie doll's original pink hula skirt packaged beside the doll's head. **$24.00.**

Wholesale Clubs (Sam's Club) 1993 **Dressing Fun Barbie Lots of Fashions Gift Set** was also sold with nine different outfits, but in this set a pink towel wrap is included and a sticker on the box front says, "Barbie Fashions and Towel Wrap Too!" The photos on the backs of the boxes picture the actual outfits found in each set. **$24.00.**

Wholesale Clubs (Sam's Club) 1993 **Holiday Gown Collection** contains green, gold, and red holiday gowns. This set is hard to find. **$35.00.**

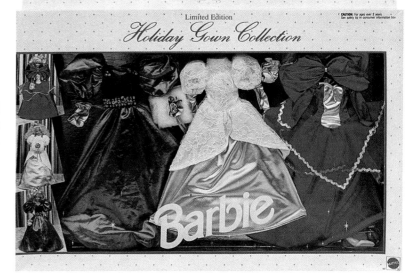

Wholesale Clubs (Sam's Club) 1993 **Hollywood Hair Barbie Deluxe Play Set** contains the playline Hollywood Hair Barbie in a satiny white jacket with gold lame sleeves, a gold lamé skirt, and matching leggings with her pink color change hair spray repackaged with an additional fashion and extra hair stencils. **$18.00.**

Wholesale Clubs 1993 **Island Fun Barbie & Ken Sizzlin' Beach Party** contains Barbie wearing a blue swimsuit with a pink wrap skirt and a pink lei with Ken wearing blue floral trunks and a green tank top. The Island Fun name was used on a 1988 series of beach dolls, but these dolls are different. **$20.00.**

Wholesale Clubs (Sam's Club) 1993 **Paint N' Dazzle Barbie Deluxe Play Set** contains the playline Paint N' Dazzle Barbie wearing a pink jacket, a pink top, and a pink skirt repackaged with an extra outfit to decorate, three bottles of fabric paint, and decorations. **$17.00.**

Wholesale Clubs (Sam's Club) 1993 **Secret Hearts Barbie Deluxe Gift Set** contains the playline Secret Hearts Barbie and Ken dolls wearing white dance costumes. However, the Ken doll in this set uses the 1992 Ken head mold with blonde hair and his tuxedo jacket is white. **$24.00.** The playline Secret Hearts Ken has a different, new head sculpt with side-part brown hair, and he wears a magenta lamé jacket. He is shown for comparison with the blonde Ken doll used in the gift set. **$12.00.**

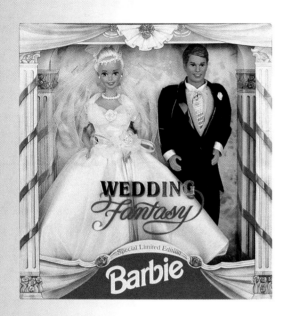

Wholesale Clubs (Sam's Club) 1993 **Wedding Fantasy Barbie Gift Set** is the first wedding set since 1964 to package Barbie doll as a bride with Ken doll as a groom. Of course, the wedding is just Barbie doll's fantasy. If Mattel ever officially married Barbie and Ken dolls, many play possibilities would be lost to children. This set should not be confused with the playline 1990 Wedding Fantasy Barbie. **$50.00.**

Wholesale Clubs (Sam's Club) 1993 **Western Stampin' Barbie Deluxe Play Set** offers the playline Western Stampin' Barbie with her blue western jacket, silver and blue top, silver lamé skirt, and blue boots with an additional red and silver lamé ensemble with red boots and a stamp pad. **$28.00.**

Wholesale Clubs (Pace Club) 1993 **Winter Royale Barbie** wears a royal purple gown with flocked velvet pattern and white faux fur trim and cap. **$30.00.**

Wholesale Clubs (Pace Club) 1994 **Beach Fun Barbie & Ken** features Barbie in a yellow swimsuit with a floral-print skirt and trim and Ken in purple shorts with a yellow and purple tank top; his tank top has the same pattern as K-Mart's Fashion Friends Casual Wear fashions #7484 and #7485. Two pairs of sunglasses are included. **$18.00.**

Wholesale Clubs (Sam's Club) 1994 **Bedtime Barbie with Bed** is a European set sold exclusively in the U.S. by Sam's Club. Barbie doll wears a pink nightgown with a lacy white collar. Her eyes open and close with water. She is the first soft-bodied Barbie doll. **$20.00.**

Wholesale Clubs (Sam's Club) 1994 **Holiday Gown Collection** includes three different holiday gowns in a green box; the 1993 set has a white box. The fashions' colors are similar in both sets — green, gold, white, and red. $30.00.

Wholesale Clubs (Sam's Club) 1994 **Season's Greetings Barbie** is Sam's Club's first holiday-themed glamour doll. She wears a velvety red jacket, a red and green metallic shag dress, and a matching hat with a green leaf. Her dress material is the same as used in General Growth Management's 1992 Holiday Sensation Barbie Evening Gown Fashion. $25.00.

Wholesale Clubs 1995 **Barbie 10-Fashion Gift Set**. Four styles were available. $20.00 each.

Wholesale Clubs (Sam's Club) 1995 **Deluxe Gown Collection** contains eight holiday gowns in one large box. The size of the package and the original price led many collectors to reconsider purchasing it. $45.00.

Wholesale Clubs (B.J.'s Club) 1995 **Denim 'n Ruffles Barbie Western Gift Set** comes with Denim 'n Ruffles Barbie, sold separately outside the U.S., and her battery-operated High Stepper horse. The horse was sold separately in the U.S. $25.00.

Wholesale Clubs (Pace Club) 1995 **Hot Skatin' Barbie Deluxe Gift Set** pairs the playline Hot Skatin' Barbie with one of six Happy Holidays Barbie fashion greeting cards. This set is hard to find. $24.00.

Wholesale Clubs (Sam's Club) 1995 **Winter's Eve Barbie** is the second Sam's Club holiday-themed glamour doll. With an upswept hairdo, Barbie doll has a satiny green bodice accented with white faux fur trim, and her gown is a red, green, and gold plaid. $20.00.

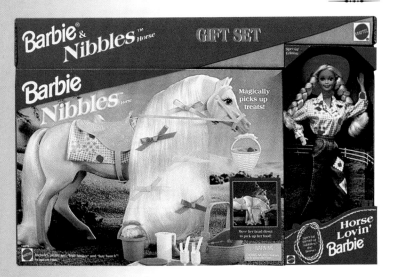

Wholesale Clubs (B.J.'s Club) 1996 **Barbie & Nibbles Horse Gift Set** pairs Horse Lovin' Barbie wearing jeans, an apple-print shirt in the same fabric as the horse's saddle blanket, a pink scarf, boots, and a pink hat with Nibbles, the horse that picks up its own food. **$30.00.**

Wholesale Clubs 1996 **Barbie Fashion Gift Set**. Four styles were available. **$18.00 each.**

Wholesale Clubs (Sam's Club) 1996 **Fifties Fun Barbie** wears a blue sweater, a white belt, a sheer white scarf, and a satiny pink poodle skirt featuring a blue poodle with a shiny collar. Collectors may note some similarity between this doll and the Toys "R" Us 1993 Malt Shoppe Barbie. **$22.00.**

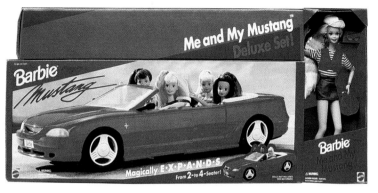

Wholesale Clubs (B.J.'s Club) 1996 **Me and My Mustang Deluxe Set** contains Me and My Mustang Barbie, sold separately outside the U.S., and Barbie doll's red Mustang, which converts from a two-seater to a four-seater. Her cardboard driver's license lists her height as 11½". **$28.00.**

Wholesale Clubs 1996 **Ocean Friends Barbie Gift Set** pairs the playline Ocean Friends Barbie with disappearing wet suit and Baby Keiko whale with an Adventure Dress 'N Play fashion. **$25.00.**

Wholesale Clubs 1996 **Barbie Special Occasion Gift Set** includes the playline Ruffle Fun Barbie with a "You're Special!" fashion greeting card. **$20.00.**

Wholesale Clubs (B.J.'s Club) 1996 **Olympic Gymnast Barbie Gift Set** features the playline doll packaged with a "You're Special!" fashion greeting card. **$24.00.**

Wholesale Clubs (B.J.'s Club) 1996 **Rose Bride Barbie** wears a satin and lace wedding gown. The box back teases collectors with the story, "Barbie is the blushing bride, with handsome Ken standing by her side; alas it's just a dream for two, but someday, Barbie, it will come true." After 44 years of courtship, Barbie and Ken dolls aren't officially married yet. **$28.00.**

Wholesale Clubs (Pace Club) 1996 **Silver Royale Barbie** wears a beautiful silver lamé gown with white marabou feather trim and a large white satin bow. **$40.00.**

Wholesale Clubs (B.J.'s Club) 1996 **Sparkle Beach Barbie Playset** offers Sparkle Beach Barbie with long braided hair wearing a sparkly blue bikini packaged with Pool Day accessories; the doll and the Pool Day set were also sold separately. **$20.00.**

Wholesale Clubs (Sam's Club) 1996 **Starlight Splendor Fashions** include six holiday gowns in one box. Some of these fashions were sold separately in 1995 as Fantasy Evening Fashions. The initial expense and oversized box have forced collectors and dealers alike to reconsider purchasing this set. **$32.00.**

Wholesale Clubs

Wholesale Clubs (Sam's Club) 1996 **Winter Fantasy Barbie**, blonde, is Sam's Club's third holiday-themed glamour doll. She has green eyes and wears a gold and white gown trimmed in white faux fur. **$18.00.**

Wholesale Clubs (Sam's Club) 1996 **Winter Fantasy Barbie**, brunette, was produced in much smaller quantities than the blonde doll; reportedly as few as one in six dolls is a brunette. Since many collectors already favor brunette Barbie dolls over blondes, this doll sold out quickly. **$20.00.**

Wholesale Clubs (Sam's Club) 1997 **Sixties Fun Barbie**, blonde, wears a Pucci-style minidress with a matching cap, a pink belt, pink fishnet stockings, tall white boots, and silver hoop earrings. She carries a pink vinyl handbag. **$18.00.**

Wholesale Clubs (Sam's Club) 1997 **Sixties Fun Barbie**, redhead, is more desirable to collectors than the blonde. The Sixties Fun dolls have stiff hair due to Mattel's styling gel. **$18.00.**

Wholesale Club's (B.J.'s Club) 1997 Sparkle Beauty Barbie wears a slim purple gown with a purple tulle train and a pink, blue, and purple tulle collar, and purple pumps. **$20.00.**

Wholesale Clubs 1997 Splash 'n Color Barbie Gift Set pairs the playline Splash 'n Color Barbie with a pink swimsuit and a color-change braid with one of three playpacks: Floatin' Fun, Sports Play Fun, or Windsurfin' Fun. **$18.00.**

Wholesale Clubs 1997 Splash 'n Color Barbie Sun Wheeler Vehicle & Speedboat (Sam's Club) includes a pink vehicle with roll bar, windshield, and safety belts with a white and pink speedboat with a life vest. This boxed set is 35" long, so few collectors have the space to add this to their collections. **$20.00.**

Wholesale Clubs (Sam's Club) 1997 Sweet Moments Barbie wears a pink and white checked jumper, a white T-shirt, a pink hairbow, and white shoes. She carries a backpack, a white basket of flowers, and a white dog with blue eyes. This dog was first used with 1992's Pet Pals Skipper. **$15.00.**

Wholesale Clubs 1997 **Jewelry Fun My First Barbie Deluxe Gift Set** pairs the playline doll with the Barbie Folding Pretty House, both of which were sold separately. **$48.00.**

Wholesale Clubs (Sam's Club) 1997 **Winter Fantasy Barbie**, black, is harder to find than the white versions. Value City sold excess Winter Fantasy Barbie dolls for $12.99. **$22.00.**

Wholesale Clubs (Sam's Club) 1997 **Winter Fantasy Barbie**, brunette. **$18.00.**

Wholesale Clubs (Sam's Club) 1997 **Winter Fantasy Barbie**, blonde, wears a maroon gown with velvety dark purple overskirt and sleeves decorated with silver glitter. Her eyes are an unusual olive and brown, set off by her pale skin tone and dark lips. **$18.00.**

Wholesale Clubs 1997 **Workin' Out Barbie Fashions Gift Set** contains the playline Workin' Out Barbie with pink workout fashion, music cassette tape, and suction cup shoes along with two extra Sports Fashions. **$20.00.**

Wholesale Clubs 1998 **Bronze Sensation Barbie** wears a bronze metallic leopard-print gown, a velvety black jacket, black pumps, a beaded choker, and dangle earrings. Her hair is a lovely shade of bronze. **$30.00.**

Wholesale Clubs (Sam's Club) 1998 **Dinner Date Barbie**, blonde or redhead, wears a lovely golden dress with white collar and cuffs, pearl buttons, sheer white pantyhose, and white pumps. She carries a golden purse in the same material as her dress. **$12.00.**

Wholesale Clubs 1998 **Pearl Beach Barbie Gift Set** contains the playline Pearl Beach Barbie wearing a blue bikini with pearl accents packaged with one water activity Play Pak: Floatin' Fun, Pool Day Fun, or Windsurfin' Fun, each also sold separately. **$18.00.**

Wholesale Clubs (Sam's Club) 1998 **70s Disco Barbie**, blonde, pays tribute to the classic Saturday Night Fever movie with a fashion similar to the one worn by John Travolta. 70s Disco Barbie wears a shimmering white bell-bottom pantsuit with a matching vest, a multicolored striped shirt, and white shoes. She carries a purple purse. The box back shows Barbie doll on the dance floor and mentions some popular 1970s terms — "Boogie Down," "Do the Hustle," "Freak-out," and "Funky!" **$22.00.**

Wholesale Clubs (Sam's Club) 1998 **Pearl Beach Barbie Sun Wheeler Vehicle & Speedboat** includes a white vehicle with purple roll bar, windshield, and seatbelts with a pink speedboat with life vest. **$20.00.**

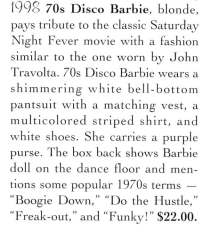

Wholesale Clubs (Sam's Club) 1998 **'70s Disco Barbie**, brunette, is even more popular than the blonde. The brunette version has brown eyes, while the blonde has blue eyes. Both dolls have been found with tightly-curled hair and fuller, loosely styled hair. Dolls with the fuller hair style appear to have the Farrah Fawcett hairstyle popular in the late 1970s. **$22.00.**

Wholesale Clubs 1998 **Starlight Splendor** contains four lovely gowns. **$22.00.**

Wholesale Clubs (Sam's Club) 1998 **Winter Evening Barbie**, blonde or brunette, wears a sparkly white jacket with faux fur collar, cuffs, and hat, and a matching skirt. She carries a snowflake ornament. **$18.00.**

Wholesale Clubs 1999 **Florida Vacation Beach Time Fun Barbie** pairs the playline Florida Vacation Barbie wearing a pink swimsuit and sunglasses with one of three Pearl Beach Barbie play packs: Floatin' Fun, Pool Day Fun, or Windsurfin' Fun. **$20.00.**

Wholesale Clubs (Sam's Club) 1999 **Pilot Barbie & Traveling Kelly & Tommy Gift Set** includes the playline Pilot Barbie and Barbie Airplane with unique versions of Kelly and Tommy in travel attire. **$85.00.**

Wholesale Clubs 1999 **Golden Waltz Barbie**, redhead, was produced in smaller quantities than the blonde. **$20.00.**

Wholesale Clubs 1999 **Golden Waltz Barbie**, blonde, wears a brilliant golden gown with a diamond-design bodice, marabou collar and cuffs, and a golden purse. **$18.00.**

Wholesale Clubs 2000 **Sisters' Celebration Barbie with Krissy** features Barbie, wearing a purple gown with velvety bodice and trim, a sheer shawl, and purple necklace, with her new baby sister, Krissy, in a purple dress with hair ribbon and booties. **$20.00.**

Wholesale Clubs 2001 **Winter Classic Barbie** (blonde or brunette) wears a lovely gown with golden floral designs and faux fur trim, a faux fur hat, and a muff. **$20.00.**

Wholesale Clubs (Costco) 2002 **Princess Barbie Gift Set** includes the blonde playline Princess Barbie packaged with the child-size Barbie Princess Dress-Up Set. **$32.00.**

Wholesale Clubs 2003 **At The Car Wash! Playset** was shrink-wrapped with the **Barbie Ford Thunderbird Convertible** using an extra pink cardboard insert. **$22.00.**

Winn-Dixie 1989 **Party Pink Barbie** wears a short pink dress with silver accents. **$14.00.**

Winn-Dixie 1990 **Pink Sensation Barbie** wears a short pink and white dress. **$12.00.**

Winn-Dixie 1991 **Southern Beauty Barbie** is called "today's Southern belle," and is wearing a satiny coral dress with white lace collar and a hair ribbon. **$15.00.**

1991 **Fashion Play Barbie**, a foreign-market doll, wears a purple and white version of Winn-Dixie's Pink Sensation Barbie doll's dress. **$16.00.**

Woodward's 1993 **Woodward's 100 Anniversary Barbie Exclusive Anniversary Collection** contains a shrink-wrapped Ibiza Barbie with a Barbie six-fashion gift set. Note the "WOODWARD'S 100 ANNIVERSARY" sticker on the package. This set was only sold at Woodward's stores in Canada. **$50.00.**

Woolworth 1989 **Special Expressions Barbie** wears a white tricot halter dress with a metallic ruffle overskirt. **$14.00.**

Woolworth 1989 **Special Expressions Barbie**, black, is the first retail store exclusive black Barbie doll. All of Woolworth's exclusive black Barbie dolls use the Christie head mold. **$14.00.**

Woolworth 1989 **Barbie Dance Club Fashions**, widely available in the U.S., were exclusive to Woolworth stores in Canada and have an "Exclusive to Woolworth's" sicker. **$10.00.**

1989 **Fashion Play Barbie** from Europe wears a pink version of the 1989 Special Expressions Barbie doll's gown. **$18.00.**

Woolworth 1990 **Special Expressions Barbie** (white or black) is dressed in a one-piece pink dress with a cloth flower at the waist and on the bodice. **$10.00.**

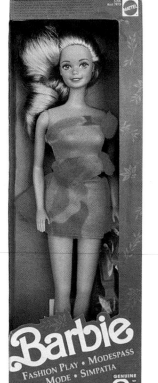

1990 **Fashion Play Barbie** from Europe is the same doll as the 1990 Caucasian Special Expressions Barbie in a different box. **$12.00.**

Woolworth 1991 **Special Expressions Barbie** (white or black) wears a short blue dress with white lace on the bodice, a sheer overskirt, and a blue hair bow. **$10.00.**

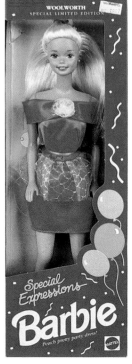

Woolworth 1991 **Special Expressions Barbie Dance Cafe** contains a play piano and snack bar. This is very hard to find. **$35.00.**

Woolworth 1992 **Special Expressions Barbie** wears a satiny peach party dress with a flower on the bodice. **$12.00.**

Woolworth 1992 **Special Expressions Barbie**, Hispanic, is the first Hispanic retail store exclusive Barbie doll. She uses the Steffie head mold. **$15.00.**

Woolworth 1992 **Sweet Lavender Barbie** (white or black) wears a lavender ball gown over a shimmering jewel-speckled bodice. While the ongoing series of Special Expressions dolls all sold for $8.97, the Sweet Lavender dolls cost $14.97 and were therefore seen in smaller quantities than the less expensive dolls. **$18.00.**

Woolworth 1992 **Special Expressions Barbie**, black, is one of the hardest to find of all black retail store exclusive dolls. **$18.00.**

Woolworth 1993 **Special Expressions Barbie** (white or black) wears a blue floral-print dress with a blue hairbow. **$10.00.**

Woolworth 1993 **Special Expressions Barbie**, Hispanic, now uses the 1992 Teresa head mold. **$12.00.**

Zayre's 1987 **My First Barbie**, Hispanic, uses the Spanish Barbie head mold. She wears a pink ballerina costume with a pink hairbow and ballet slippers. The Caucasian and African American My First Barbie dolls of 1987 are widely available playline dolls, but this Hispanic version in a two-language box was offered only at Zayre's. **$20.00.**

Zellers 1994 **Rollerskating Barbie and Her Roll-Along Puppy** is an extremely limited gift set for the Zellers store in Canada. The Barbie doll has the head and hairstyle of the 1992 Rollerblade Barbie doll, but her outfit is different. The puppy rolls along as Barbie doll skates. **$50.00.**

Zellers 1996 **Fashion Avenue Barbie** wears one of the Fashion Avenue series of fashions, a pink top and yellow skirt with flowers at the waist, lacy white leggings, and a pink beret. She was sold in Canada, only at Zellers. **$16.00.**

1996 **Fashion Date Barbie** from Japan wears the same fashion as Fashion Avenue Barbie, but she has the Mackie head mold in contrast to the SuperStar head mold used on the Zellers doll. **$20.00.**

1996 **Ruffle Fun Barbie** wears a purple mini-dress with a pink ruffle. Zellers sold this unique version, while U.S. retailers sold Ruffle Fun Barbie wearing a pink minidress with a yellow ruffle. **$14.00.**

Zellers 1997 **Splash 'n Color Barbie Bonus Barbie Bubble Bath!** includes the Canadian boxed Splash 'n Color Barbie with a color-change braid packaged with a 16 oz. bottle of Kid Care Barbie Bubble Bath. **$18.00.**

Zellers 1996 **Sparkle Beach Barbie Free Barbie Bubble Bath!** includes the Canadian boxed Sparkle Beach Barbie with a straight hairstyle packaged with a 16 oz. bottle of Kid Care Barbie Bubble Bath. **$18.00.**

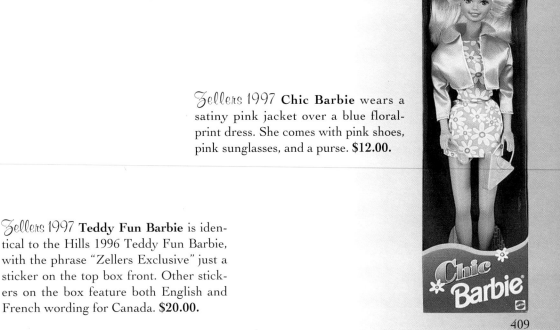

Zellers 1997 **Chic Barbie** wears a satiny pink jacket over a blue floral-print dress. She comes with pink shoes, pink sunglasses, and a purse. **$12.00.**

Zellers 1997 **Teddy Fun Barbie** is identical to the Hills 1996 Teddy Fun Barbie, with the phrase "Zellers Exclusive" just a sticker on the top box front. Other stickers on the box feature both English and French wording for Canada. **$20.00.**

Zellers 1998 **Barbie Loves Zellers** wears a denim miniskirt with a white belt and a pink top with print cuffs, collar, and matching headband. She carries a "Barbie (heart) Zellers" shopping bag. **$20.00.**

Zellers 2000 **Cherokee Style Barbie** has the Generation Girl Barbie head mold with blonde hair and brown eyes. She wears an ankle-length Cherokee-label skirt, a cream-colored top with a red vest, and brown boots. She carries a Cherokee portfolio containing a first-place ribbon and a report card indicating she earned an A+ in Math, English, Science, and History. **$24.00.**

Zellers 2003 **Barbie Fun in the Sun Pack** packages the playline Rio de Janeiro Barbie in a large vinyl tote bag with a carded Barbie fashion, a child-size Frisbee, a flutter board, and water wings. **$20.00.**

Trademarks

The word mark BARBIE, the Barbie doll and character likenesses, the color "Barbie pink" and associated trademarks are owned by and used under license from Mattel, Inc. © 2004 Mattel, Inc. All Rights Reserved. Mattel makes no representation as to the authenticity of the materials contained herein. All opinions are those of the author and not of Mattel.

ANNE KLEIN is a registered trademark of Anne Klein & Company.

AVON and MRS. P.F.E. ALBEE are trademarks of Avon products.

CABOODLES is a trademark of Plano Molding Company.

CAMPBELL'S, the Red & White label design, and M'm! M'm! Good! are trademarks licensed by Campbell Soup Company.

Carnival Cruise and the Reverse-C logo are service marks of Carnival Corporation.

CHEROKEE ® is a trademark owned by Cherokee Inc.

CHUCK E CHEESE © 2000 CEC Entertainment.

"CK/Calvin Klein Jeans" is a logo form of the trademark owned by CKTT.

COCA-COLA, COKE, the Dynamic Ribbon device, and the design of the contour bottle are trademarks of The Coca-Cola Company. © 1996 The Coca-Cola Company.

Disney Characters © The Walt Disney Company.

Disney's Animal Kingdom is a trademark of Disney Enterprises, Inc.

Donna Karan New York Barbie fashions designed by Donna Karan.

FASHION AVENUE is a registered trademark of Newport News, Inc., a member of the Spiegel Group.

The Flintstones™ © 1994 Hanna-Barbera Productions, Inc.

GAP and GAP KIDS are U.S. trademarks of Gap (Apparel) Inc.

GOT MILK? is a registered trademark of California Milk Processor Board.

Hallmark name and Hallmark Gold Crown logo owned by Hallmark Cards, Inc.

Happy Meal ® /McDonald's ® The following are trademarks owned by McDonald's Corporation: Golden Arches (logo), Happy Meal, Happy Meal box design, Happy Meal logo, and the McDonaldland characters, names and designs.

HARD ROCK and HARD ROCK CAFÉ are trademarks owned by Hard Rock Café International (USA), Inc. © 2003 Hard Rock Café International (USA), Inc.

HARLEY DAVIDSON ® Barbie ® Doll 1997 H-D.

KRAFT ® and the logos KRAFT TREASURES™ and KRAFT CHEESASAURUS REX™ are registered trademarks of Kraft General Foods, Inc.

Kool-Aid ® and Wacky Warehouse ® are registered trademarks of Kraft General Foods, Inc.

Little Debbie is a trademark of McKee Foods Corporation.

LOONEY TUNES, the characters, names, and all related indicia are trademarks of Warner Bros.

"March of Dimes" and "WalkAmerica" are registered trademarks of the March of Dimes Birth Defects Foundation.

MARY KAY ® is a registered trademark of Mary Kay Inc., Dallas, Texas. "Inspiring Beauty. Enriching Lives.™" and the 40th Anniversary logo are trademarks of Mary Kay Inc.

Mustang is a trademark of Ford Motor Company.

Nicole Miller trademark used by Mattel under license.

OREO™ and the OREO wafer design are trademarks of Nabisco Brands Company.

THE ORIGINAL ARIZONA JEAN CO. and ARIZONA JEAN COMPANY names and logos are trademarks of JCPenney Co., Inc.

"Pepsi" and "Pepsi-Cola" are registered trademarks of PepsiCo., Inc.

POG™ is a trademark of the World POG Federation™.

POLLY POCKET and associated trademarks owned by Bluebird Toys (UK) Ltd., England.

REEBOK and the Stripecheck Design are registered trademarks of Reebok International.

ROLLERBLADE, ROLLERBLADE logo and Skate Smart logo are trademarks of Rollerblade, Inc.

SPONGEBOB SQUAREPANTS © 2003 Viacom International, Inc. Nickelodeon, SpongeBob SquarePants, and all related titles, logos, and characters are trademarks of Viacom International Inc. Created by Stephen Hillenburg.

SWAROVSKI ® is a registered trademark of Swarovski Triesen AG.

About the Author

Introduced to Barbie doll as a child, J. Michael Augustyniak played with his older sisters' Barbie dolls alongside traditional boys' toys such as superhero dolls and the original Star Wars action figures. His most beloved childhood doll, a gift from his Grandma Clara, was the 1976 Ballerina Barbie, which was the first new Barbie doll Michael owned. Childhood toys are often discarded, yet seldom forgotten, so Michael's love for Barbie was rekindled soon after graduating from high school when, in 1988, a clearance-priced Rocker Derek doll wearing a gold stage costume proved too tempting to resist. At this time, Michael was working at his first job, as an associate with Kohl's department store, and he was fascinated by how Mattel's dolls reflected current fashion trends; California Dream Ken's fish necktie looked similar to the novelty neckties sold at Kohl's! Thinking he could keep his new collection manageable by only buying Ken dolls, Michael soon found Barbie doll irresistible anyway; in 1989 he paid double the issue price for the 1988 Happy Holidays Barbie. While in college, Michael worked for Sears, so collecting Sears exclusive Barbie dolls was inevitable. Within a few years, he owned thousands of dolls and fashions. He has attended eleven national Barbie Collectors' Conventions since 1991.

Michael earned his Bachelor's degree from Indiana University in 1992, with a double major in English and social studies, and he put his love of writing and photography to use as a staff member of *Barbie Bazaar* magazine, beginning in 1995. He also contributed to *Dolls In Print* magazine, where he collaborated on the first collectors' fashion doll photo soap opera, "Pink Intentions," from 2000 to 2001. Michael was promoted to *Barbie Bazaar Price Guide* editor in 2002, and is now considered a leading authority on Barbie.

Michael's books include *The Barbie Doll Boom* (1996), *Thirty Years of Mattel Fashion Dolls* (1998), the best-selling *Collector's Encyclopedia of Barbie Doll Exclusives and More* (1997, 2000, 2001, 2004), and *Collector's Encyclopedia of Barbie Doll Collector's Editions* (2004). Michael welcomes comments at Dollboy@aol.com.

Author J. Michael Augustyniak

Index

414

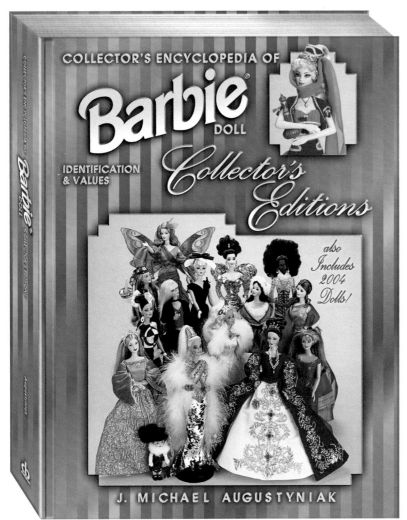